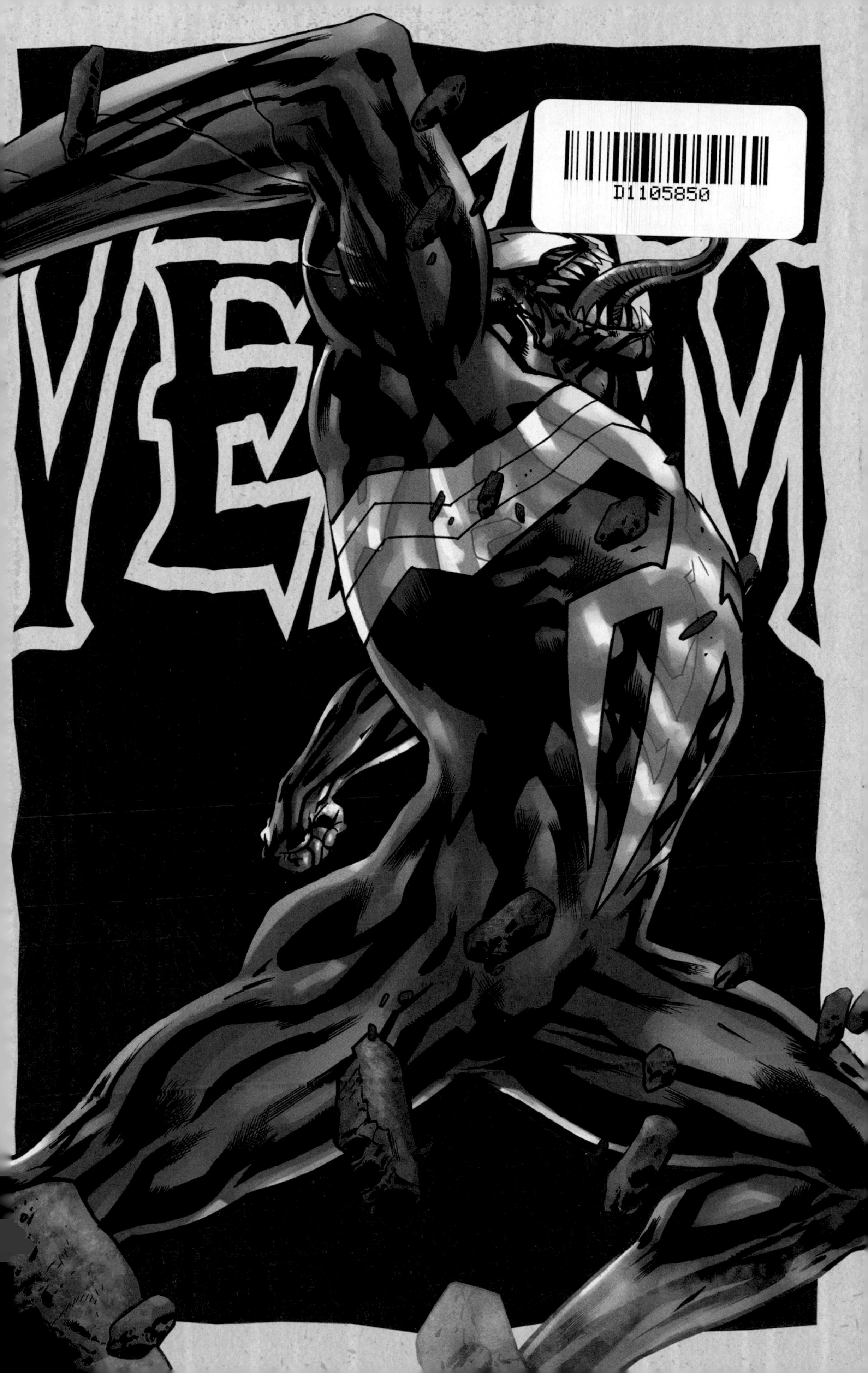

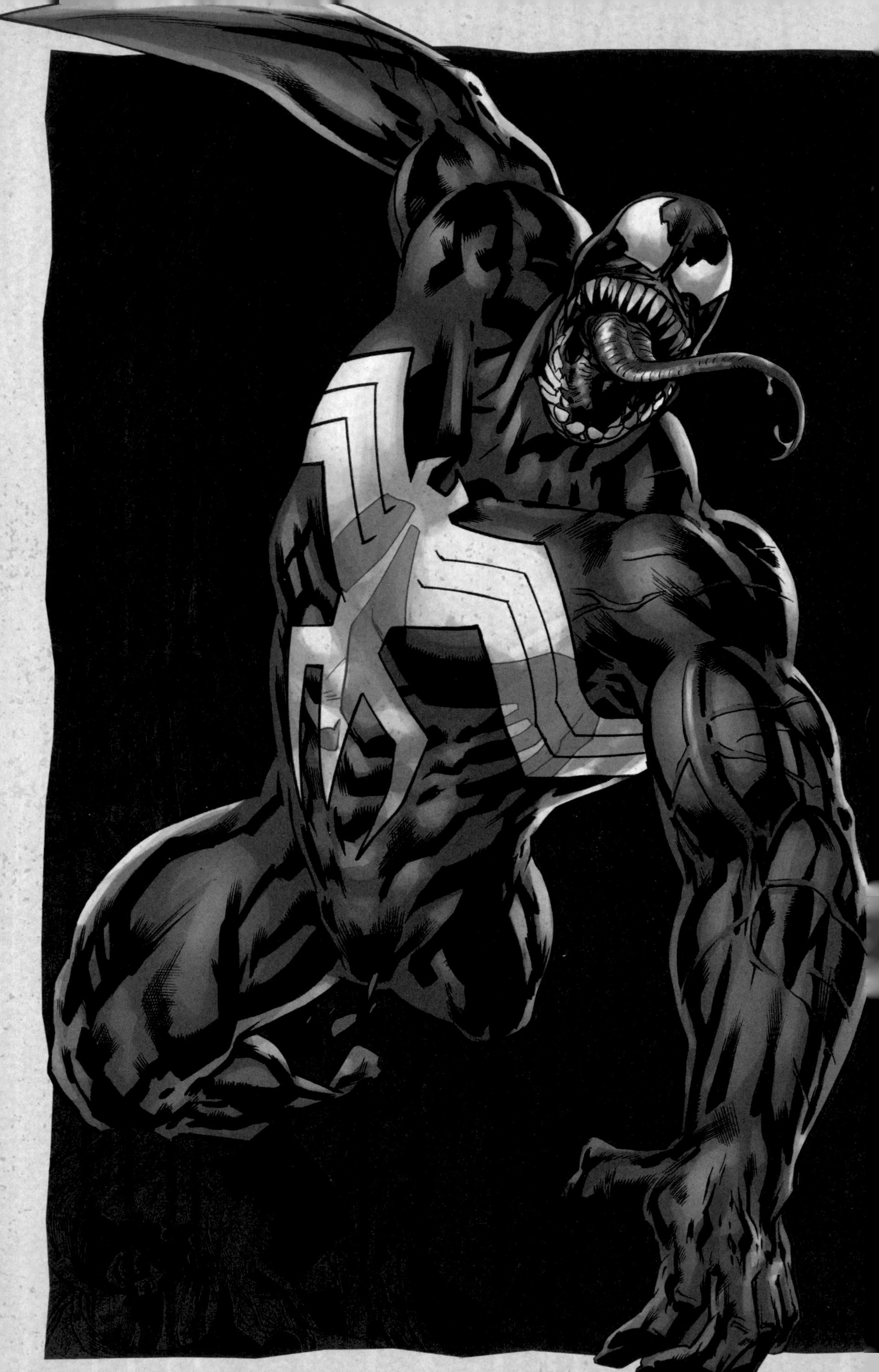

YEARS AGO, **EDDIE BROCK** WAS A REPORTER WHOSE CAREER WAS RUINED AFTER **THE AMAZING SPIDER-MAN** REVEALED THAT HE HAD FALSIFIED A STORY. DISTRAUGHT, BROCK CONTEMPLATED SUICIDE AND WENT TO HIS CHURCH TO ASK FORGIVENESS IN PREPARATION FOR TAKING HIS OWN LIFE.

INSTEAD, HE FOUND AN EXTRATERRESTRIAL PARASITIC ALIEN CALLED A **SYMBIOTE** THAT SPIDER-MAN HAD INADVERTENTLY BROUGHT TO EARTH AND REJECTED AFTER DISCOVERING ITS TRUE NATURE. SENSING BROCK'S SHARED HATRED OF THE WALL-CRAWLER, THE CREATURE BONDED WITH HIM AND THE TWO BECAME...

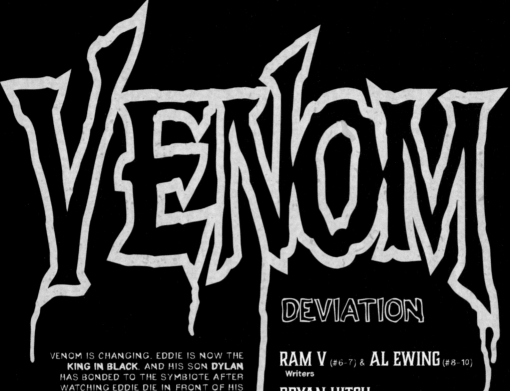

VENOM

DEVIATION

VENOM IS CHANGING. EDDIE IS NOW THE **KING IN BLACK**, AND HIS SON **DYLAN** HAS BONDED TO THE SYMBIOTE AFTER WATCHING EDDIE DIE IN FRONT OF HIS EYES. NOW DYLAN IS ON THE RUN FROM THE **LIFE FOUNDATION**, WHILE EDDIE'S CONSCIOUSNESS SURVIVED AND ARRIVED AT MERIDIUS' GARDEN AT THE END OF TIME. MERIDIUS IS ALSO A KING IN BLACK, LIKE THE MANY OTHER SYMBIOTE-CLAD BEINGS WHO INHABIT HIS GARDEN, AND MERIDIUS HAS PLANS FOR EDDIE, DYLAN AND THE SYMBIOTE!

RAM V (#6-7) & **AL EWING** (#8-10)
Writers

BRYAN HITCH
Penciler

ANDREW CURRIE with
WADE VON GRAWBADGER (#6) &
ANDY OWENS (#8)
Inkers

ALEX SINCLAIR with **PETER PANTAZIS** (#6, #8)
Color Artists

VC's **CLAYTON COWLES**
Letterer

BRYAN HITCH & **ALEX SINCLAIR**
Cover Art

THOMAS GRONEMAN
Assistant Editor

DEVIN LEWIS
Editor

DANIEL KIRCHHOFFER
Collection Editor

MAIA LOY
Assistant Managing Editor

LISA MONTALBANO
Associate Manager, Talent Relations

JENNIFER GRÜNWALD
Director, Production & Special Projects

JEFF YOUNGQUIST
VP Production & Special Projects

ANTHONY GAMBINO
Book Designer

ADAM DEL RE
Senior Designer

DAVID GABRIEL
SVP Print, Sales & Marketing

C.B. CEBULSKI
Editor in Chief

VENOM BY AL EWING & RAM V VOL. 2: DEVIATION. Contains material originally published in magazine form as VENOM (2021) #6-10. First printing 2022. ISBN 978-1-302-93256-5. Published by MARVEL WORLDWIDE, INC., a subsidiary of MARVEL ENTERTAINMENT, LLC. OFFICE OF PUBLICATION: 1290 Avenue of the Americas, New York, NY 10104. © 2022 MARVEL No similarity between any of the names, characters, persons, and/or institutions in this book with those of any living or dead person or institution is intended, and any such similarity which may exist is purely coincidental. **Printed in Canada.** KEVIN FEIGE, Chief Creative Officer; DAN BUCKLEY, President, Marvel Entertainment; DAVID BOGART, Associate Publisher & SVP of Talent Affairs; TOM BREVOORT, VP, Executive Editor; NICK LOWE, Executive Editor, VP of Content, Digital Publishing; DAVID GABRIEL, VP of Print & Digital Publishing; SVEN LARSEN, VP of Licensed Publishing; MARK ANNUNZIATO, VP of Planning & Forecasting; JEFF YOUNGQUIST, VP of Production & Special Projects; ALEX MORALES, Director of Publishing Operations; DAN EDINGTON, Director of Editorial Operations; RICKEY PURDIN, Director of Talent Relations; JENNIFER GRUNWALD, Director of Production & Special Projects; SUSAN CRESPI, Production Manager; STAN LEE, Chairman Emeritus. For information regarding advertising in Marvel Comics or on Marvel.com, please contact Vit DeBellis, Custom Solutions & Integrated Advertising Manager, at vdebellis@marvel.com. For Marvel subscription inquiries, please call 888-511-5480. **Manufactured between 8/19/2022 and 9/20/2022 by SOLISCO PRINTERS, SCOTT, QC, CANADA.**

10 9 8 7 6 5 4 3 2 1

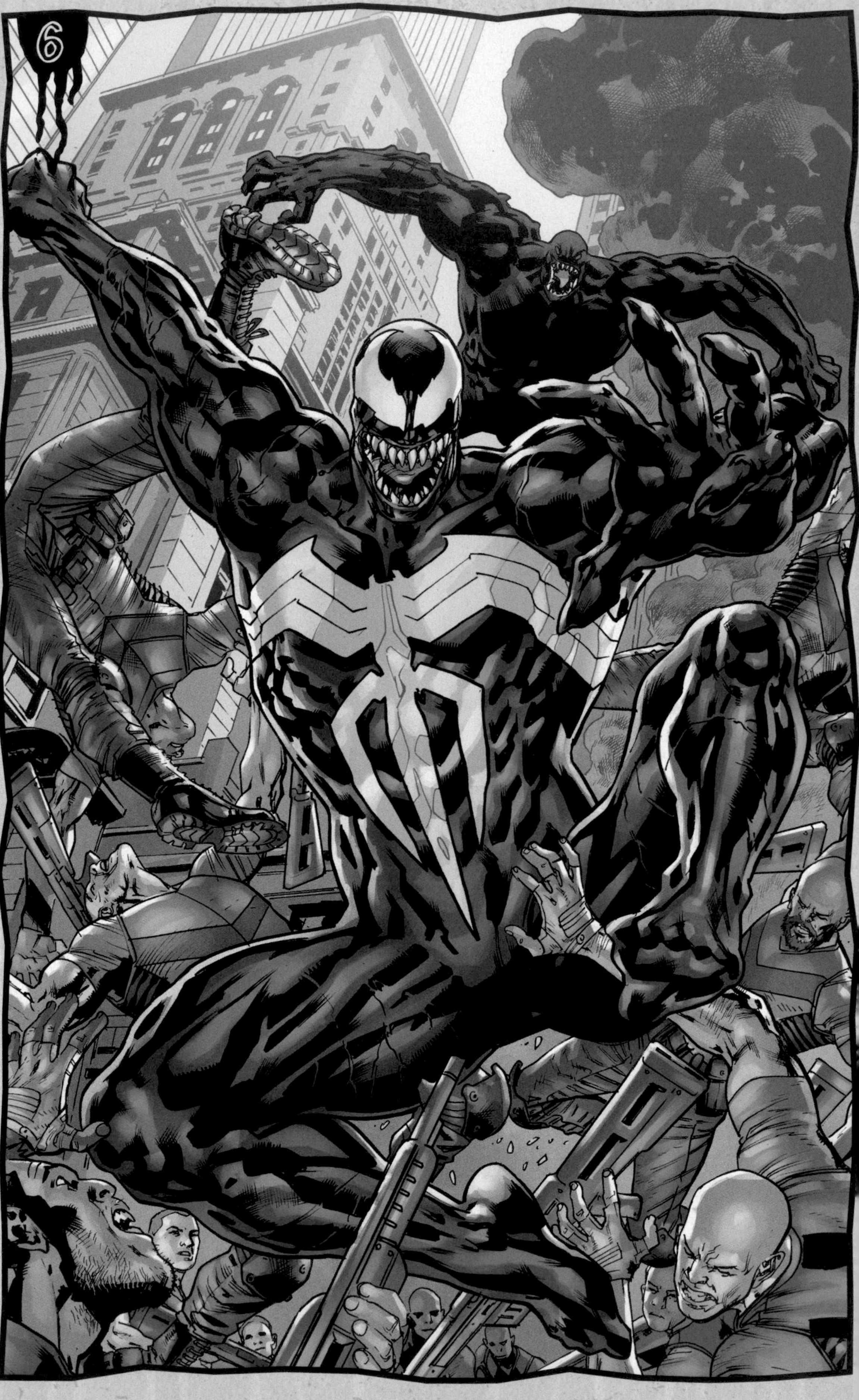
6

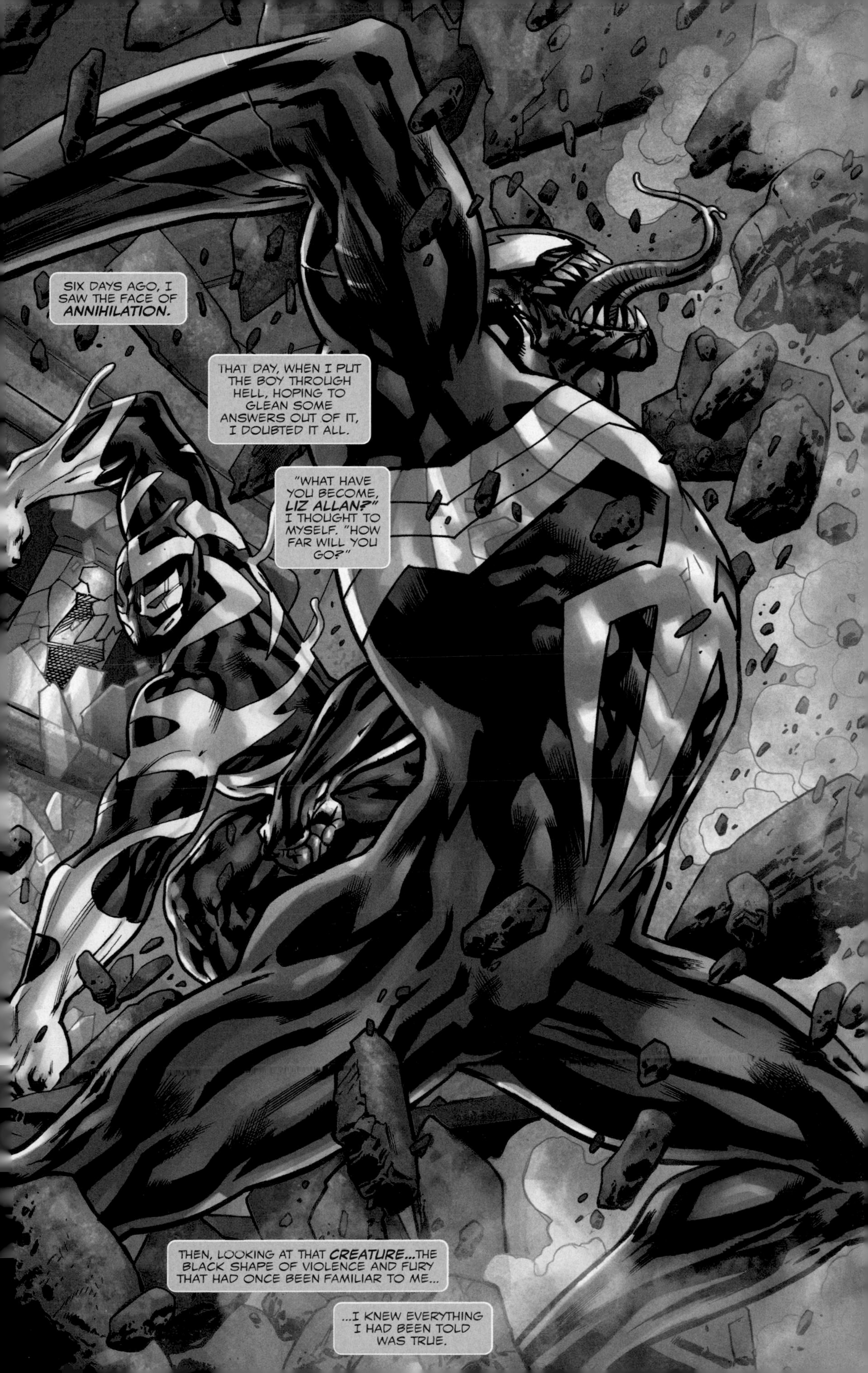
SIX DAYS AGO, I SAW THE FACE OF ANNIHILATION.
THAT DAY, WHEN I PUT THE BOY THROUGH HELL, HOPING TO GLEAN SOME ANSWERS OUT OF IT, I DOUBTED IT ALL.
"WHAT HAVE YOU BECOME, LIZ ALLAN?" I THOUGHT TO MYSELF. "HOW FAR WILL YOU GO?"
THEN, LOOKING AT THAT CREATURE...THE BLACK SHAPE OF VIOLENCE AND FURY THAT HAD ONCE BEEN FAMILIAR TO ME...
...I KNEW EVERYTHING I HAD BEEN TOLD WAS TRUE.

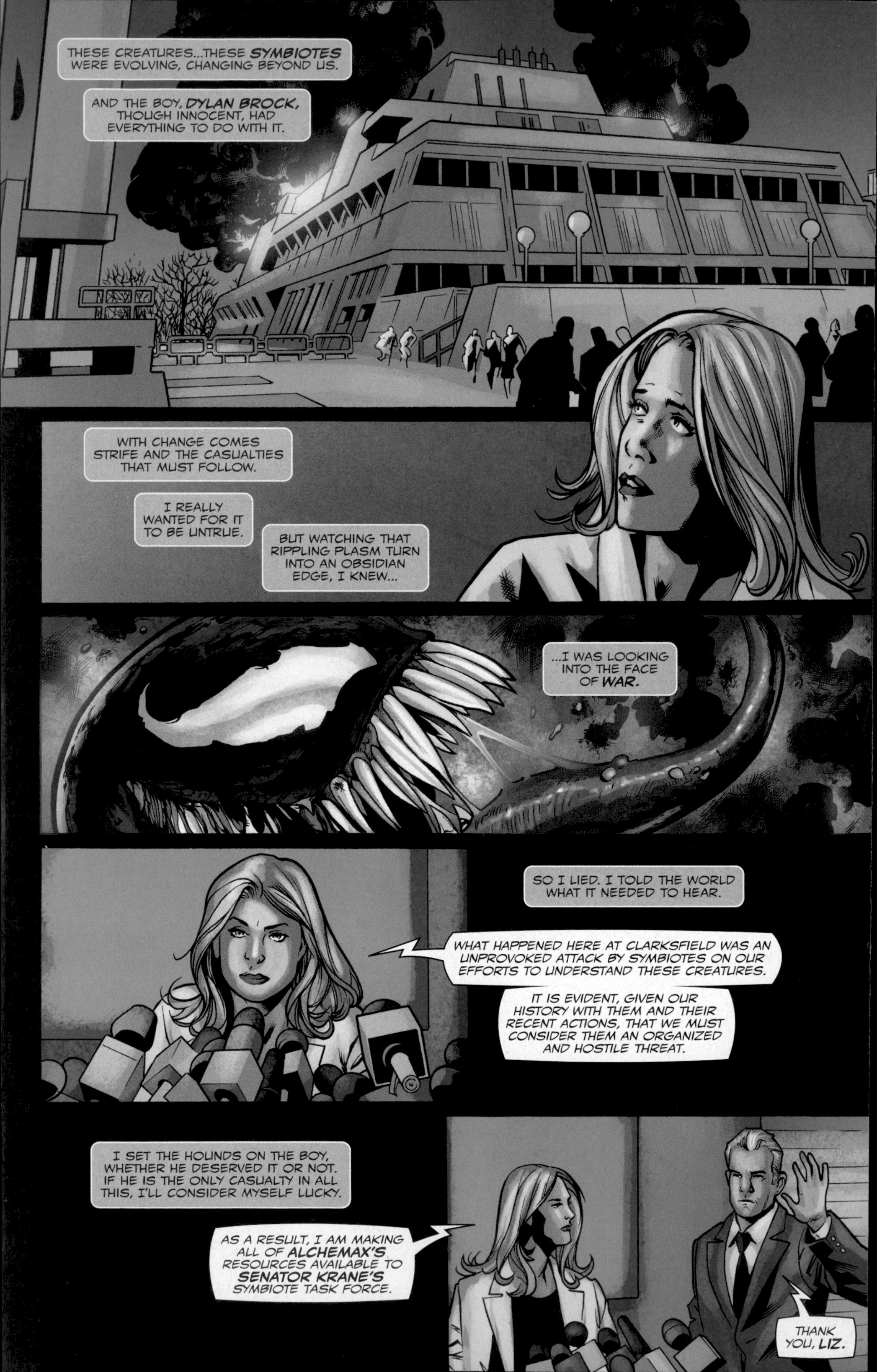
THESE CREATURES...THESE SYMBIOTES WERE EVOLVING, CHANGING BEYOND US.
AND THE BOY, DYLAN BROCK, THOUGH INNOCENT, HAD EVERYTHING TO DO WITH IT.
WITH CHANGE COMES STRIFE AND THE CASUALTIES THAT MUST FOLLOW.
I REALLY WANTED FOR IT TO BE UNTRUE.
BUT WATCHING THAT RIPPLING PLASM TURN INTO AN OBSIDIAN EDGE, I KNEW...
...I WAS LOOKING INTO THE FACE OF WAR.
SO I LIED. I TOLD THE WORLD WHAT IT NEEDED TO HEAR.
WHAT HAPPENED HERE AT CLARKSFIELD WAS AN UNPROVOKED ATTACK BY SYMBIOTES ON OUR EFFORTS TO UNDERSTAND THESE CREATURES.
IT IS EVIDENT, GIVEN OUR HISTORY WITH THEM AND THEIR RECENT ACTIONS, THAT WE MUST CONSIDER THEM AN ORGANIZED AND HOSTILE THREAT.
I SET THE HOUNDS ON THE BOY, WHETHER HE DESERVED IT OR NOT. IF HE IS THE ONLY CASUALTY IN ALL THIS, I'LL CONSIDER MYSELF LUCKY.
AS A RESULT, I AM MAKING ALL OF ALCHEMAX'S RESOURCES AVAILABLE TO SENATOR KRANE'S SYMBIOTE TASK FORCE.
THANK YOU, LIZ.

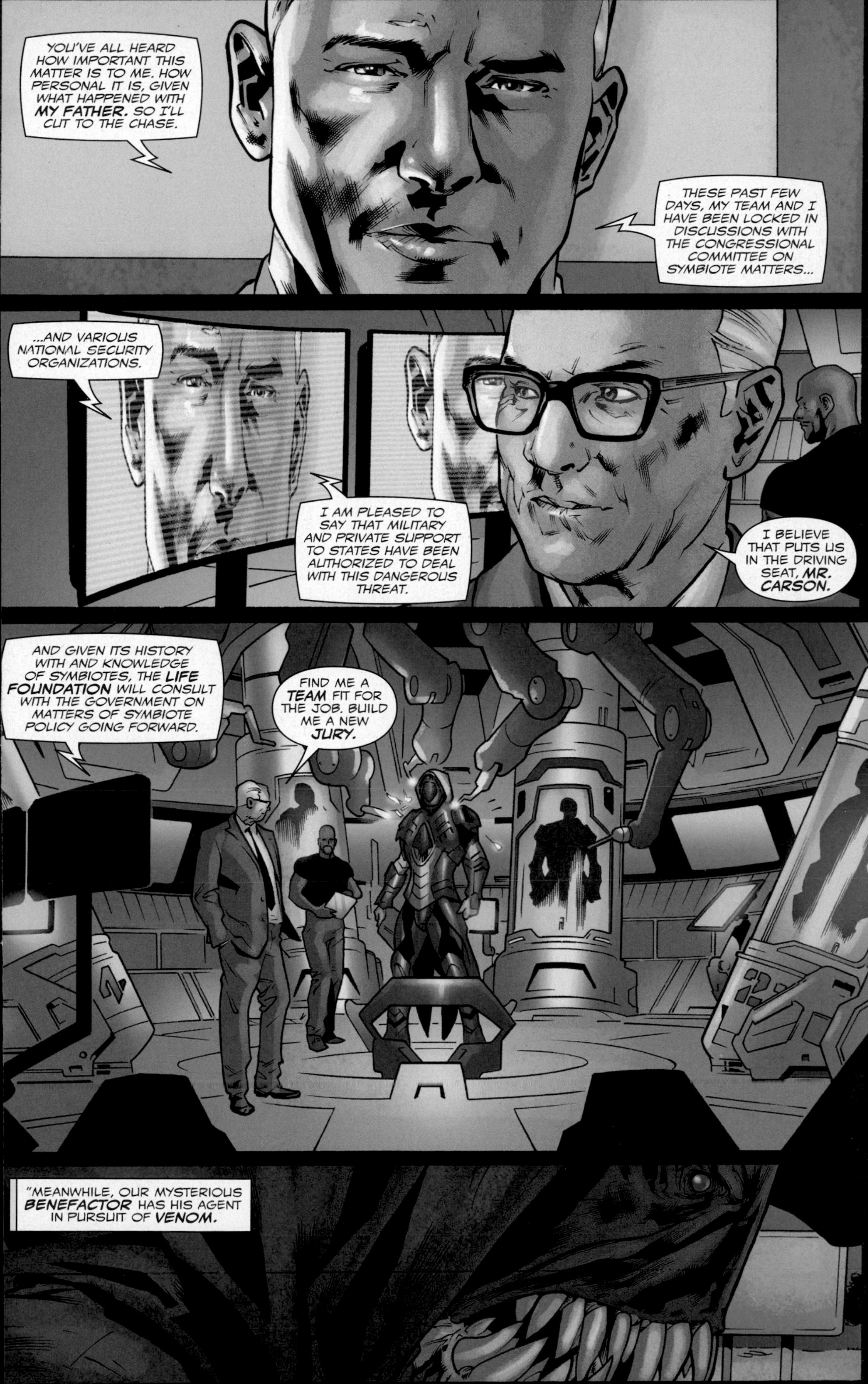
YOU'VE ALL HEARD HOW IMPORTANT THIS MATTER IS TO ME. HOW PERSONAL IT IS, GIVEN WHAT HAPPENED WITH MY FATHER. SO I'LL CUT TO THE CHASE.
THESE PAST FEW DAYS, MY TEAM AND I HAVE BEEN LOCKED IN DISCUSSIONS WITH THE CONGRESSIONAL COMMITTEE ON SYMBIOTE MATTERS...
...AND VARIOUS NATIONAL SECURITY ORGANIZATIONS.
I AM PLEASED TO SAY THAT MILITARY AND PRIVATE SUPPORT TO STATES HAVE BEEN AUTHORIZED TO DEAL WITH THIS DANGEROUS THREAT.
I BELIEVE THAT PUTS US IN THE DRIVING SEAT, MR. CARSON.
AND GIVEN ITS HISTORY WITH AND KNOWLEDGE OF SYMBIOTES, THE LIFE FOUNDATION WILL CONSULT WITH THE GOVERNMENT ON MATTERS OF SYMBIOTE POLICY GOING FORWARD.
FIND ME A TEAM FIT FOR THE JOB. BUILD ME A NEW JURY.
"MEANWHILE, OUR MYSTERIOUS BENEFACTOR HAS HIS AGENT IN PURSUIT OF VENOM.

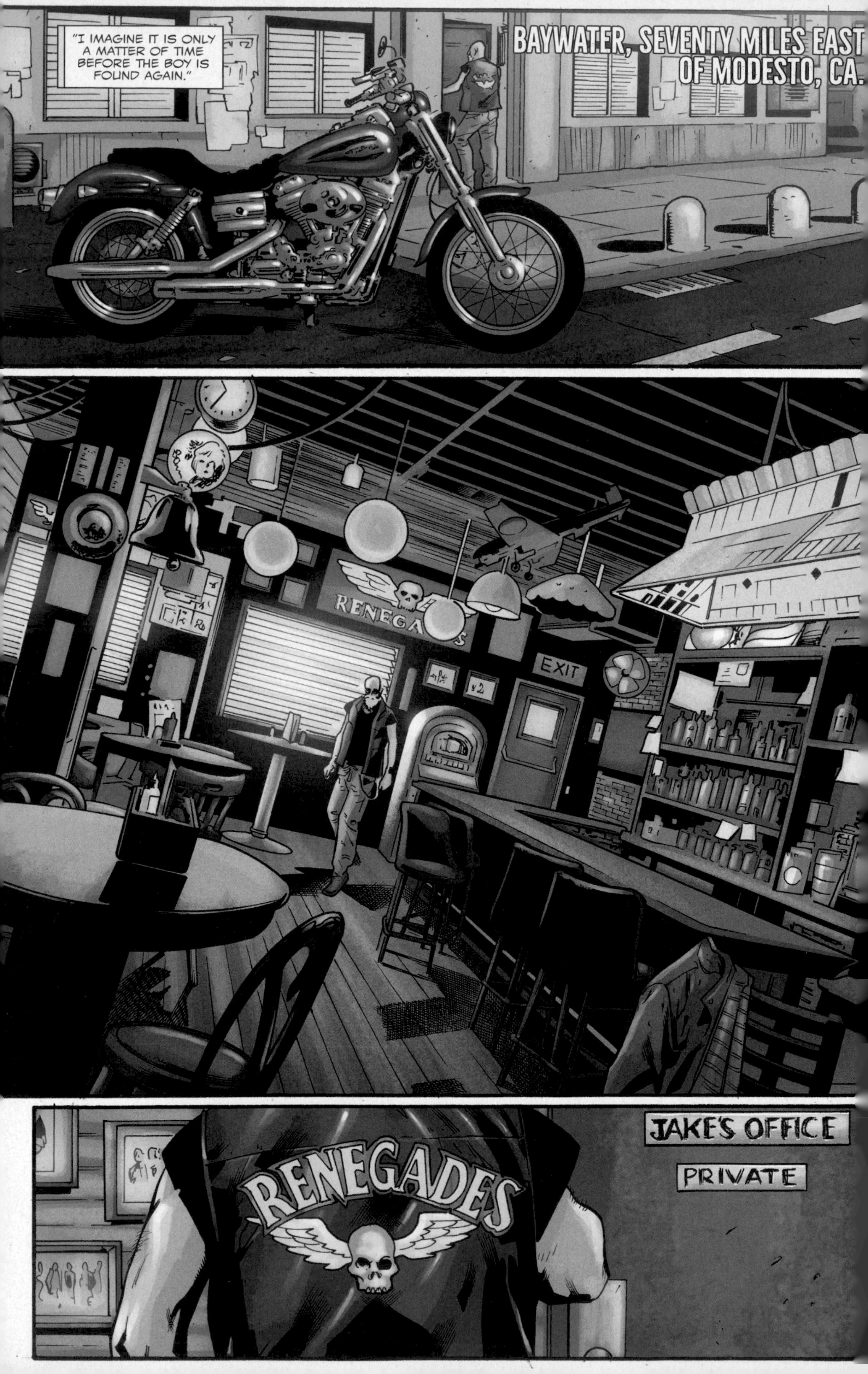

"I IMAGINE IT IS ONLY A MATTER OF TIME BEFORE THE BOY IS FOUND AGAIN."
BAYWATER, SEVENTY MILES EAST OF MODESTO, CA.
RENEGADES
EXIT
RENEGADES
JAKE'S OFFICE
PRIVATE

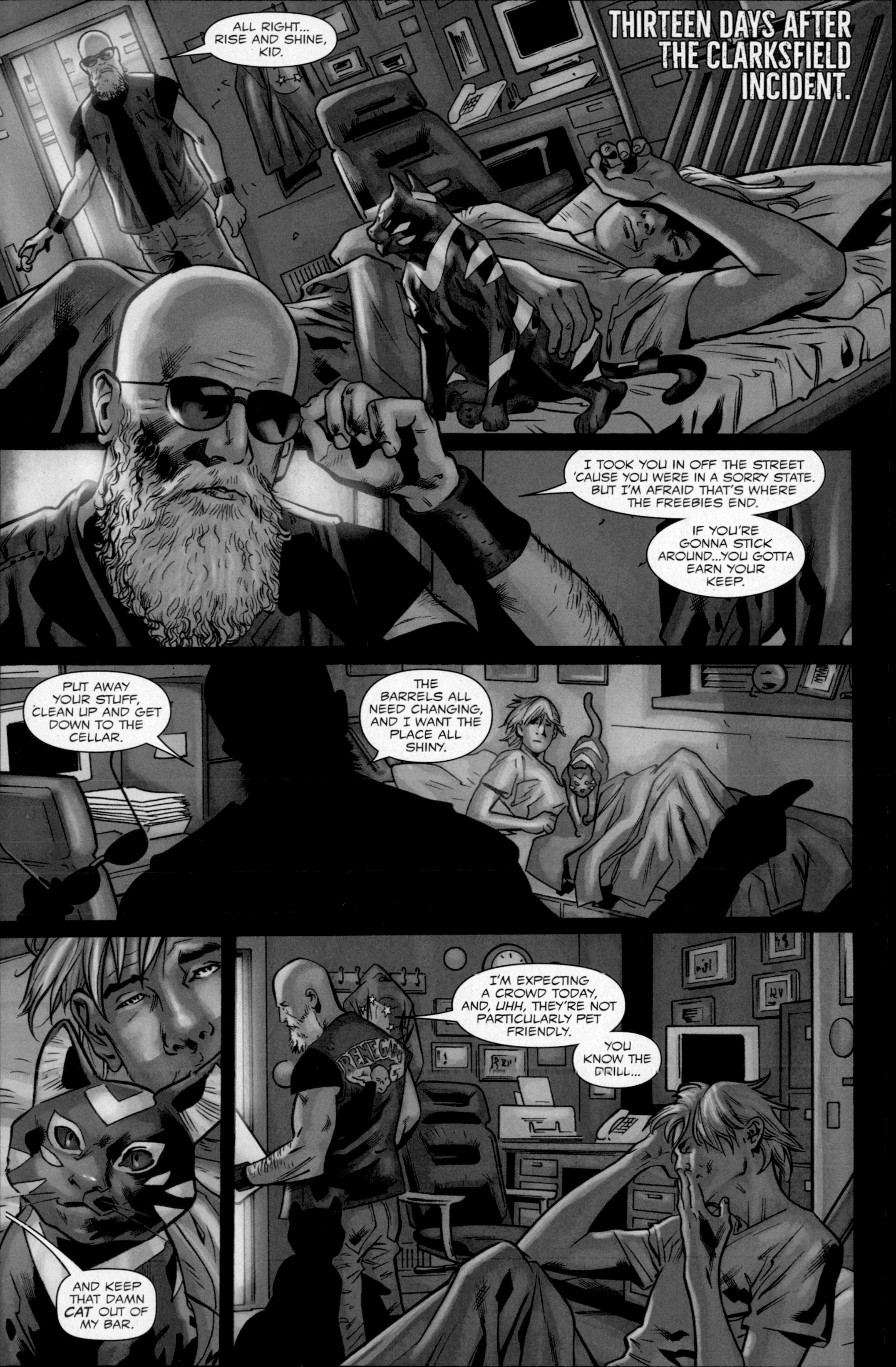
THIRTEEN DAYS AFTER THE CLARKSFIELD INCIDENT.
ALL RIGHT... RISE AND SHINE, KID.
I TOOK YOU IN OFF THE STREET 'CAUSE YOU WERE IN A SORRY STATE. BUT I'M AFRAID THAT'S WHERE THE FREEBIES END.
IF YOU'RE GONNA STICK AROUND...YOU GOTTA EARN YOUR KEEP.
PUT AWAY YOUR STUFF, CLEAN UP AND GET DOWN TO THE CELLAR.
THE BARRELS ALL NEED CHANGING, AND I WANT THE PLACE ALL SHINY.
I'M EXPECTING A CROWD TODAY, AND, UHH, THEY'RE NOT PARTICULARLY PET FRIENDLY.
YOU KNOW THE DRILL...
AND KEEP THAT DAMN CAT OUT OF MY BAR.

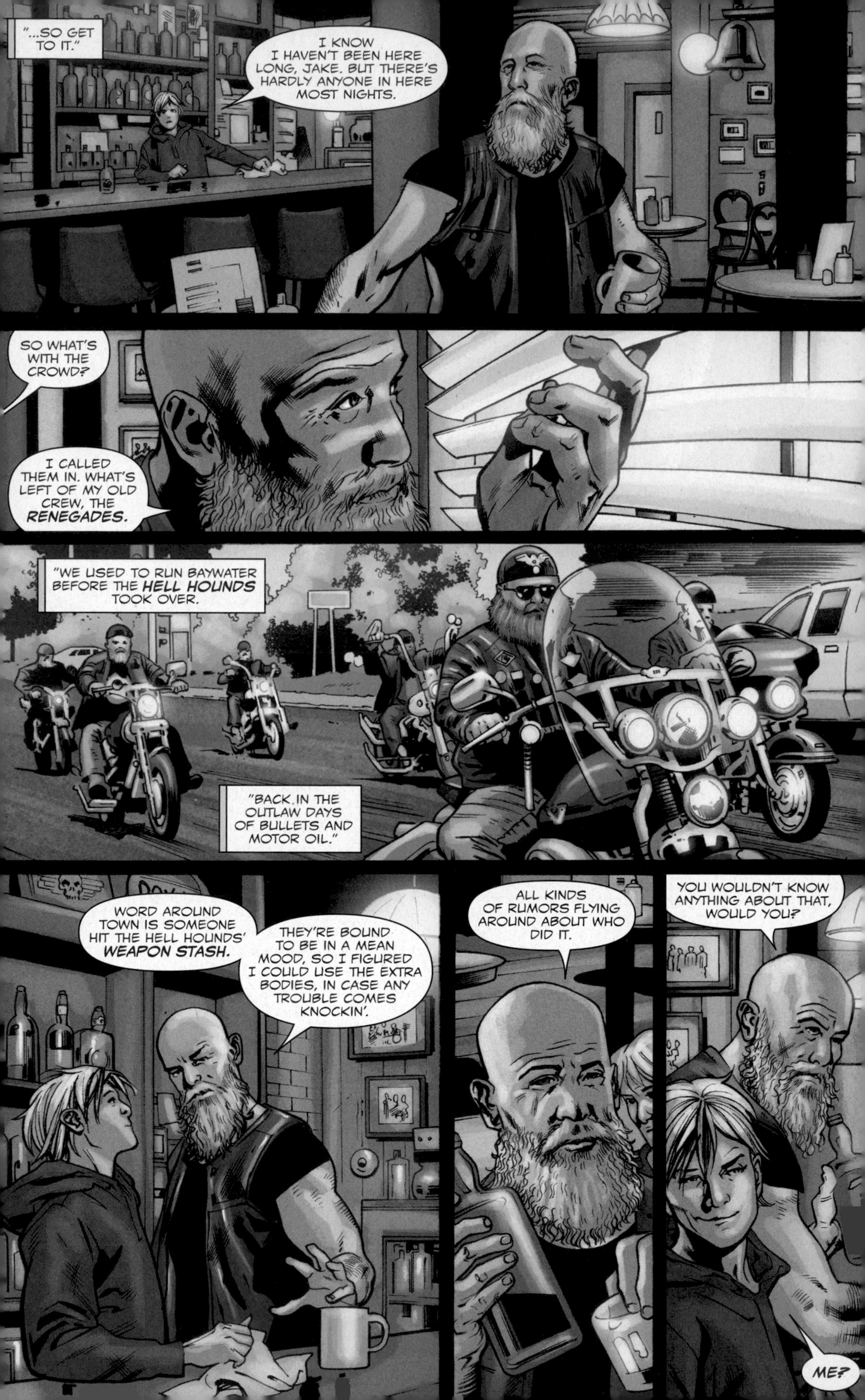
"...SO GET TO IT."
I KNOW I HAVEN'T BEEN HERE LONG, JAKE. BUT THERE'S HARDLY ANYONE IN HERE MOST NIGHTS.
SO WHAT'S WITH THE CROWD?
I CALLED THEM IN. WHAT'S LEFT OF MY OLD CREW, THE RENEGADES.
"WE USED TO RUN BAYWATER BEFORE THE HELL HOUNDS TOOK OVER.
"BACK IN THE OUTLAW DAYS OF BULLETS AND MOTOR OIL."
WORD AROUND TOWN IS SOMEONE HIT THE HELL HOUNDS' WEAPON STASH.
THEY'RE BOUND TO BE IN A MEAN MOOD, SO I FIGURED I COULD USE THE EXTRA BODIES, IN CASE ANY TROUBLE COMES KNOCKIN'.
ALL KINDS OF RUMORS FLYING AROUND ABOUT WHO DID IT.
YOU WOULDN'T KNOW ANYTHING ABOUT THAT, WOULD YOU?
ME?

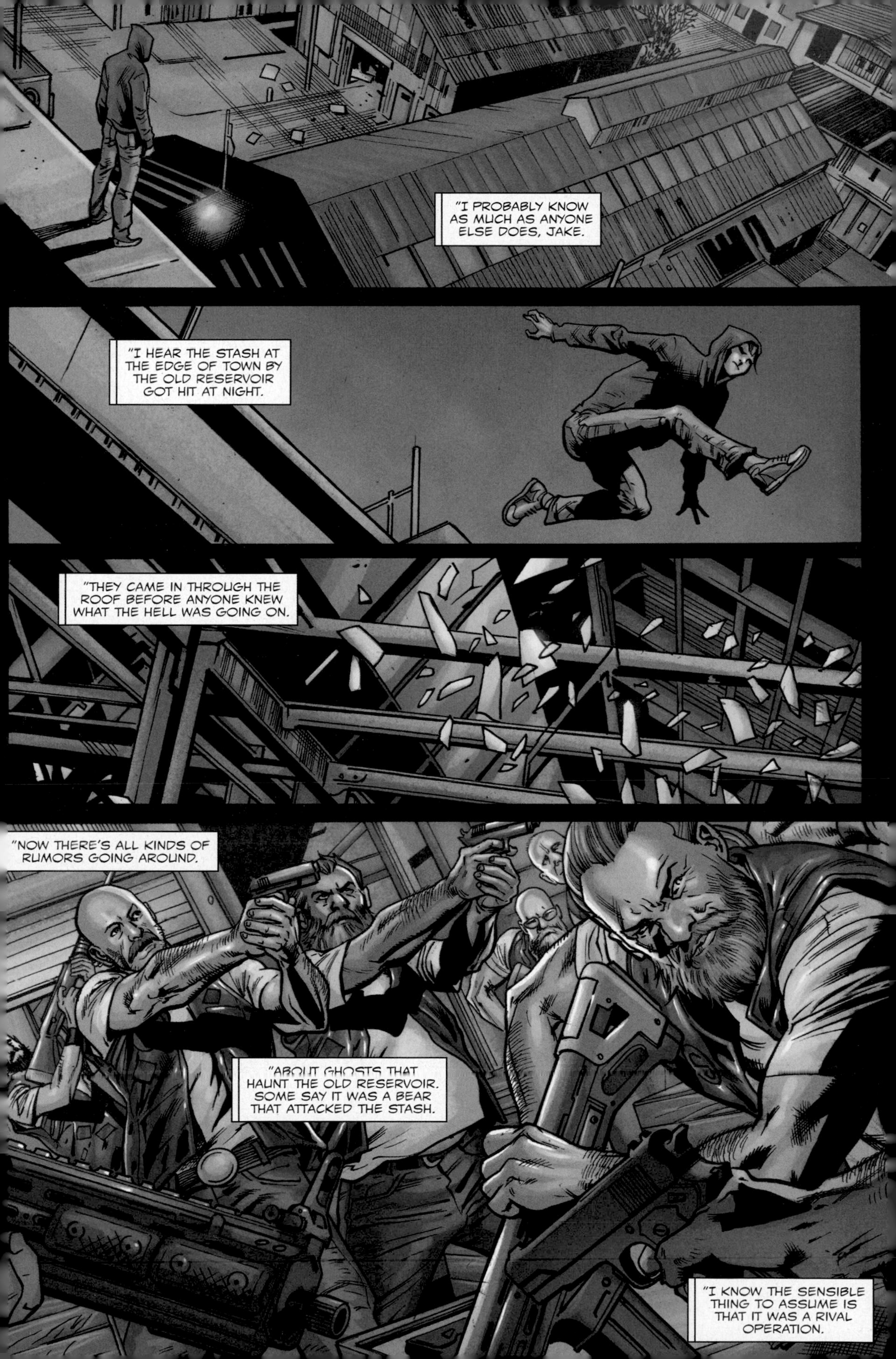
"I PROBABLY KNOW AS MUCH AS ANYONE ELSE DOES, JAKE.
"I HEAR THE STASH AT THE EDGE OF TOWN BY THE OLD RESERVOIR GOT HIT AT NIGHT.
"THEY CAME IN THROUGH THE ROOF BEFORE ANYONE KNEW WHAT THE HELL WAS GOING ON.
"NOW THERE'S ALL KINDS OF RUMORS GOING AROUND.
"ABOUT GHOSTS THAT HAUNT THE OLD RESERVOIR. SOME SAY IT WAS A BEAR THAT ATTACKED THE STASH.
"I KNOW THE SENSIBLE THING TO ASSUME IS THAT IT WAS A RIVAL OPERATION.

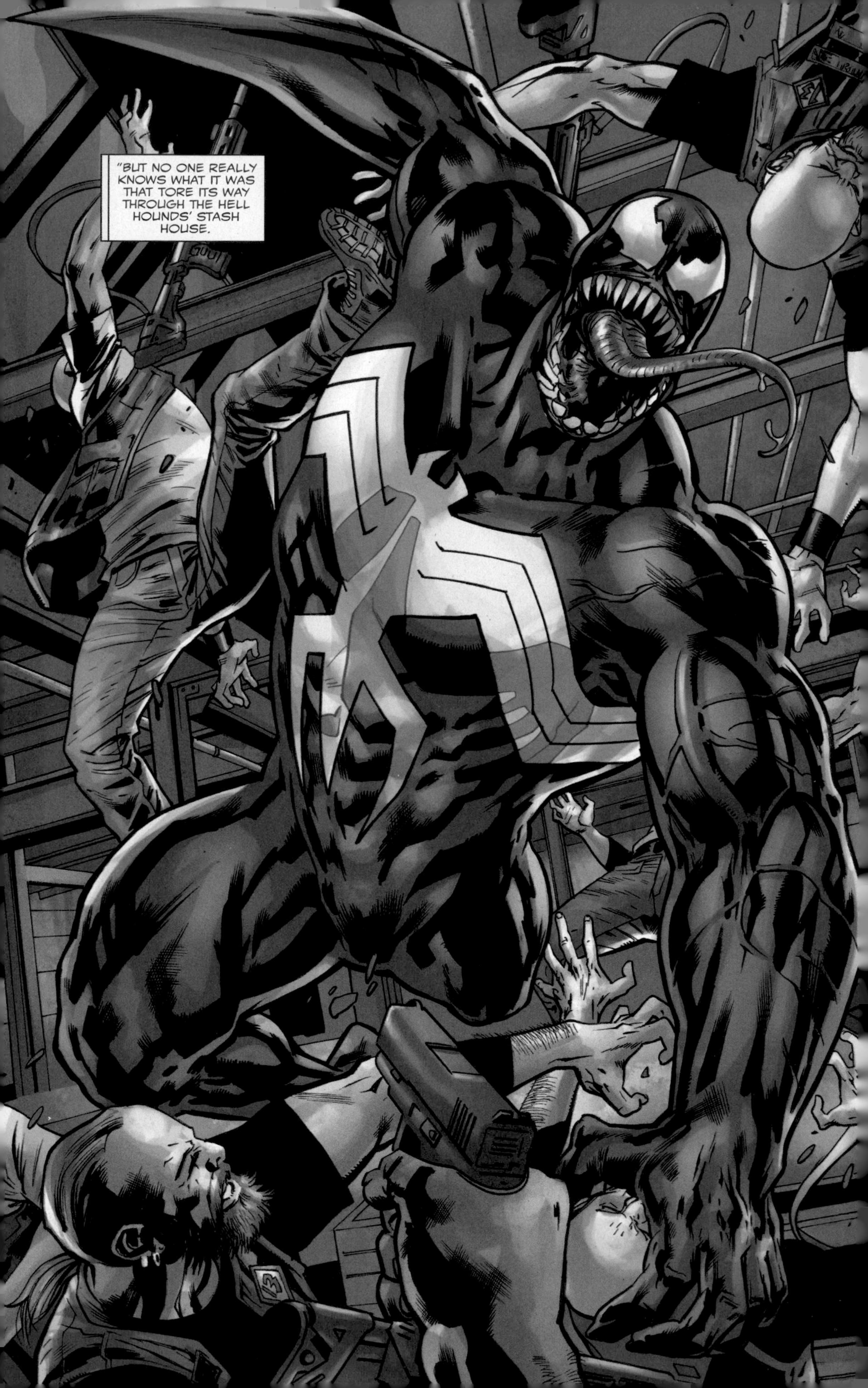
"BUT NO ONE REALLY KNOWS WHAT IT WAS THAT TORE ITS WAY THROUGH THE HELL HOUNDS' STASH HOUSE.

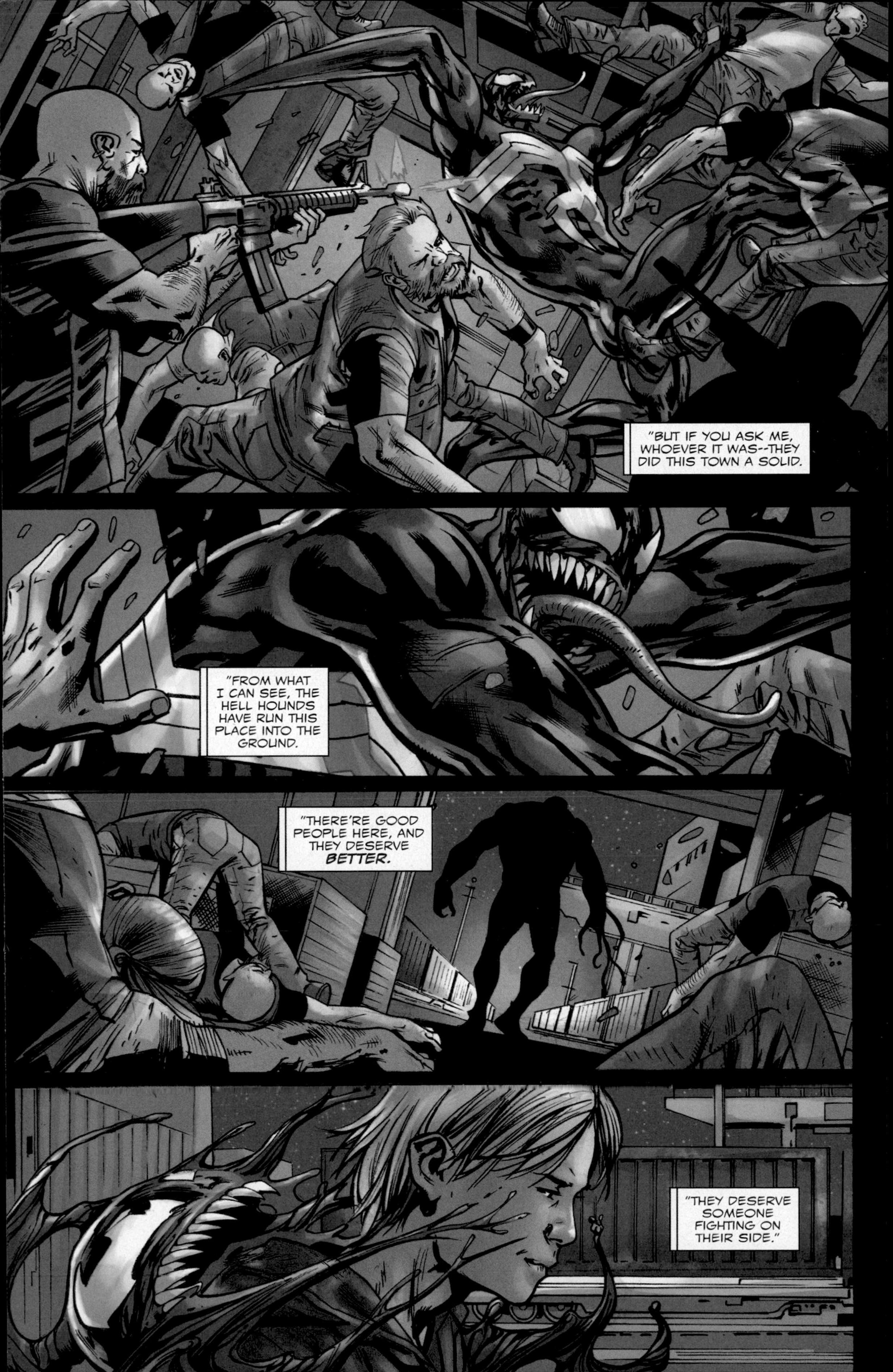
"BUT IF YOU ASK ME, WHOEVER IT WAS--THEY DID THIS TOWN A SOLID.
"FROM WHAT I CAN SEE, THE HELL HOUNDS HAVE RUN THIS PLACE INTO THE GROUND.
"THERE'RE GOOD PEOPLE HERE, AND THEY DESERVE *BETTER.*
"THEY DESERVE SOMEONE FIGHTING ON THEIR SIDE."

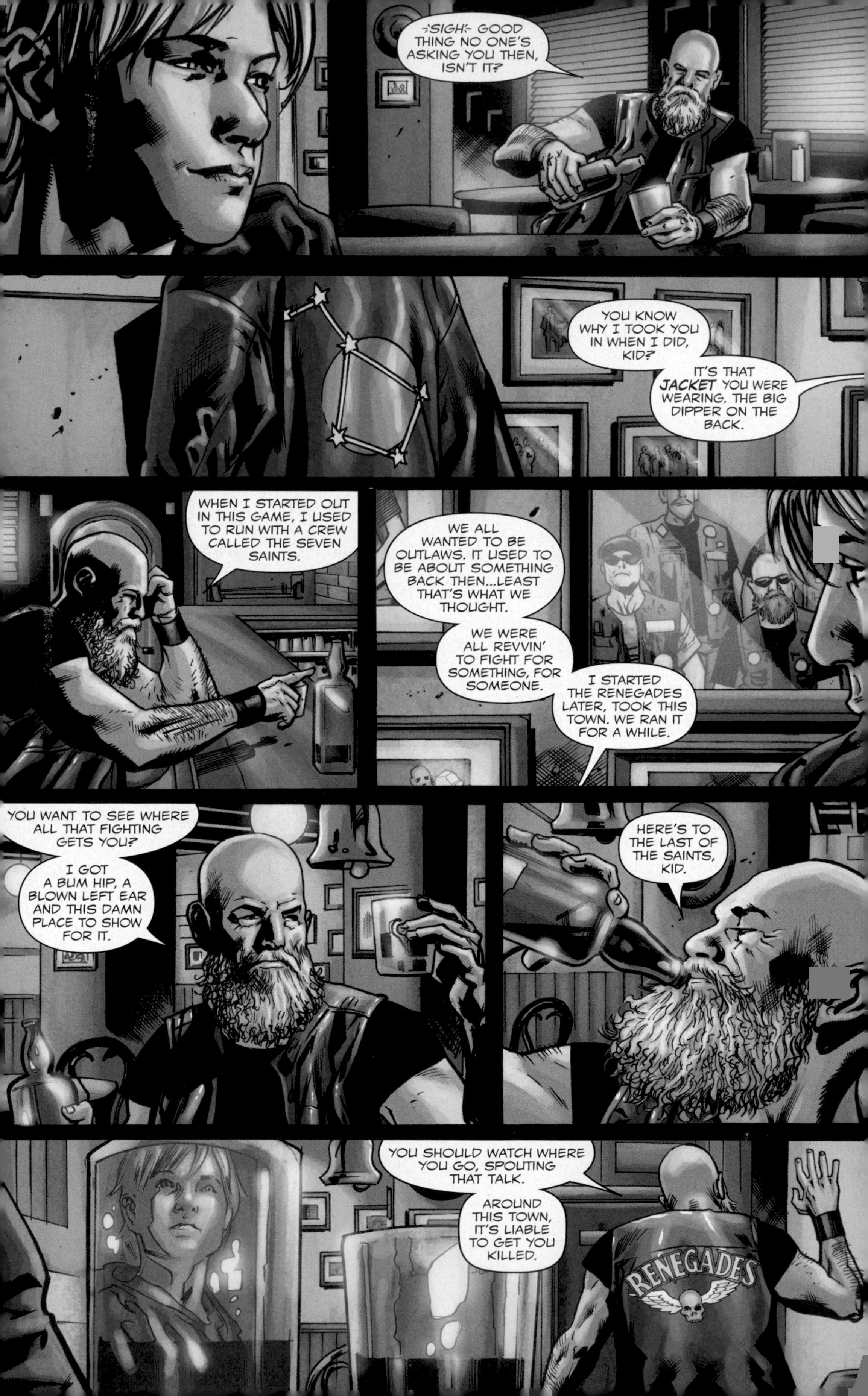
-SIGH- GOOD THING NO ONE'S ASKING YOU THEN, ISN'T IT?
YOU KNOW WHY I TOOK YOU IN WHEN I DID, KID?
IT'S THAT JACKET YOU WERE WEARING. THE BIG DIPPER ON THE BACK.
WHEN I STARTED OUT IN THIS GAME, I USED TO RUN WITH A CREW CALLED THE SEVEN SAINTS.
WE ALL WANTED TO BE OUTLAWS. IT USED TO BE ABOUT SOMETHING BACK THEN...LEAST THAT'S WHAT WE THOUGHT.
WE WERE ALL REVVIN' TO FIGHT FOR SOMETHING, FOR SOMEONE.
I STARTED THE RENEGADES LATER, TOOK THIS TOWN. WE RAN IT FOR A WHILE.
YOU WANT TO SEE WHERE ALL THAT FIGHTING GETS YOU?
I GOT A BUM HIP, A BLOWN LEFT EAR AND THIS DAMN PLACE TO SHOW FOR IT.
HERE'S TO THE LAST OF THE SAINTS, KID.
YOU SHOULD WATCH WHERE YOU GO, SPOUTING THAT TALK.
AROUND THIS TOWN, IT'S LIABLE TO GET YOU KILLED.
RENEGADES

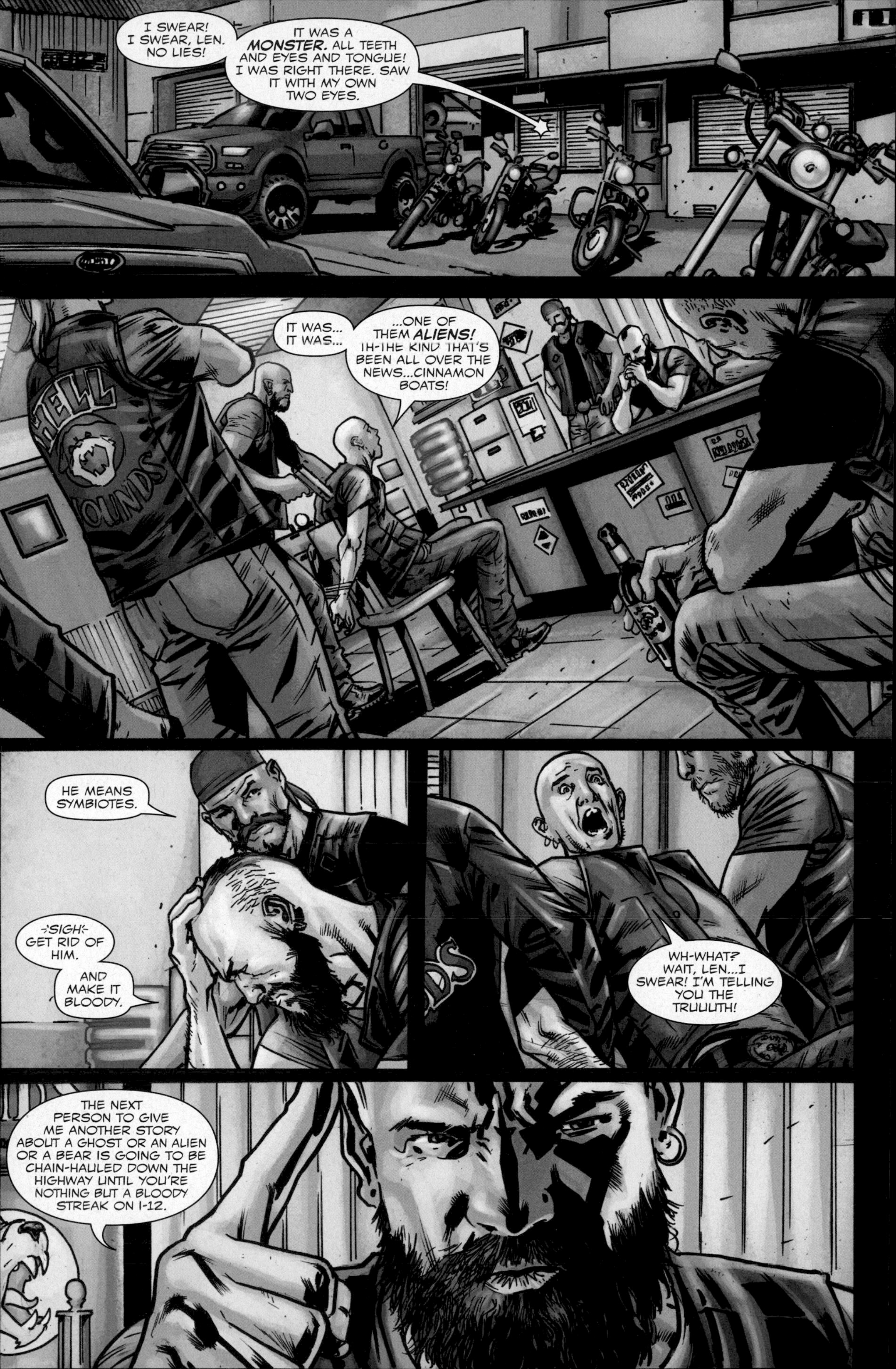
I SWEAR! I SWEAR, LEN. NO LIES!
IT WAS A MONSTER. ALL TEETH AND EYES AND TONGUE! I WAS RIGHT THERE. SAW IT WITH MY OWN TWO EYES.
IT WAS... IT WAS...
...ONE OF THEM ALIENS! TH-THE KIND THAT'S BEEN ALL OVER THE NEWS...CINNAMON BOATS!
HE MEANS SYMBIOTES.
SIGH
GET RID OF HIM.
AND MAKE IT BLOODY.
WH-WHAT? WAIT, LEN...I SWEAR! I'M TELLING YOU THE TRUUUTH!
THE NEXT PERSON TO GIVE ME ANOTHER STORY ABOUT A GHOST OR AN ALIEN OR A BEAR IS GOING TO BE CHAIN-HAULED DOWN THE HIGHWAY UNTIL YOU'RE NOTHING BUT A BLOODY STREAK ON I-12.

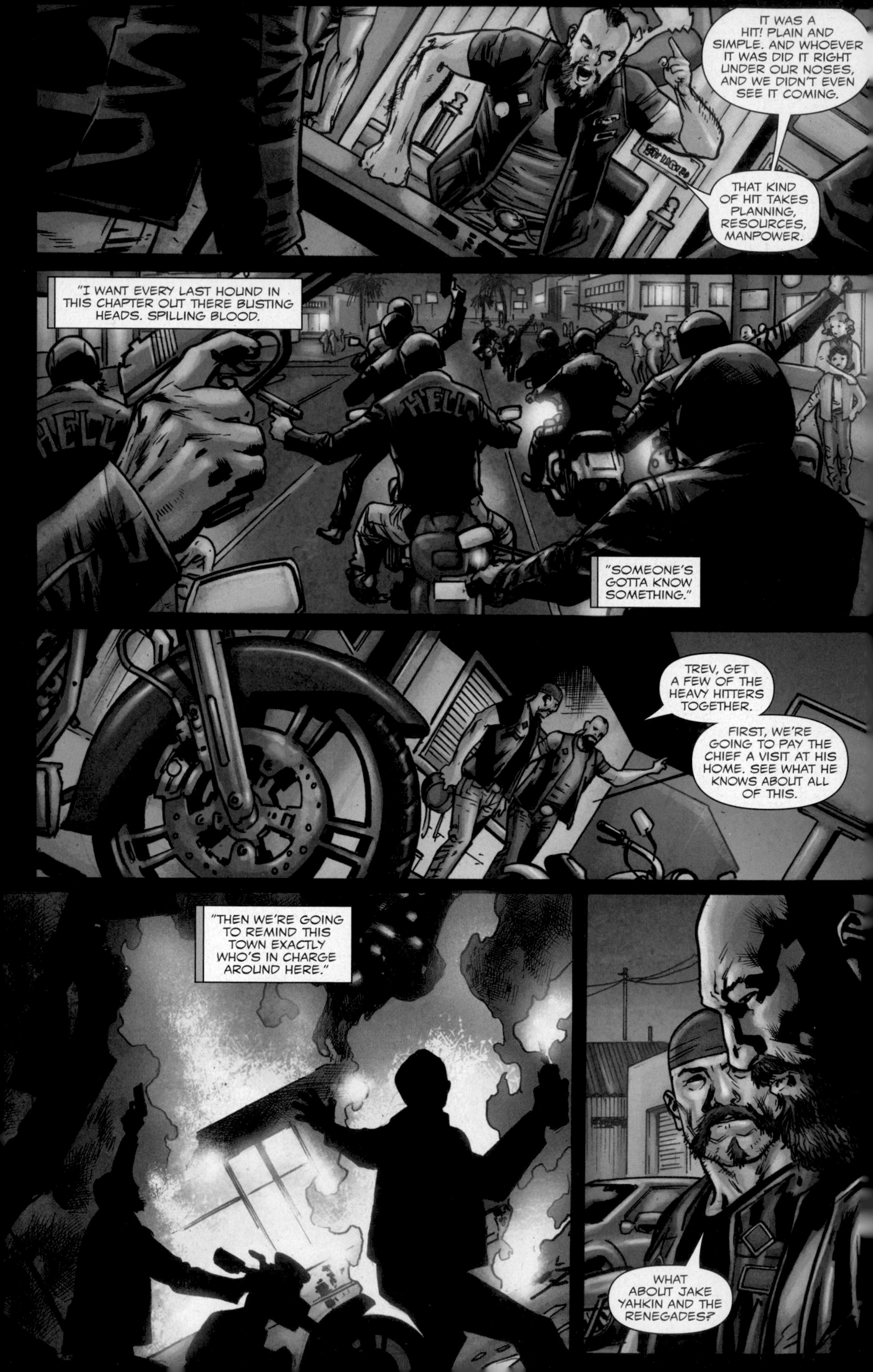
IT WAS A HIT! PLAIN AND SIMPLE. AND WHOEVER IT WAS DID IT RIGHT UNDER OUR NOSES, AND WE DIDN'T EVEN SEE IT COMING.
THAT KIND OF HIT TAKES PLANNING, RESOURCES, MANPOWER.
"I WANT EVERY LAST HOUND IN THIS CHAPTER OUT THERE BUSTING HEADS. SPILLING BLOOD.
HELL
"SOMEONE'S GOTTA KNOW SOMETHING."
TREV, GET A FEW OF THE HEAVY HITTERS TOGETHER.
FIRST, WE'RE GOING TO PAY THE CHIEF A VISIT AT HIS HOME. SEE WHAT HE KNOWS ABOUT ALL OF THIS.
"THEN WE'RE GOING TO REMIND THIS TOWN EXACTLY WHO'S IN CHARGE AROUND HERE."
WHAT ABOUT JAKE YAHKIN AND THE RENEGADES?

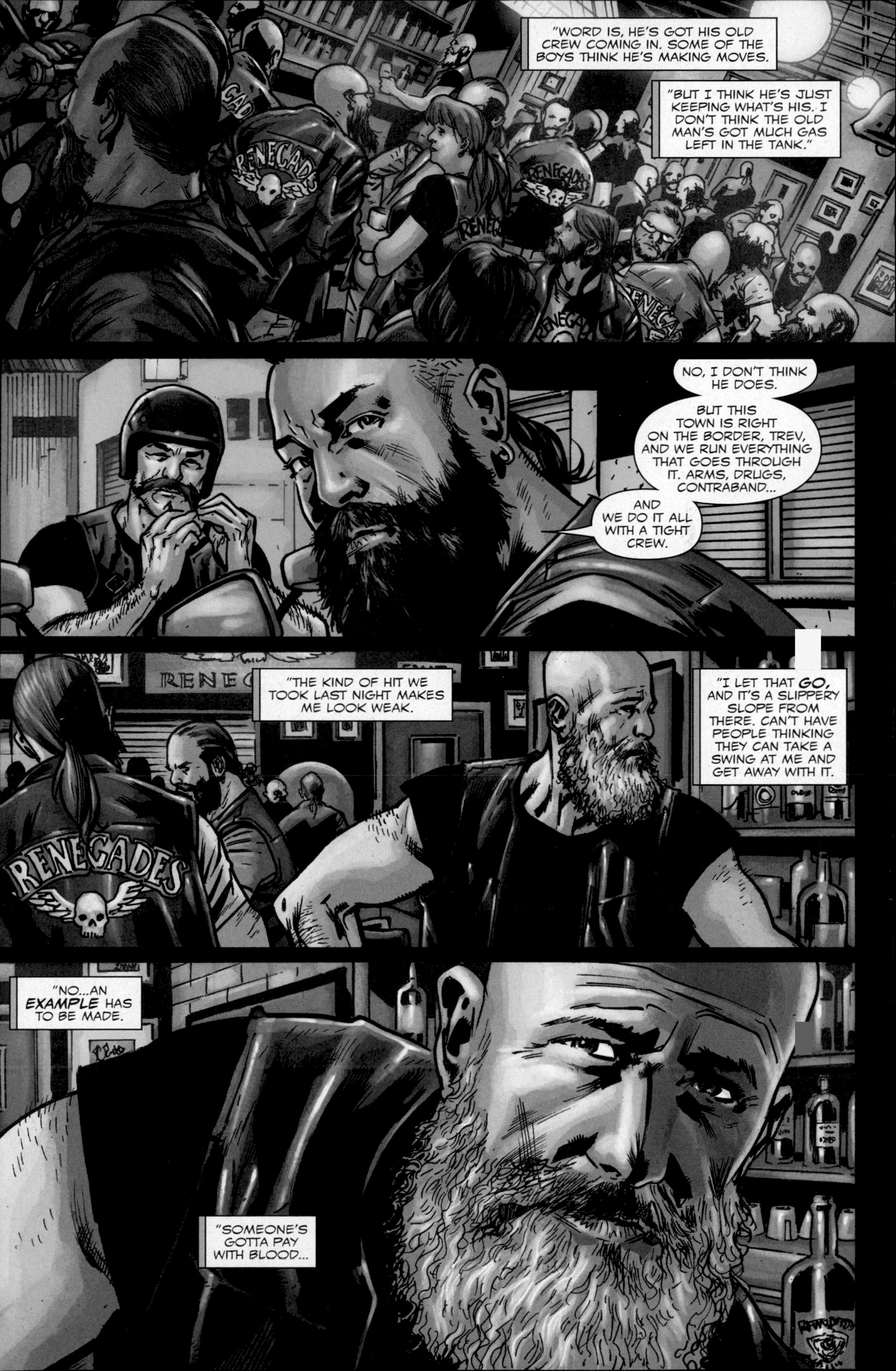
"WORD IS, HE'S GOT HIS OLD CREW COMING IN. SOME OF THE BOYS THINK HE'S MAKING MOVES.
"BUT I THINK HE'S JUST KEEPING WHAT'S HIS. I DON'T THINK THE OLD MAN'S GOT MUCH GAS LEFT IN THE TANK."
RENEGADES
NO, I DON'T THINK HE DOES.
BUT THIS TOWN IS RIGHT ON THE BORDER, TREV, AND WE RUN EVERYTHING THAT GOES THROUGH IT. ARMS, DRUGS, CONTRABAND...
AND WE DO IT ALL WITH A TIGHT CREW.
"THE KIND OF HIT WE TOOK LAST NIGHT MAKES ME LOOK WEAK.
"I LET THAT GO, AND IT'S A SLIPPERY SLOPE FROM THERE. CAN'T HAVE PEOPLE THINKING THEY CAN TAKE A SWING AT ME AND GET AWAY WITH IT.
RENEGADES
"NO...AN EXAMPLE HAS TO BE MADE.
"SOMEONE'S GOTTA PAY WITH BLOOD...

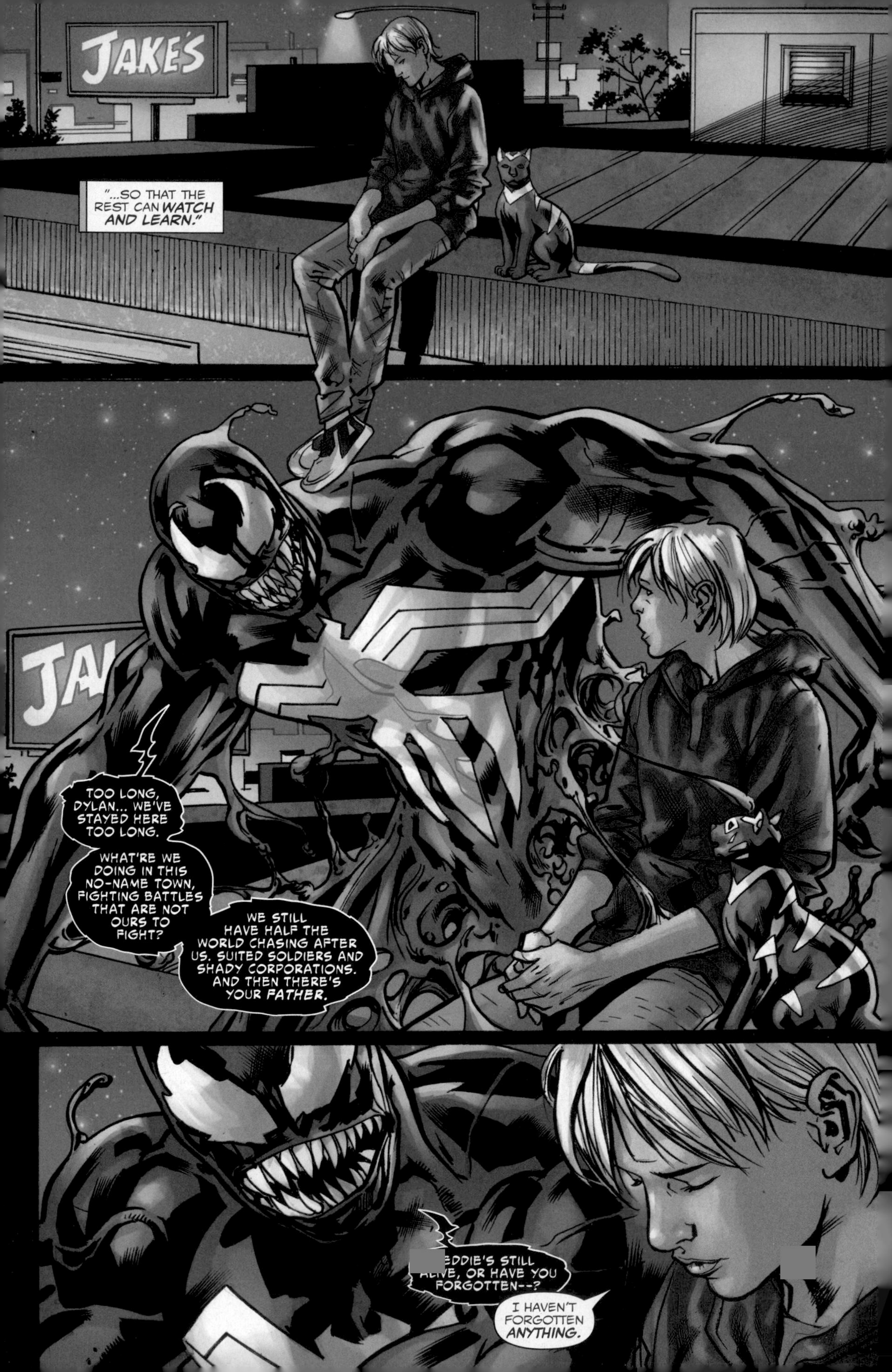
JAKE'S
"...SO THAT THE REST CAN WATCH AND LEARN."
TOO LONG, DYLAN... WE'VE STAYED HERE TOO LONG.
WHAT'RE WE DOING IN THIS NO-NAME TOWN, FIGHTING BATTLES THAT ARE NOT OURS TO FIGHT?
WE STILL HAVE HALF THE WORLD CHASING AFTER US. SUITED SOLDIERS AND SHADY CORPORATIONS. AND THEN THERE'S YOUR FATHER.
EDDIE'S STILL ALIVE, OR HAVE YOU FORGOTTEN--?
I HAVEN'T FORGOTTEN ANYTHING.

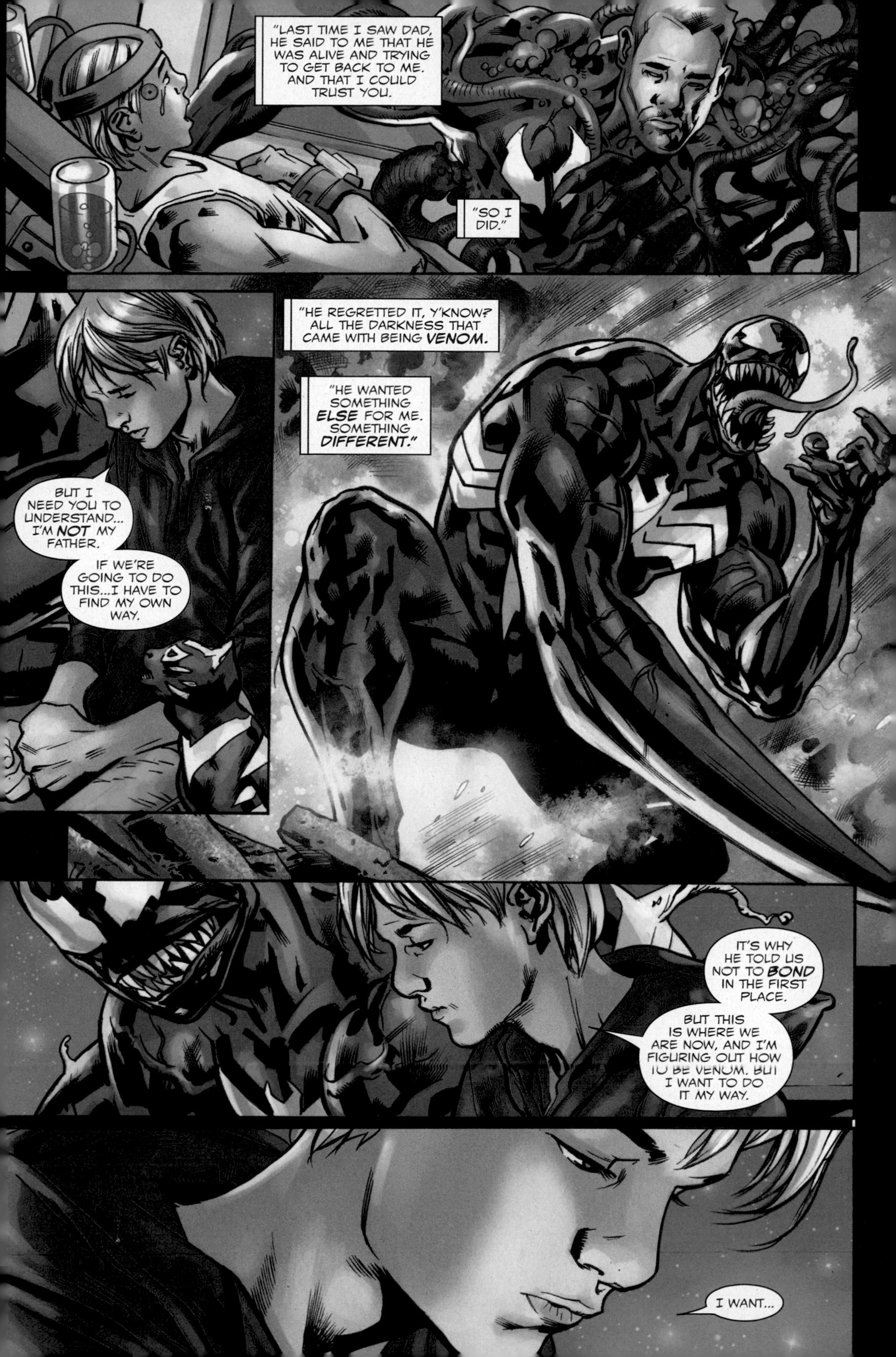
"LAST TIME I SAW DAD, HE SAID TO ME THAT HE WAS ALIVE AND TRYING TO GET BACK TO ME. AND THAT I COULD TRUST YOU.
"SO I DID."
"HE REGRETTED IT, Y'KNOW? ALL THE DARKNESS THAT CAME WITH BEING VENOM.
"HE WANTED SOMETHING ELSE FOR ME. SOMETHING DIFFERENT."
BUT I NEED YOU TO UNDERSTAND... I'M NOT MY FATHER.
IF WE'RE GOING TO DO THIS...I HAVE TO FIND MY OWN WAY.
IT'S WHY HE TOLD US NOT TO BOND IN THE FIRST PLACE.
BUT THIS IS WHERE WE ARE NOW, AND I'M FIGURING OUT HOW TO BE VENOM. BUT I WANT TO DO IT MY WAY.
I WANT...

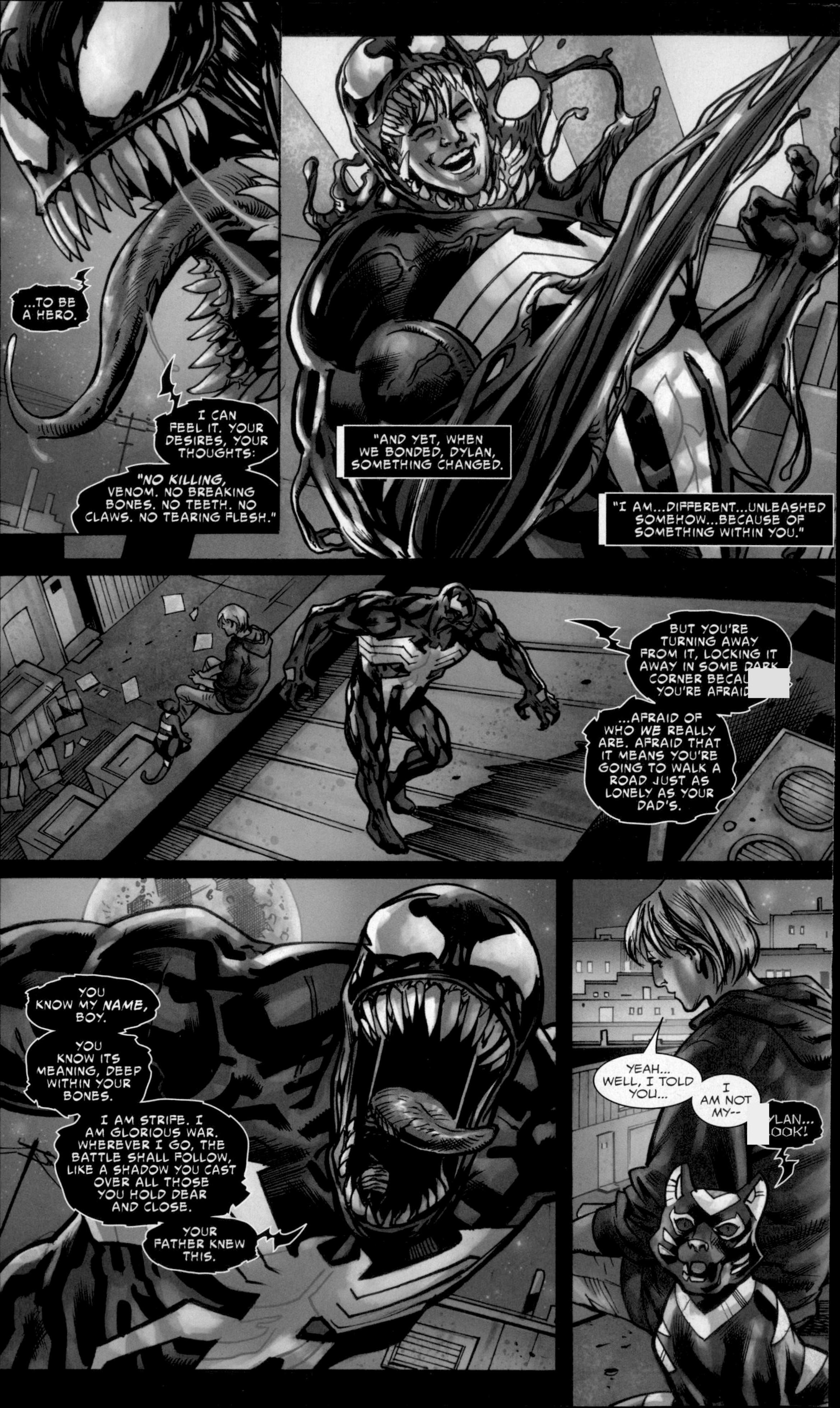
...TO BE A HERO.
I CAN FEEL IT. YOUR DESIRES, YOUR THOUGHTS:
"NO KILLING, VENOM. NO BREAKING BONES. NO TEETH. NO CLAWS. NO TEARING FLESH."
"AND YET, WHEN WE BONDED, DYLAN, SOMETHING CHANGED.
"I AM...DIFFERENT...UNLEASHED SOMEHOW...BECAUSE OF SOMETHING WITHIN YOU."
BUT YOU'RE TURNING AWAY FROM IT, LOCKING IT AWAY IN SOME DAR CORNER BECAU YOU'RE AFRAID
...AFRAID OF WHO WE REALLY ARE. AFRAID THAT IT MEANS YOU'RE GOING TO WALK A ROAD JUST AS LONELY AS YOUR DAD'S.
YOU KNOW MY NAME, BOY.
YOU KNOW ITS MEANING, DEEP WITHIN YOUR BONES.
I AM STRIFE. I AM GLORIOUS WAR. WHEREVER I GO, THE BATTLE SHALL FOLLOW, LIKE A SHADOW YOU CAST OVER ALL THOSE YOU HOLD DEAR AND CLOSE.
YOUR FATHER KNEW THIS.
YEAH... WELL, I TOLD YOU...
I AM NOT MY--
YLAN... OOK!

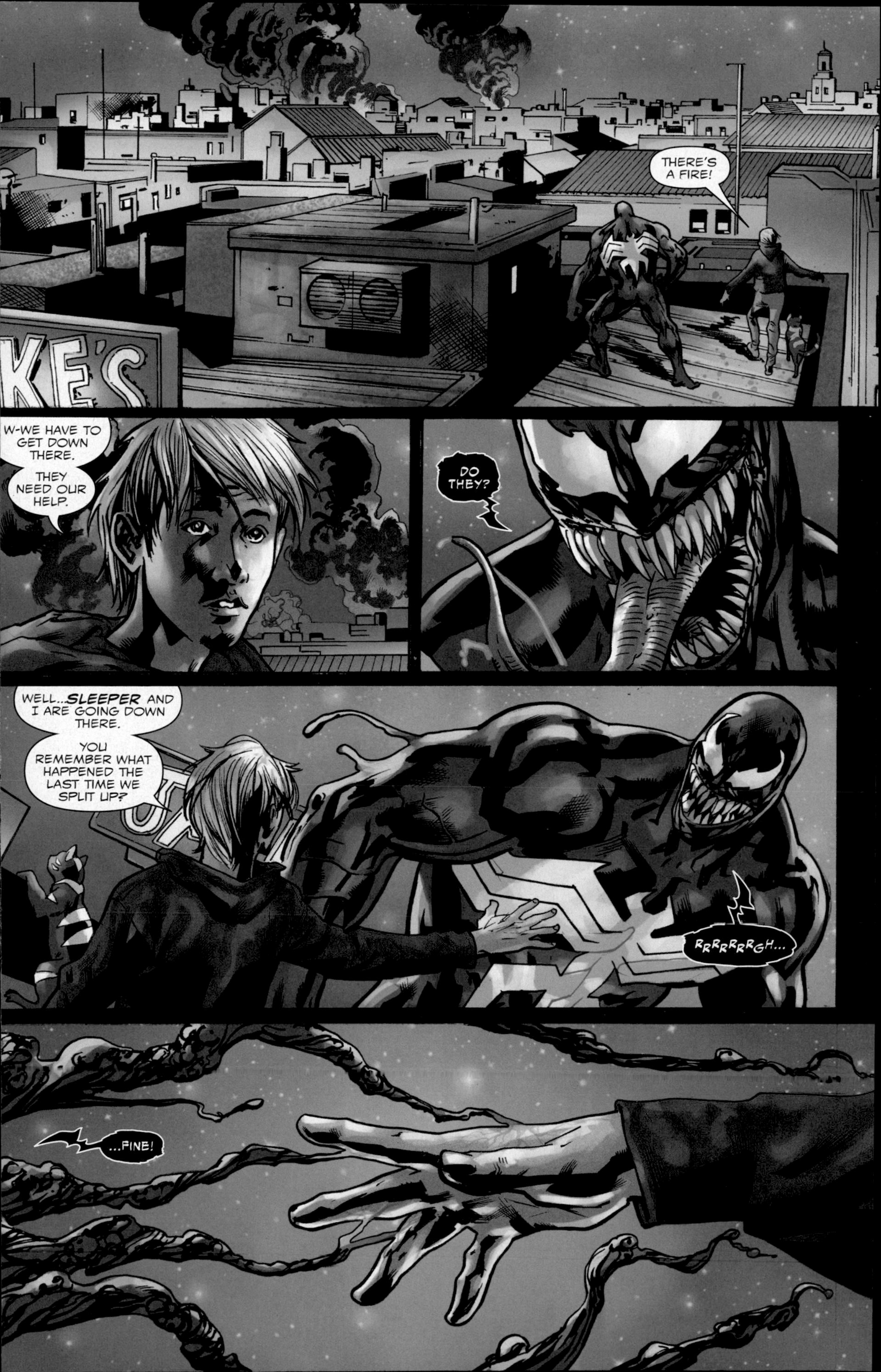
THERE'S A FIRE!
KE'S
W-WE HAVE TO GET DOWN THERE.
THEY NEED OUR HELP.
DO THEY?
WELL...SLEEPER AND I ARE GOING DOWN THERE.
YOU REMEMBER WHAT HAPPENED THE LAST TIME WE SPLIT UP?
RRRRRRGH...
...FINE!

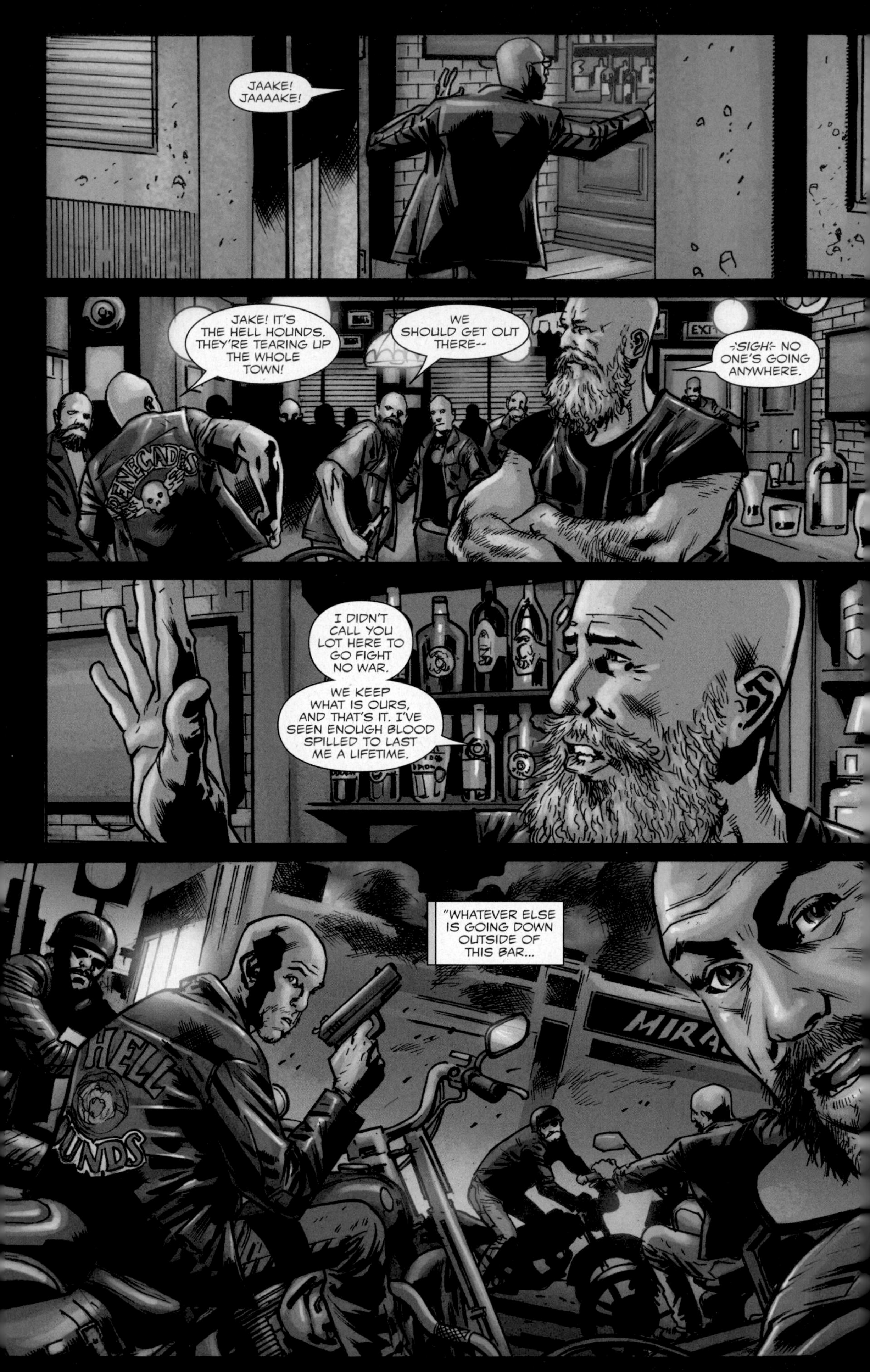
JAAKE! JAAAAKE!
JAKE! IT'S THE HELL HOUNDS. THEY'RE TEARING UP THE WHOLE TOWN!
WE SHOULD GET OUT THERE--
EXIT
RENEGADES
-SIGH- NO ONE'S GOING ANYWHERE.
I DIDN'T CALL YOU LOT HERE TO GO FIGHT NO WAR.
WE KEEP WHAT IS OURS, AND THAT'S IT. I'VE SEEN ENOUGH BLOOD SPILLED TO LAST ME A LIFETIME.
"WHATEVER ELSE IS GOING DOWN OUTSIDE OF THIS BAR...
HELL HOUNDS
MIRA

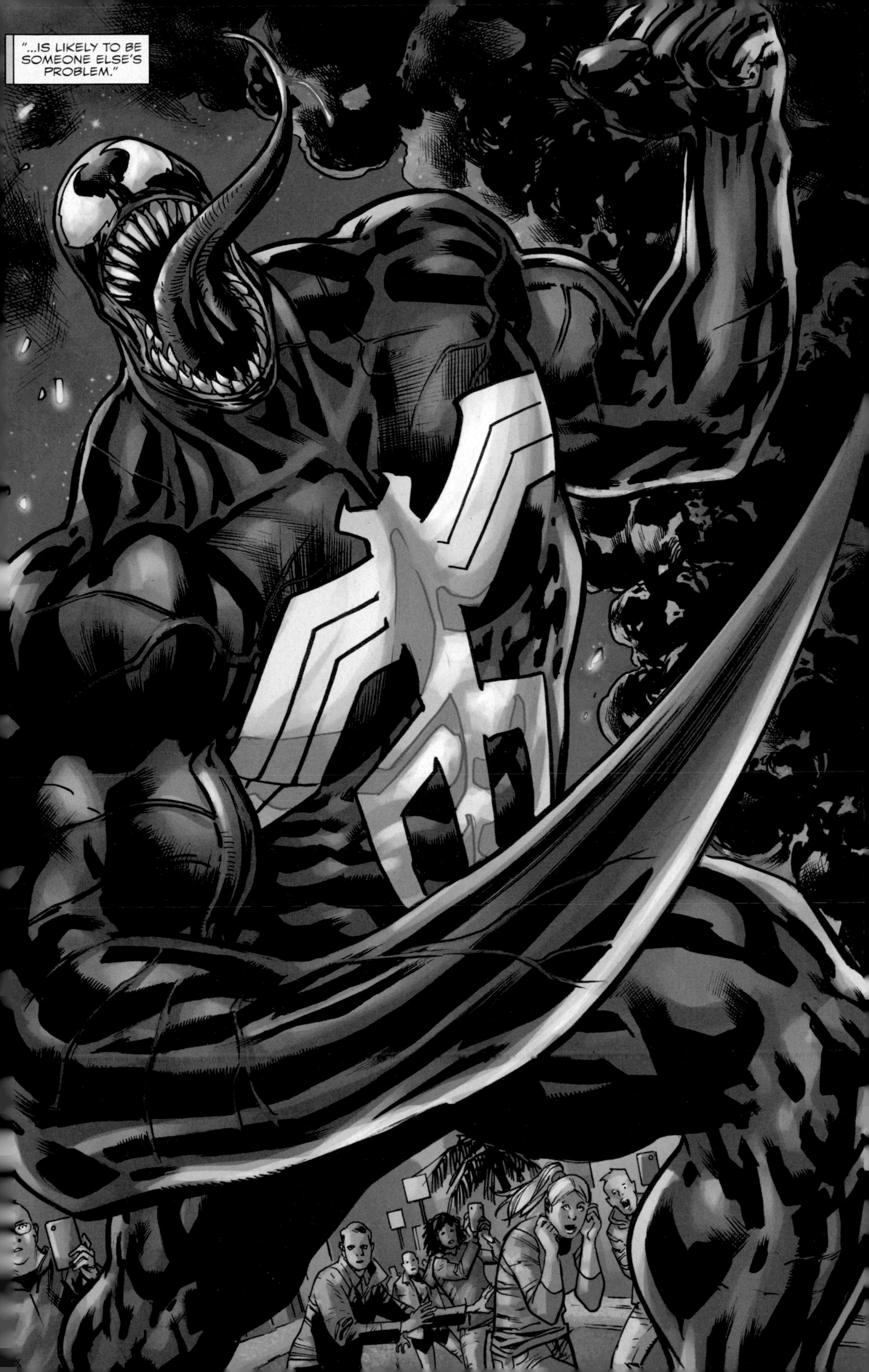
"...IS LIKELY TO BE SOMEONE ELSE'S PROBLEM."

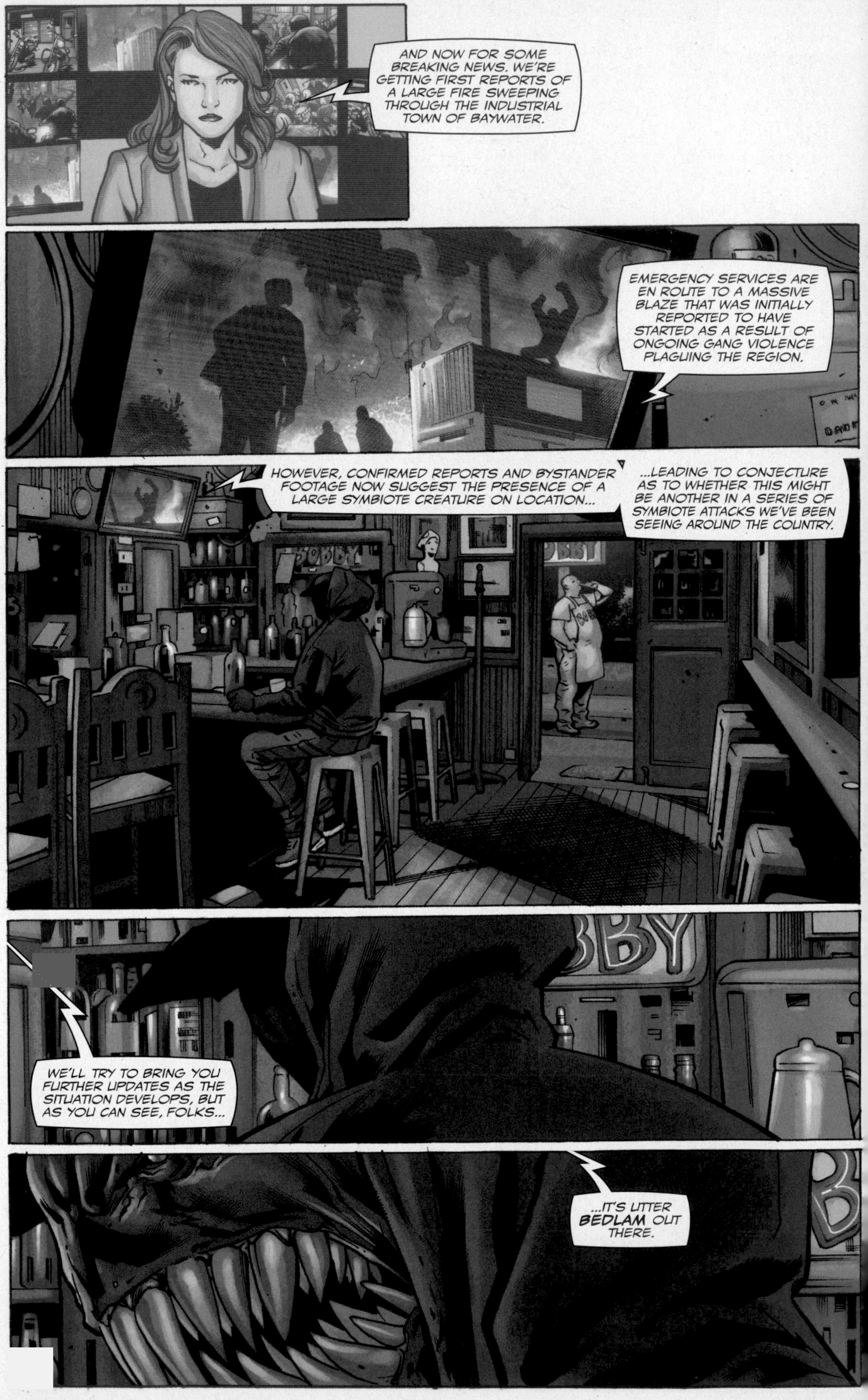
AND NOW FOR SOME BREAKING NEWS. WE'RE GETTING FIRST REPORTS OF A LARGE FIRE SWEEPING THROUGH THE INDUSTRIAL TOWN OF BAYWATER.
EMERGENCY SERVICES ARE EN ROUTE TO A MASSIVE BLAZE THAT WAS INITIALLY REPORTED TO HAVE STARTED AS A RESULT OF ONGOING GANG VIOLENCE PLAGUING THE REGION.
HOWEVER, CONFIRMED REPORTS AND BYSTANDER FOOTAGE NOW SUGGEST THE PRESENCE OF A LARGE SYMBIOTE CREATURE ON LOCATION...
...LEADING TO CONJECTURE AS TO WHETHER THIS MIGHT BE ANOTHER IN A SERIES OF SYMBIOTE ATTACKS WE'VE BEEN SEEING AROUND THE COUNTRY.
WE'LL TRY TO BRING YOU FURTHER UPDATES AS THE SITUATION DEVELOPS, BUT AS YOU CAN SEE, FOLKS...
...IT'S UTTER **BEDLAM** OUT THERE.

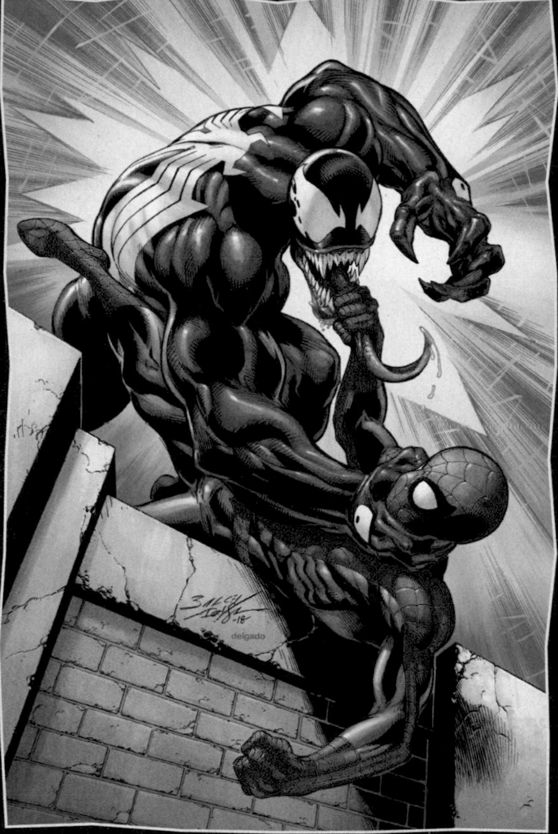

#6 variant by
MARK BAGLEY, JOHN DELL & EDGAR DELGADO

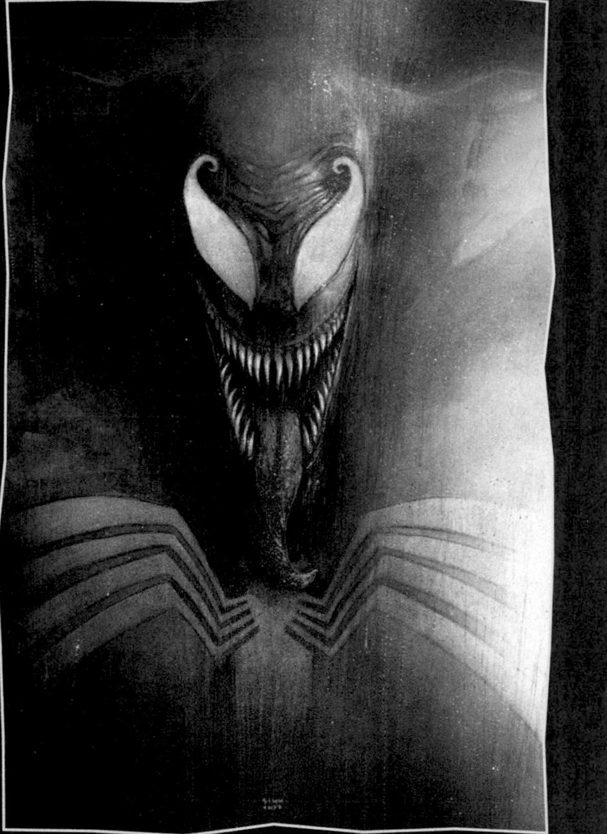

#6 variant by
MARTIN SIMMONDS

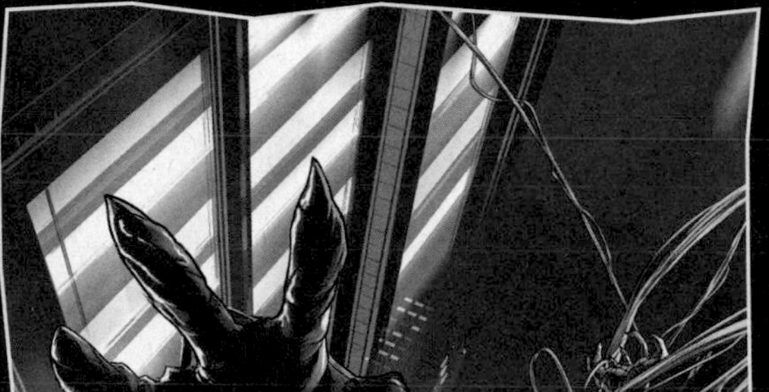

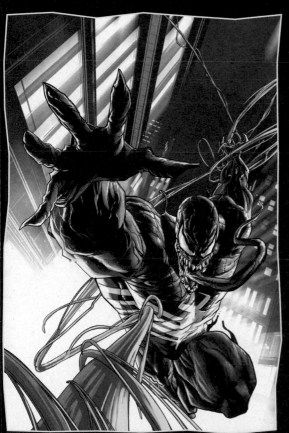

#7 Spider-Man 60th Anniversary variant by
PETE WOODS

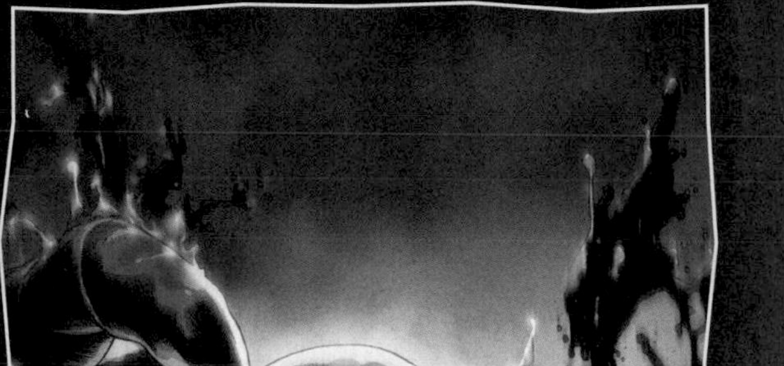

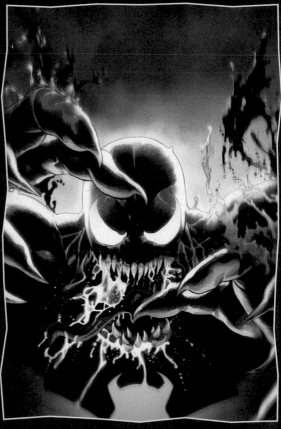

#7 variant by
CARLOS MAGNO & ROMULO FAJARDO JR.

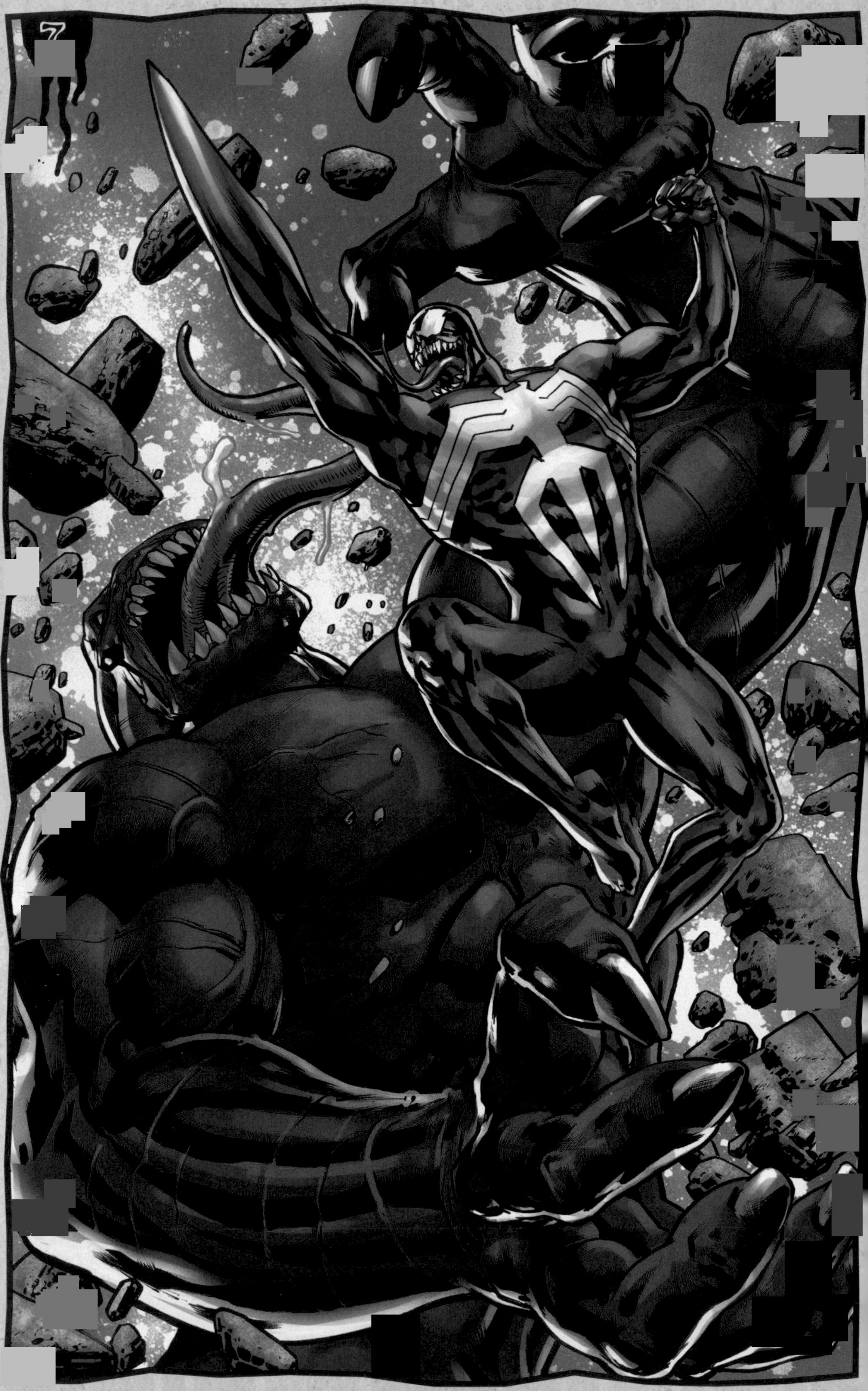

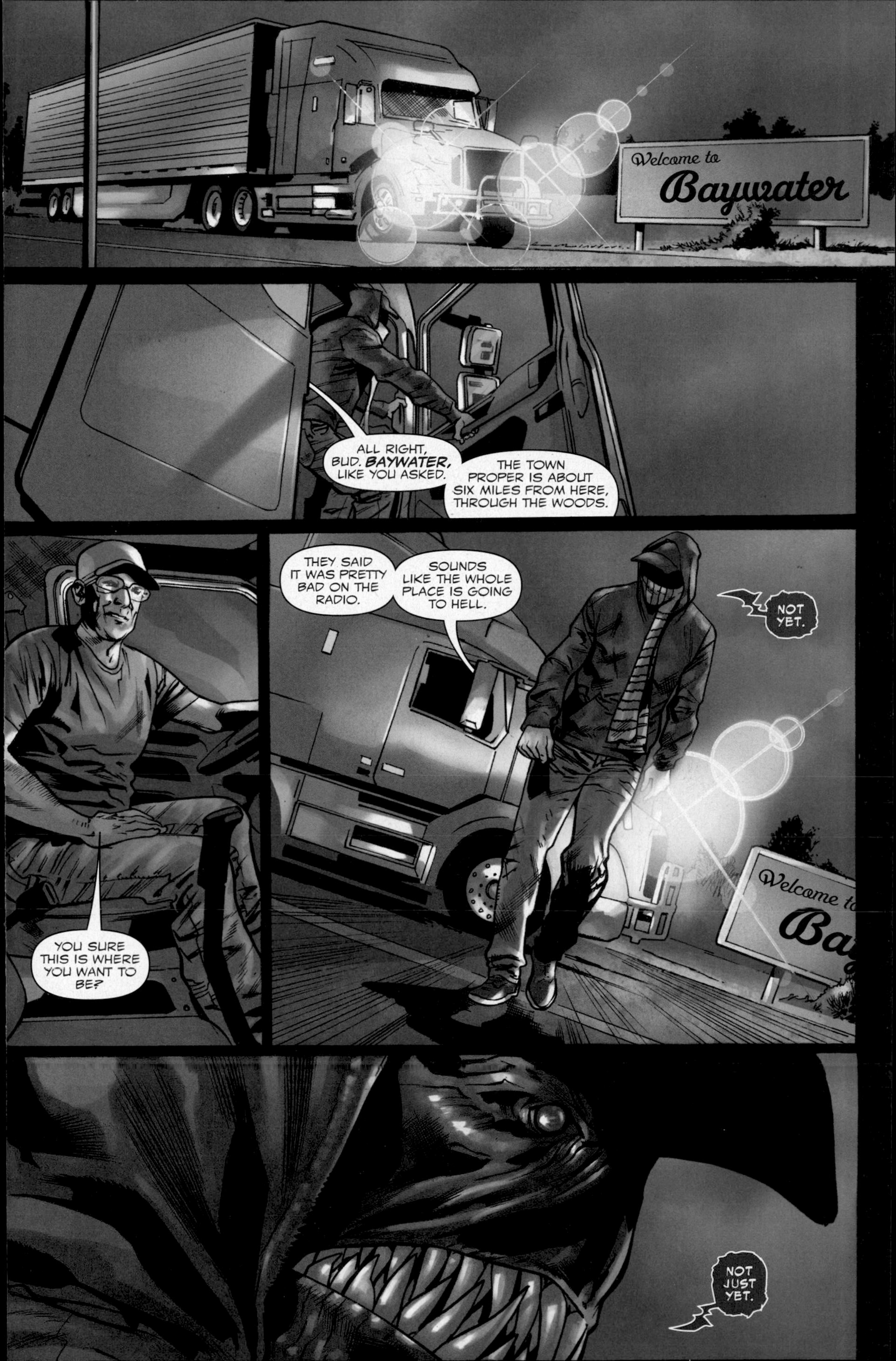
Welcome to
Baywater
ALL RIGHT, BUD. BAYWATER, LIKE YOU ASKED.
THE TOWN PROPER IS ABOUT SIX MILES FROM HERE, THROUGH THE WOODS.
YOU SURE THIS IS WHERE YOU WANT TO BE?
THEY SAID IT WAS PRETTY BAD ON THE RADIO.
SOUNDS LIKE THE WHOLE PLACE IS GOING TO HELL.
NOT YET.
NOT JUST YET.

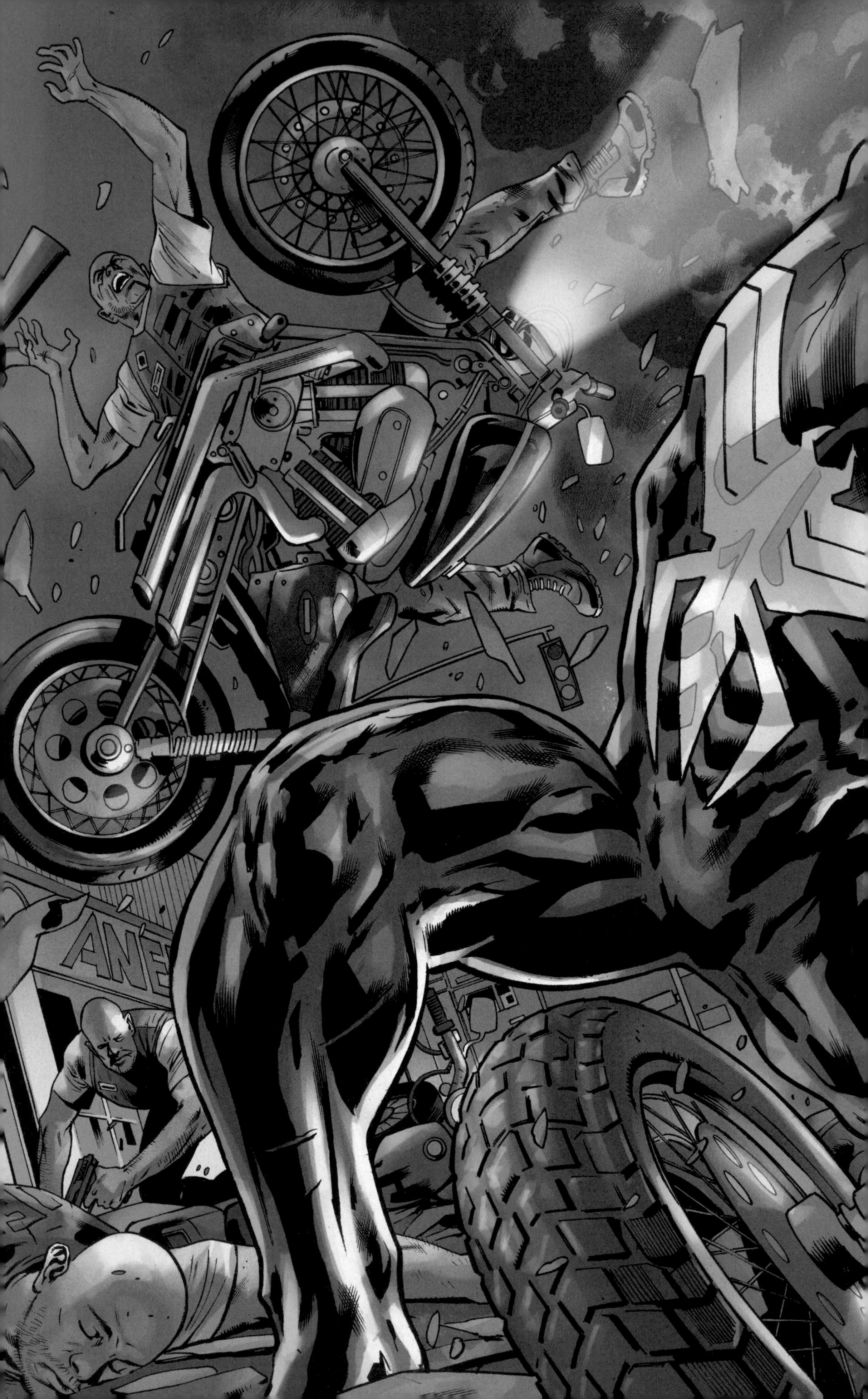

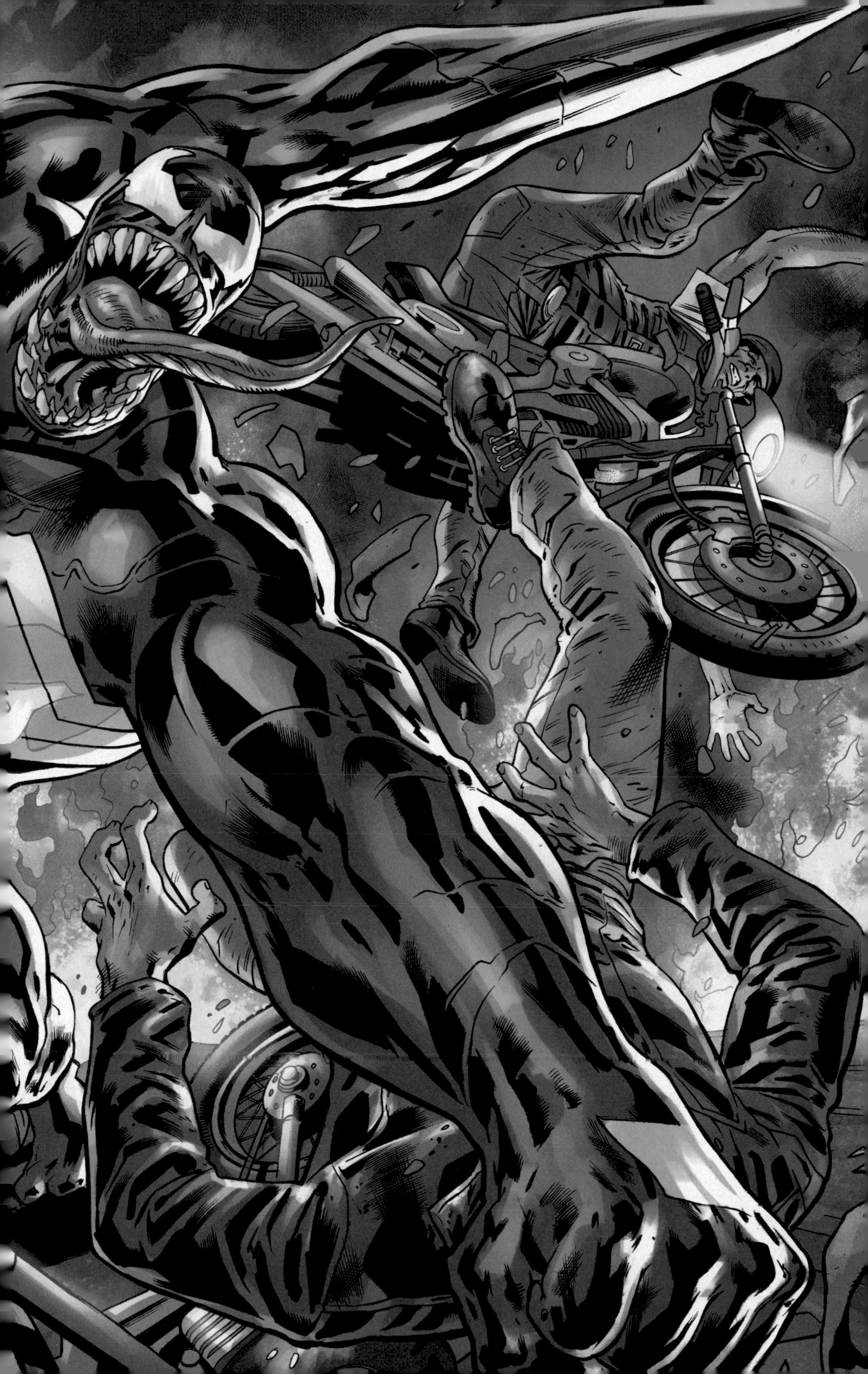

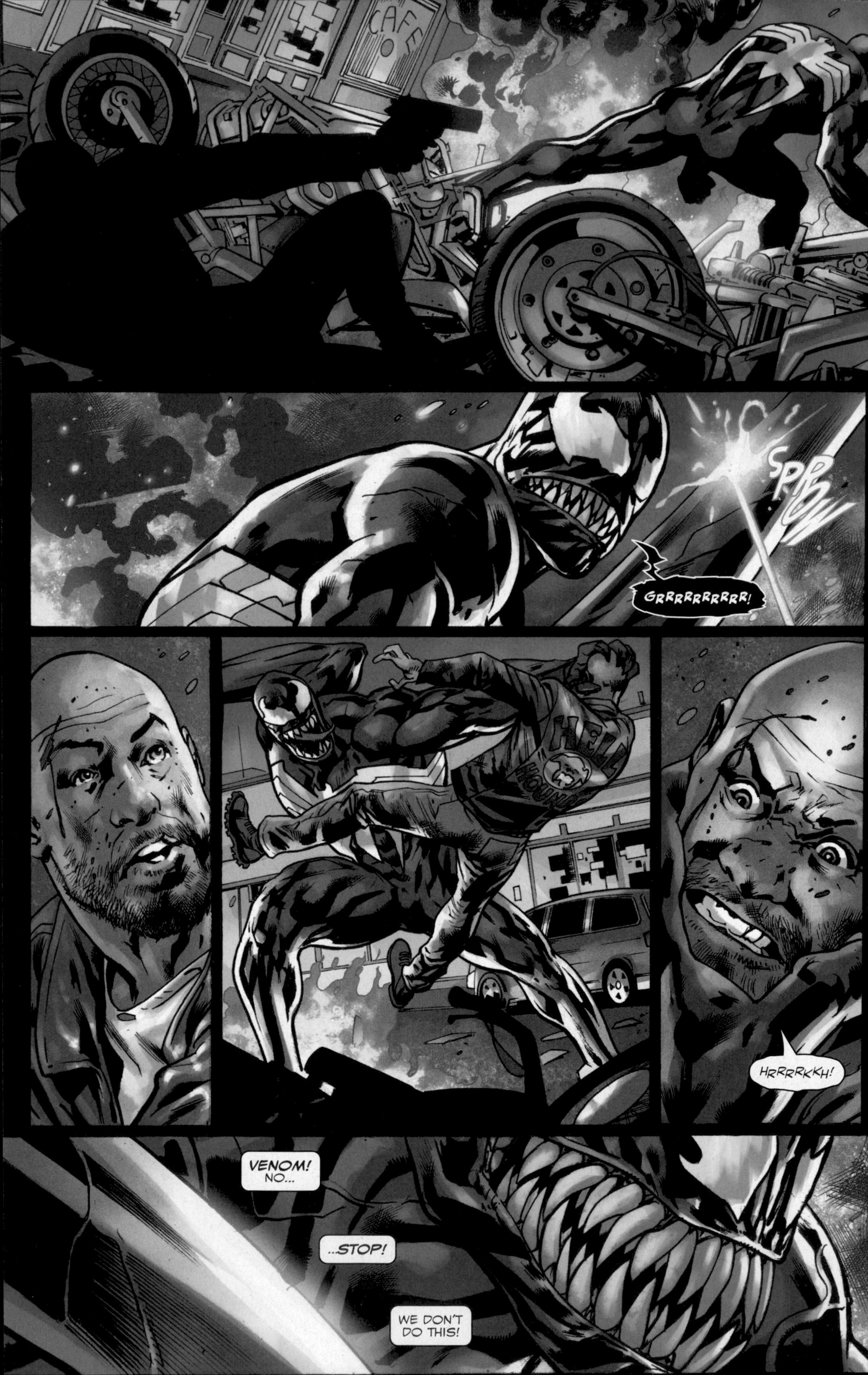
CAFE
SPROW
GRRRRRRRRRR!
HELL HOUNDS
HRRRRKKH!
VENOM! NO...
...STOP!
WE DON'T DO THIS!

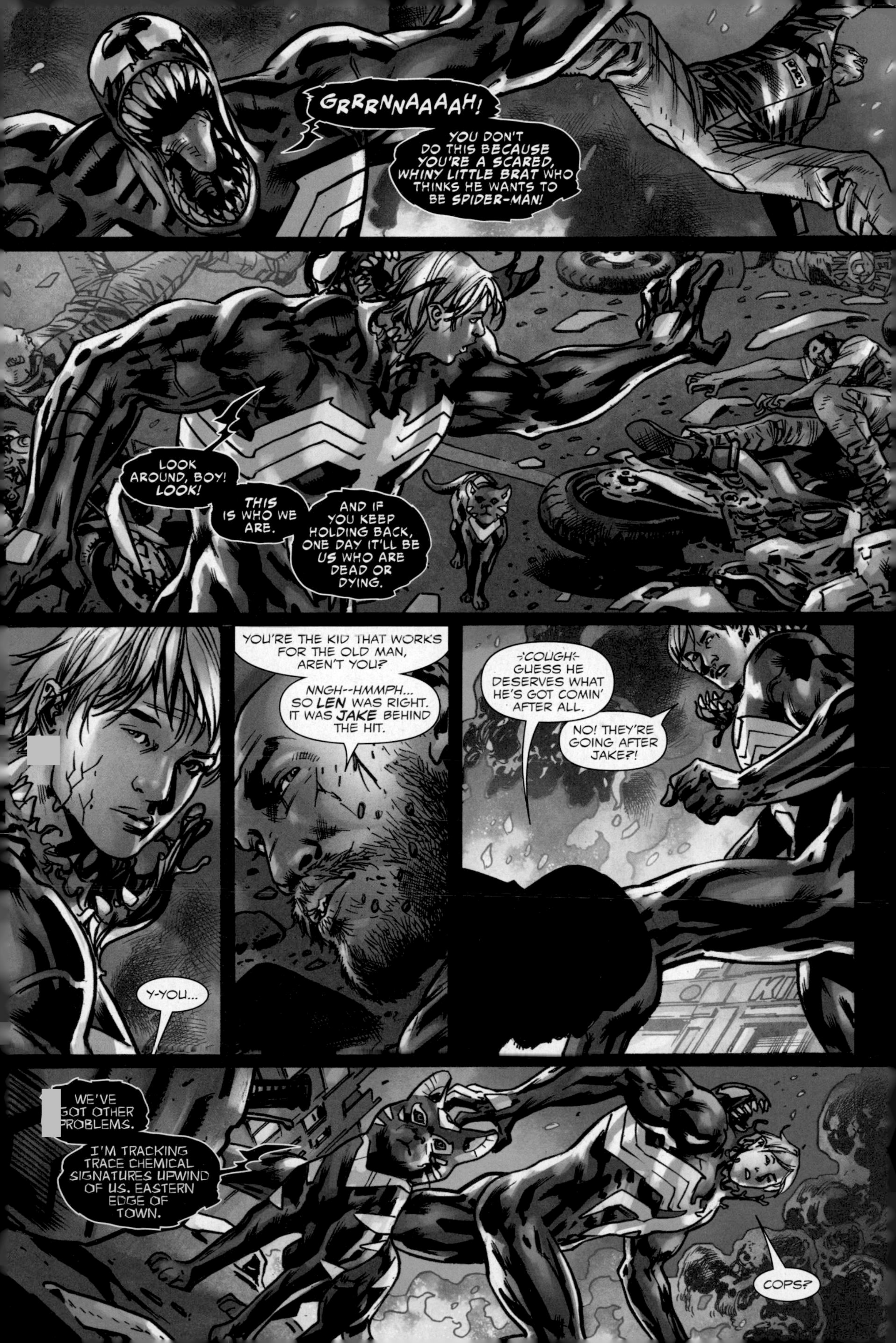
GRRRNNAAAAH!
YOU DON'T DO THIS BECAUSE YOU'RE A SCARED, WHINY LITTLE BRAT WHO THINKS HE WANTS TO BE SPIDER-MAN!
LOOK AROUND, BOY! LOOK!
THIS IS WHO WE ARE.
AND IF YOU KEEP HOLDING BACK, ONE DAY IT'LL BE US WHO ARE DEAD OR DYING.
Y-YOU...
YOU'RE THE KID THAT WORKS FOR THE OLD MAN, AREN'T YOU?
NNGH--HMMPH... SO LEN WAS RIGHT. IT WAS JAKE BEHIND THE HIT.
COUGH GUESS HE DESERVES WHAT HE'S GOT COMIN' AFTER ALL.
NO! THEY'RE GOING AFTER JAKE?!
WE'VE OT OTHER ROBLEMS.
I'M TRACKING TRACE CHEMICAL SIGNATURES UPWIND OF US. EASTERN EDGE OF TOWN.
COPS?

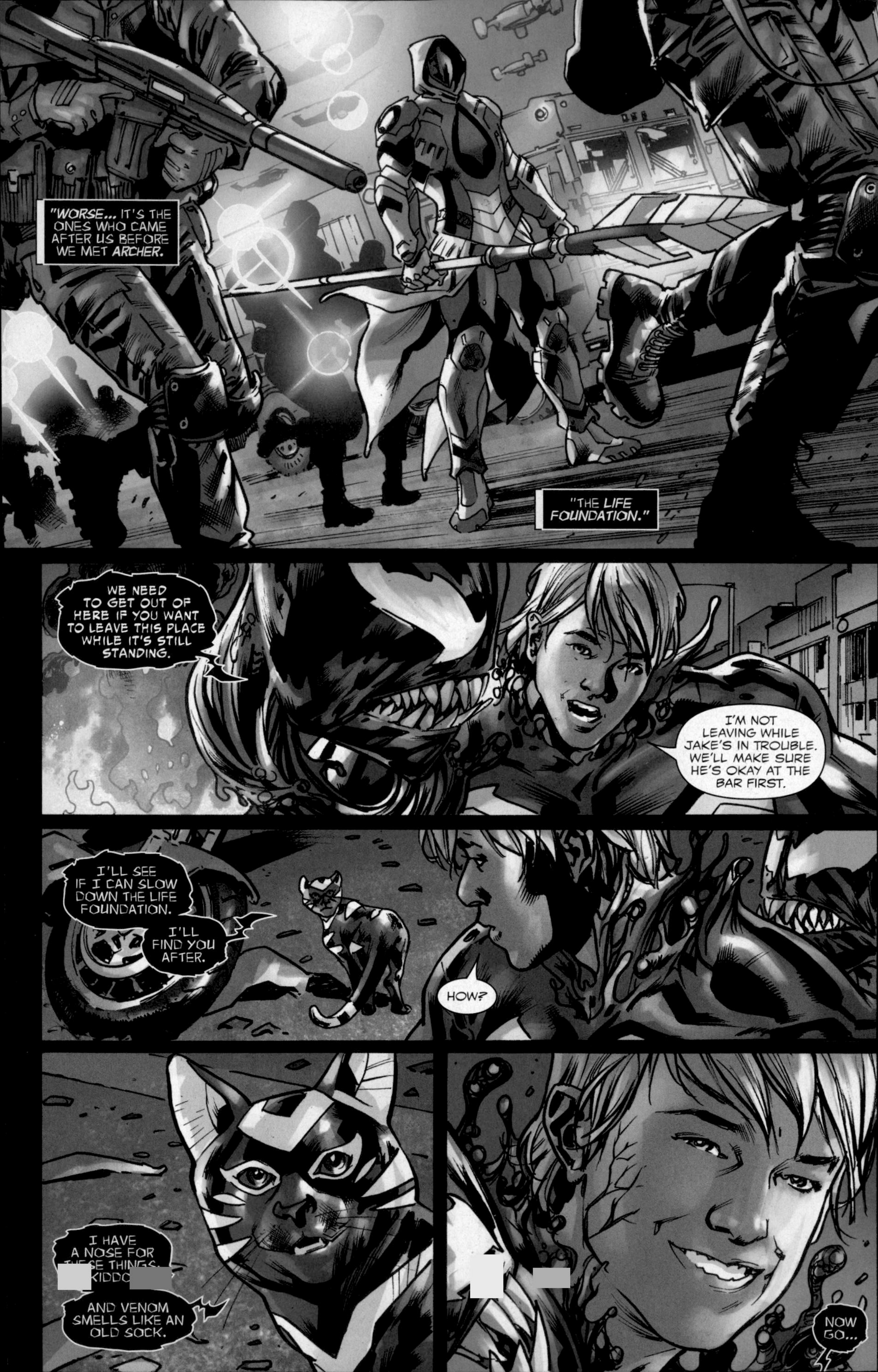
"WORSE... IT'S THE ONES WHO CAME AFTER US BEFORE WE MET ARCHER.
"THE LIFE FOUNDATION."
WE NEED TO GET OUT OF HERE IF YOU WANT TO LEAVE THIS PLACE WHILE IT'S STILL STANDING.
I'M NOT LEAVING WHILE JAKE'S IN TROUBLE. WE'LL MAKE SURE HE'S OKAY AT THE BAR FIRST.
I'LL SEE IF I CAN SLOW DOWN THE LIFE FOUNDATION.
I'LL FIND YOU AFTER.
HOW?
I HAVE A NOSE FOR THESE THINGS, KIDDO.
AND VENOM SMELLS LIKE AN OLD SOCK.
NOW GO...

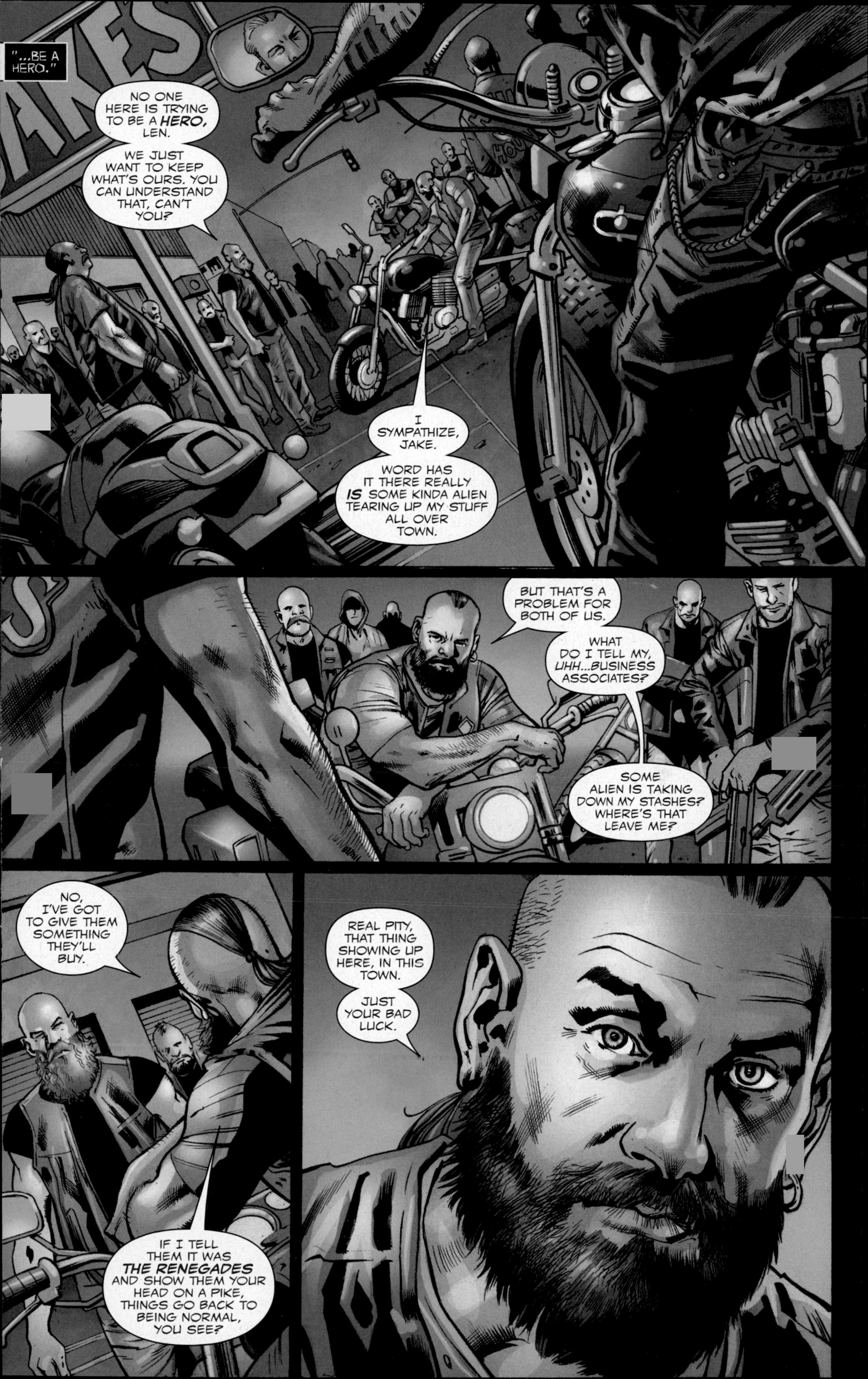
"...BE A HERO."
NO ONE HERE IS TRYING TO BE A HERO, LEN.
WE JUST WANT TO KEEP WHAT'S OURS. YOU CAN UNDERSTAND THAT, CAN'T YOU?
I SYMPATHIZE, JAKE.
WORD HAS IT THERE REALLY IS SOME KINDA ALIEN TEARING UP MY STUFF ALL OVER TOWN.
BUT THAT'S A PROBLEM FOR BOTH OF US.
WHAT DO I TELL MY, UHH...BUSINESS ASSOCIATES?
SOME ALIEN IS TAKING DOWN MY STASHES? WHERE'S THAT LEAVE ME?
NO, I'VE GOT TO GIVE THEM SOMETHING THEY'LL BUY.
IF I TELL THEM IT WAS THE RENEGADES AND SHOW THEM YOUR HEAD ON A PIKE, THINGS GO BACK TO BEING NORMAL, YOU SEE?
REAL PITY, THAT THING SHOWING UP HERE, IN THIS TOWN.
JUST YOUR BAD LUCK.

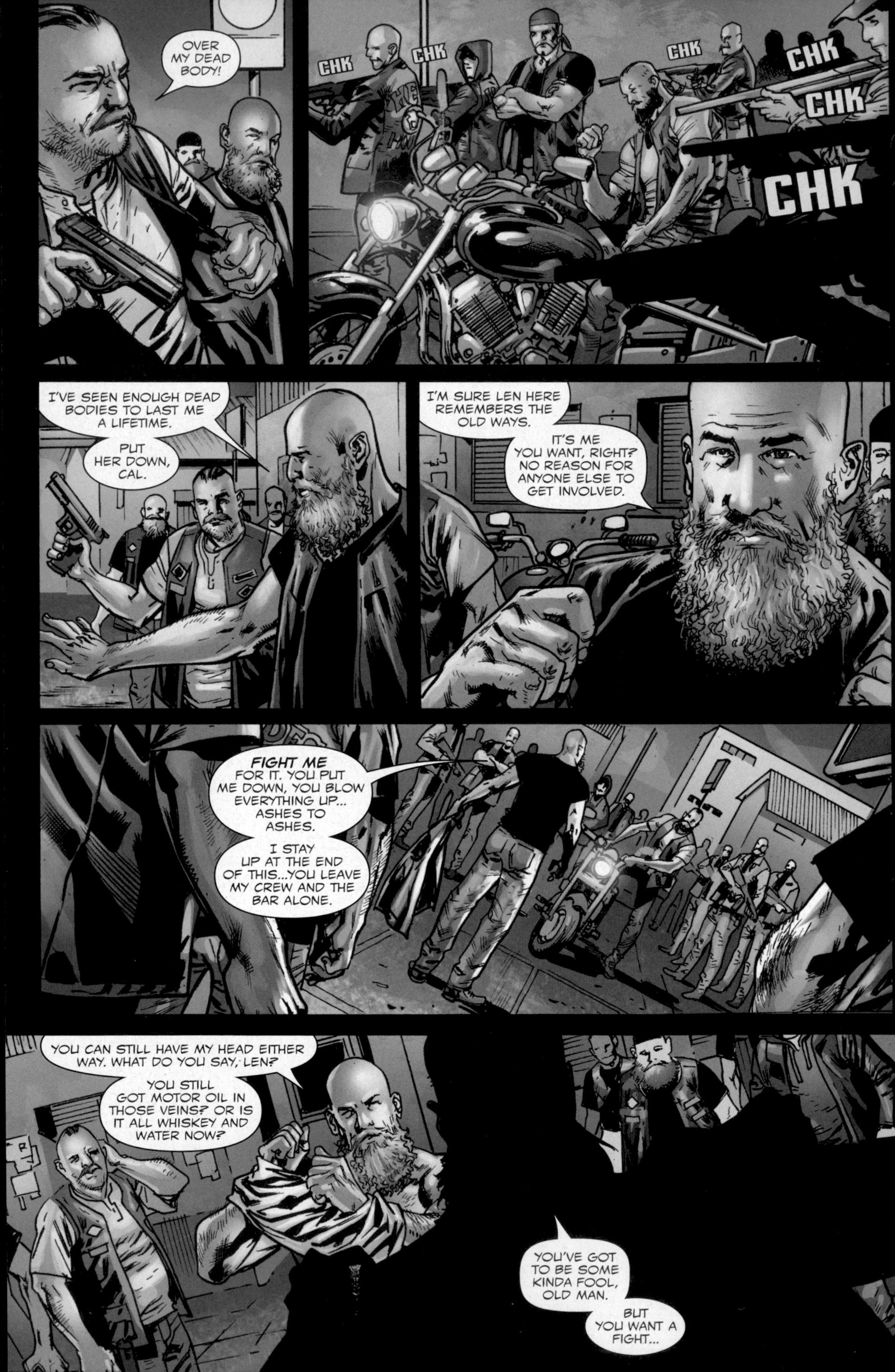
OVER MY DEAD BODY!
CHK
CHK
CHK
CHK
CHK
CHK
I'VE SEEN ENOUGH DEAD BODIES TO LAST ME A LIFETIME.
PUT HER DOWN, CAL.
I'M SURE LEN HERE REMEMBERS THE OLD WAYS.
IT'S ME YOU WANT, RIGHT? NO REASON FOR ANYONE ELSE TO GET INVOLVED.
FIGHT ME FOR IT. YOU PUT ME DOWN, YOU BLOW EVERYTHING UP... ASHES TO ASHES.
I STAY UP AT THE END OF THIS...YOU LEAVE MY CREW AND THE BAR ALONE.
YOU CAN STILL HAVE MY HEAD EITHER WAY. WHAT DO YOU SAY, LEN?
YOU STILL GOT MOTOR OIL IN THOSE VEINS? OR IS IT ALL WHISKEY AND WATER NOW?
YOU'VE GOT TO BE SOME KINDA FOOL, OLD MAN.
BUT YOU WANT A FIGHT...

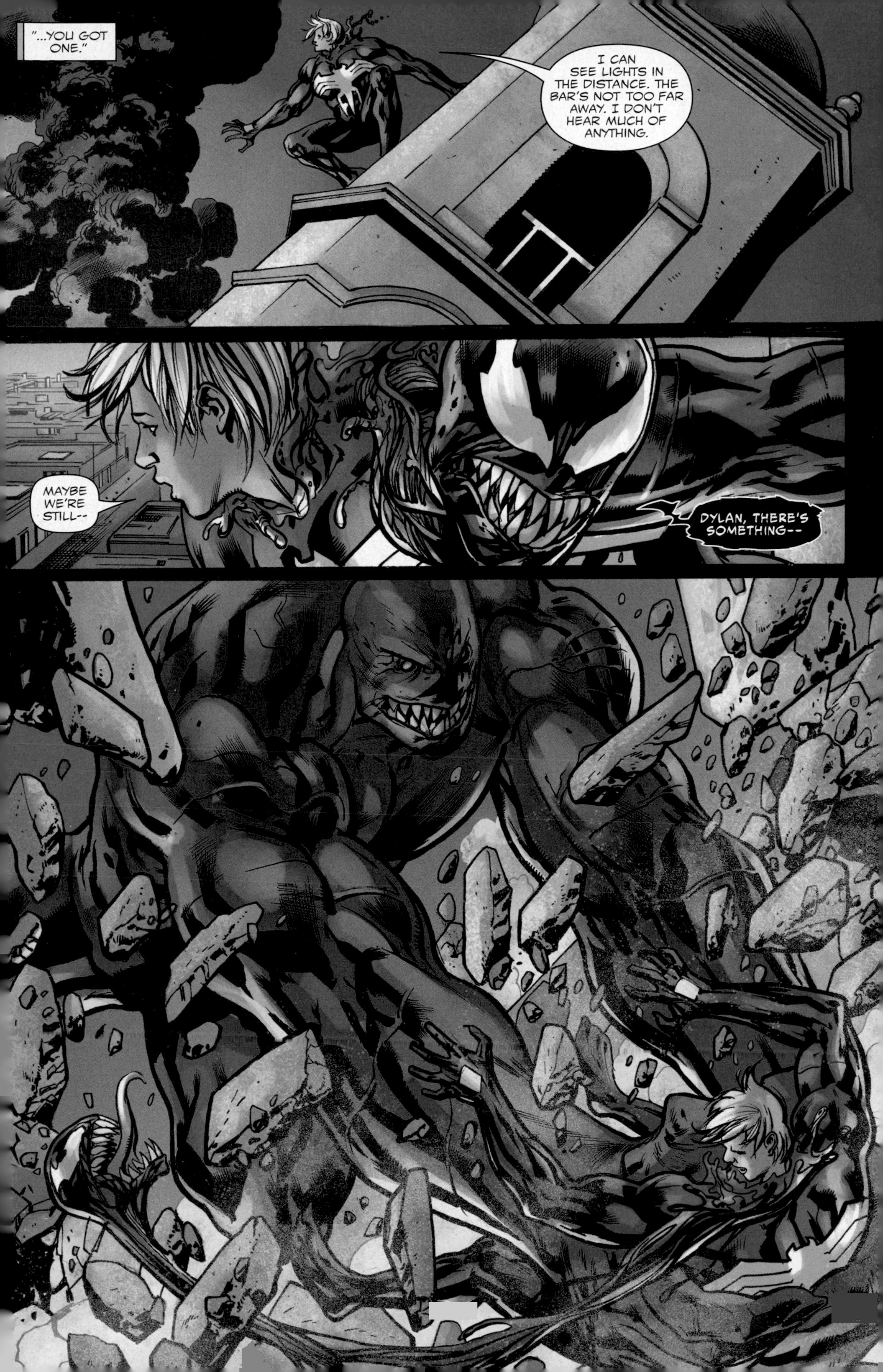
"...YOU GOT ONE."
I CAN SEE LIGHTS IN THE DISTANCE. THE BAR'S NOT TOO FAR AWAY. I DON'T HEAR MUCH OF ANYTHING.
MAYBE WE'RE STILL--
DYLAN, THERE'S SOMETHING--

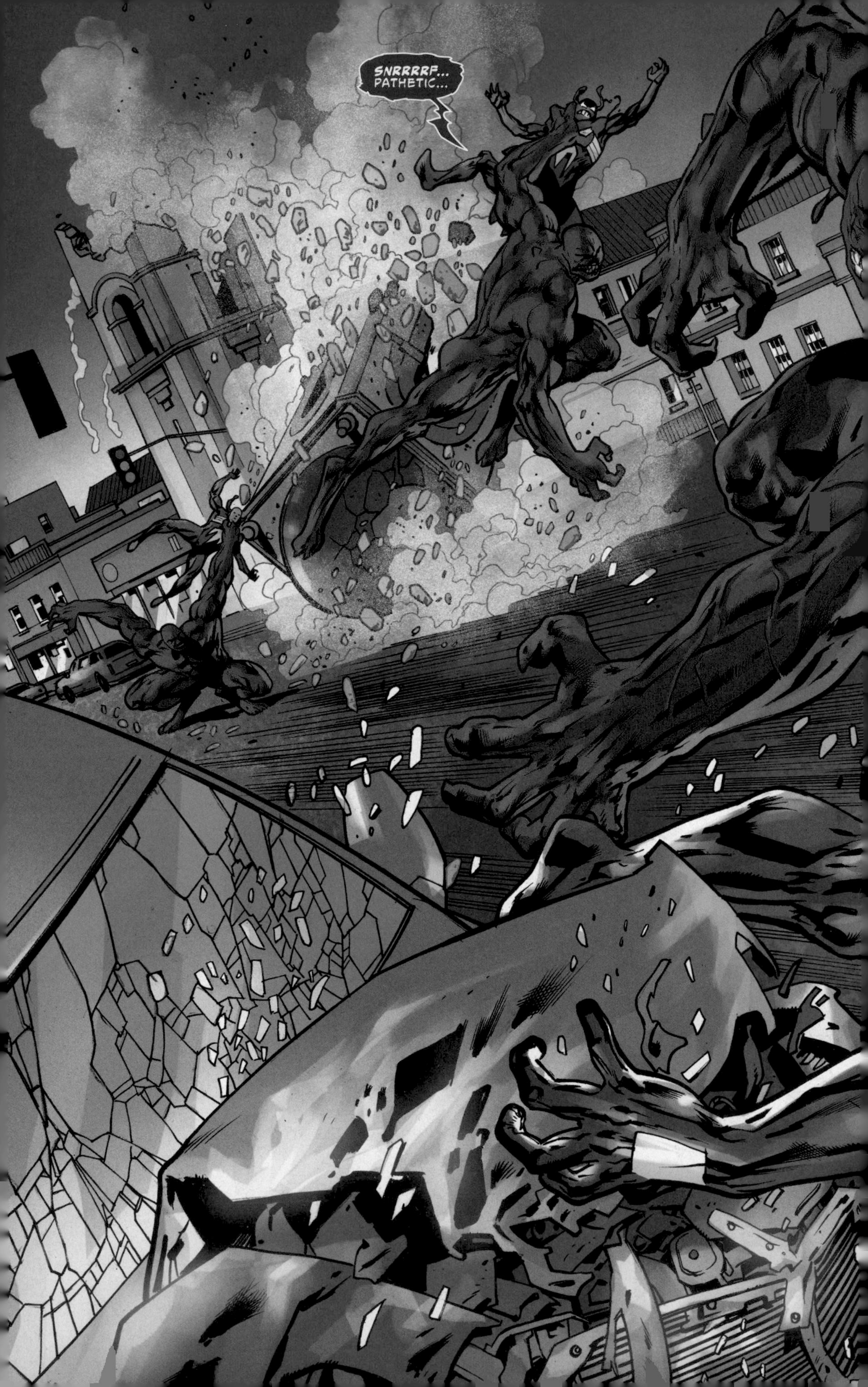
SNRRRRF... PATHETIC...

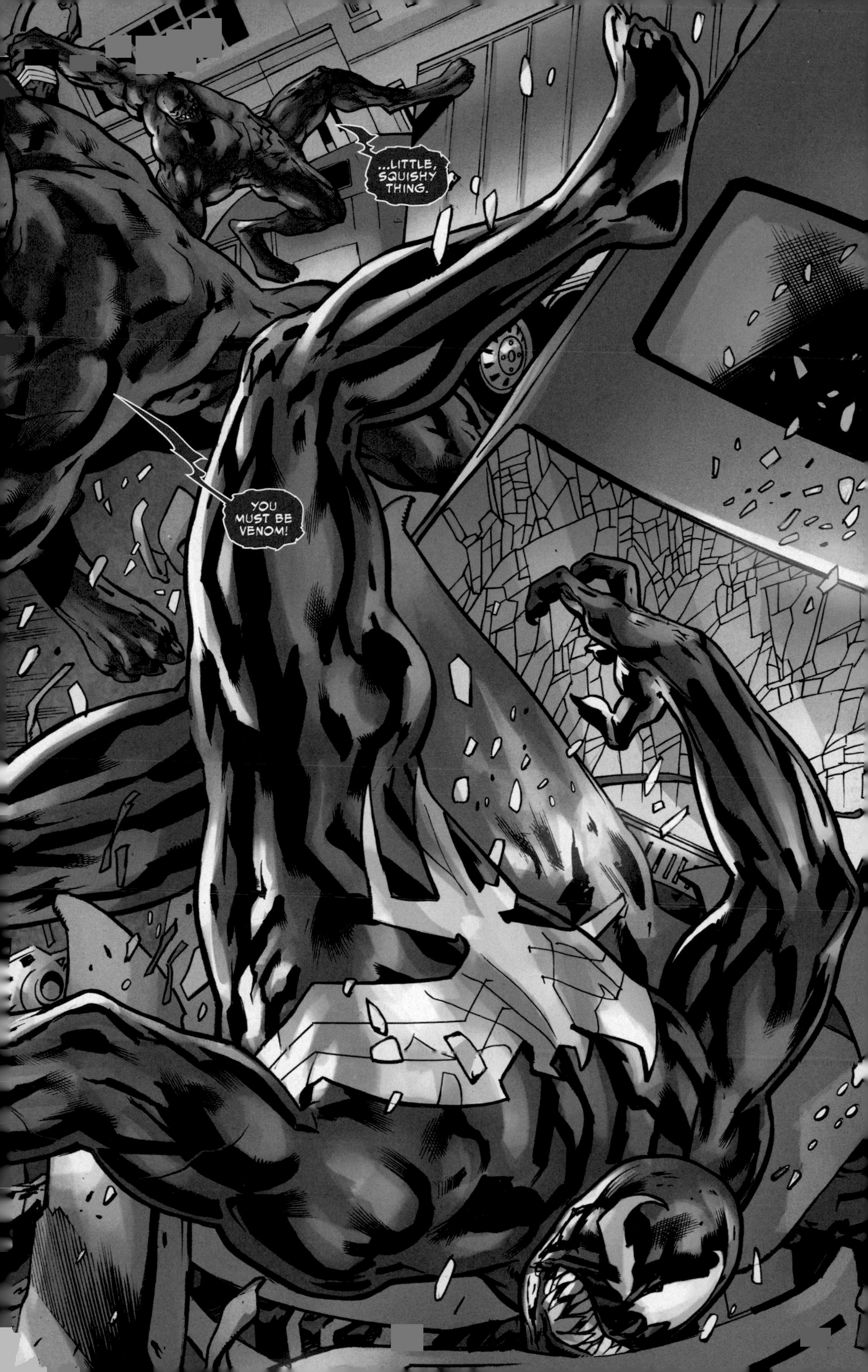
...LITTLE, SQUISHY THING.
YOU MUST BE VENOM!

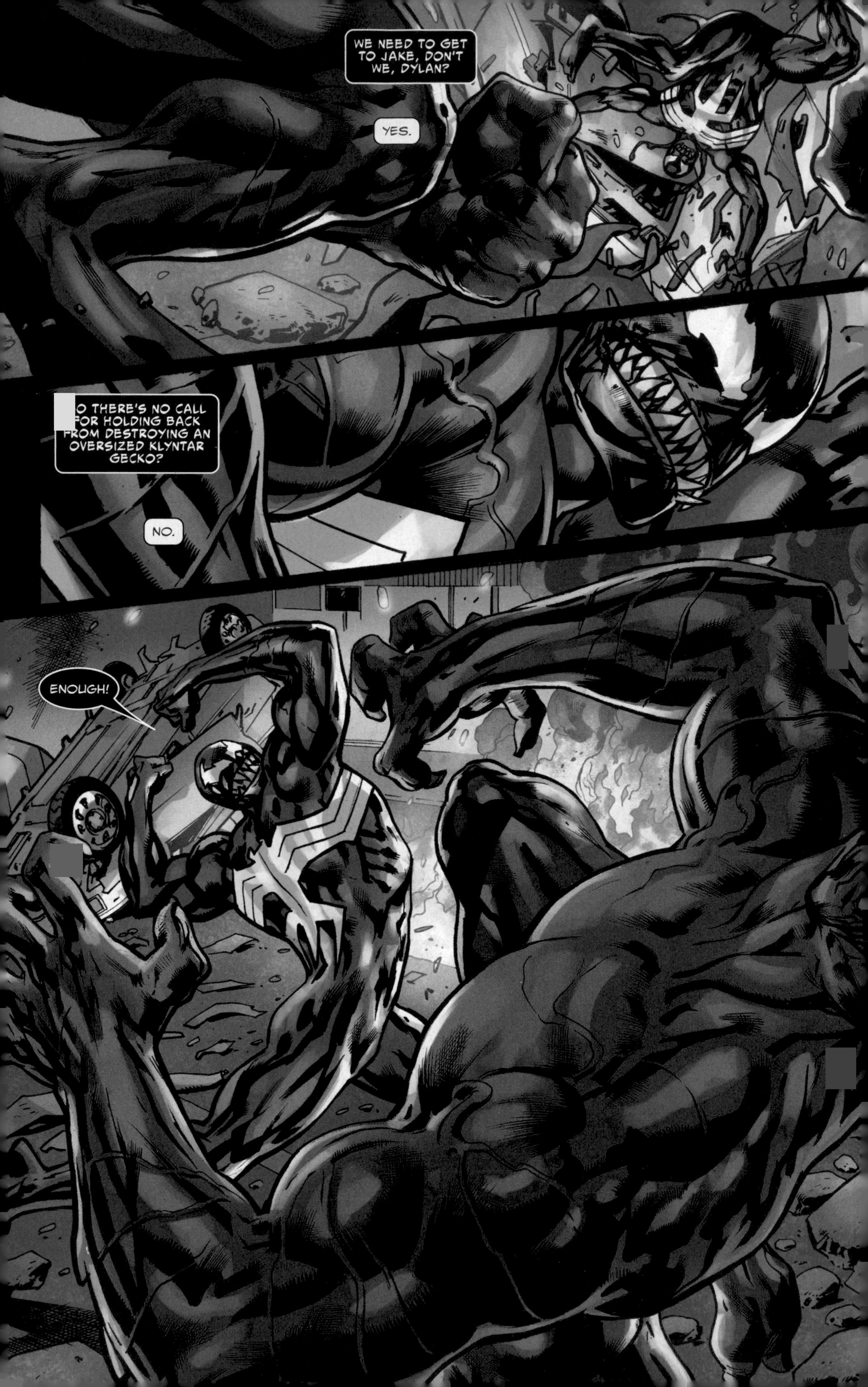
WE NEED TO GET TO JAKE, DON'T WE, DYLAN?
YES.
O THERE'S NO CALL FOR HOLDING BACK FROM DESTROYING AN OVERSIZED KLYNTAR GECKO?
NO.
ENOUGH!

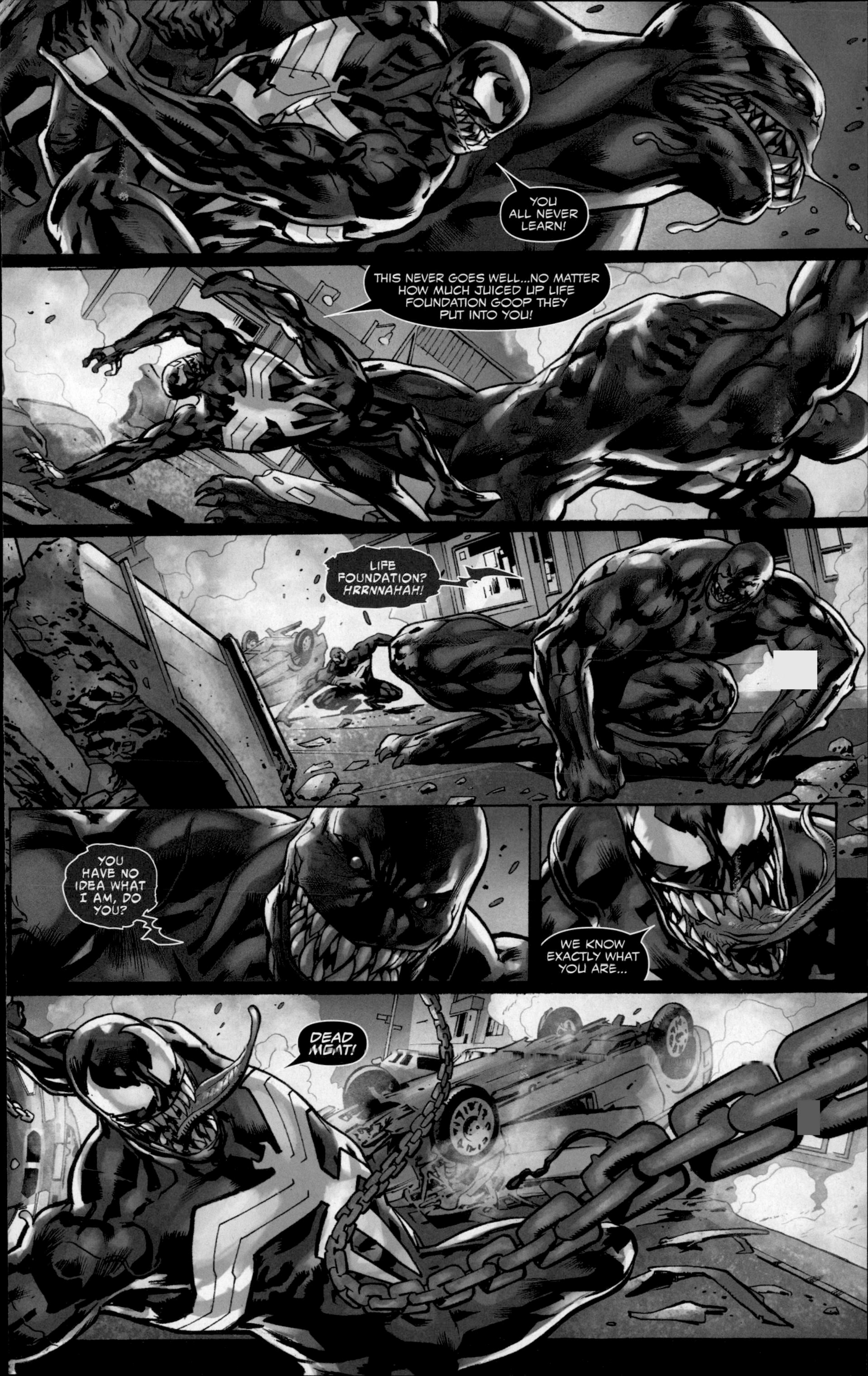
YOU ALL NEVER LEARN!
THIS NEVER GOES WELL...NO MATTER HOW MUCH JUICED UP LIFE FOUNDATION GOOP THEY PUT INTO YOU!
LIFE FOUNDATION? HRRNNAHAH!
YOU HAVE NO IDEA WHAT I AM, DO YOU?
WE KNOW EXACTLY WHAT YOU ARE...
DEAD MEAT!

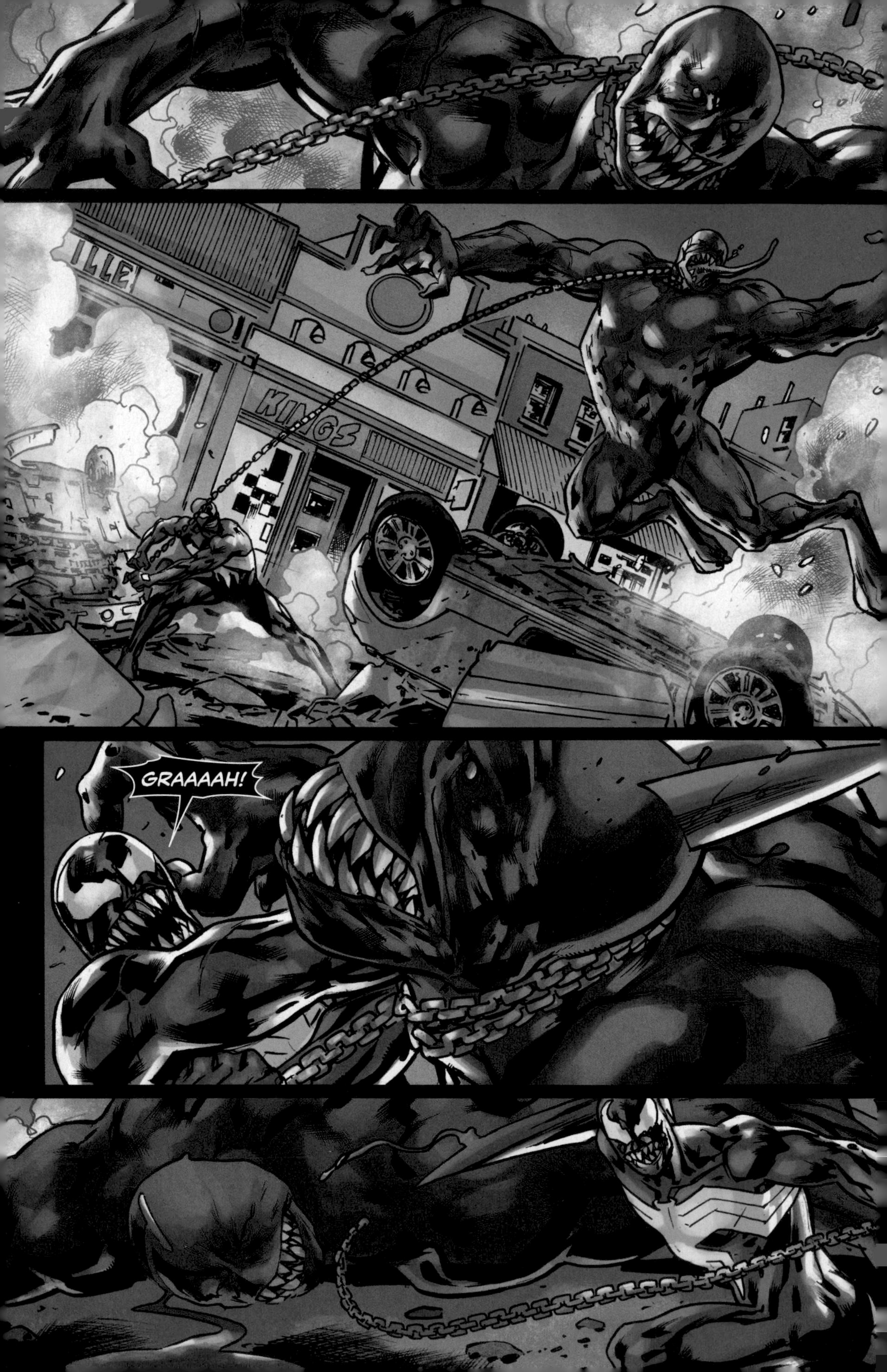
KINGS
GRAAAAH!

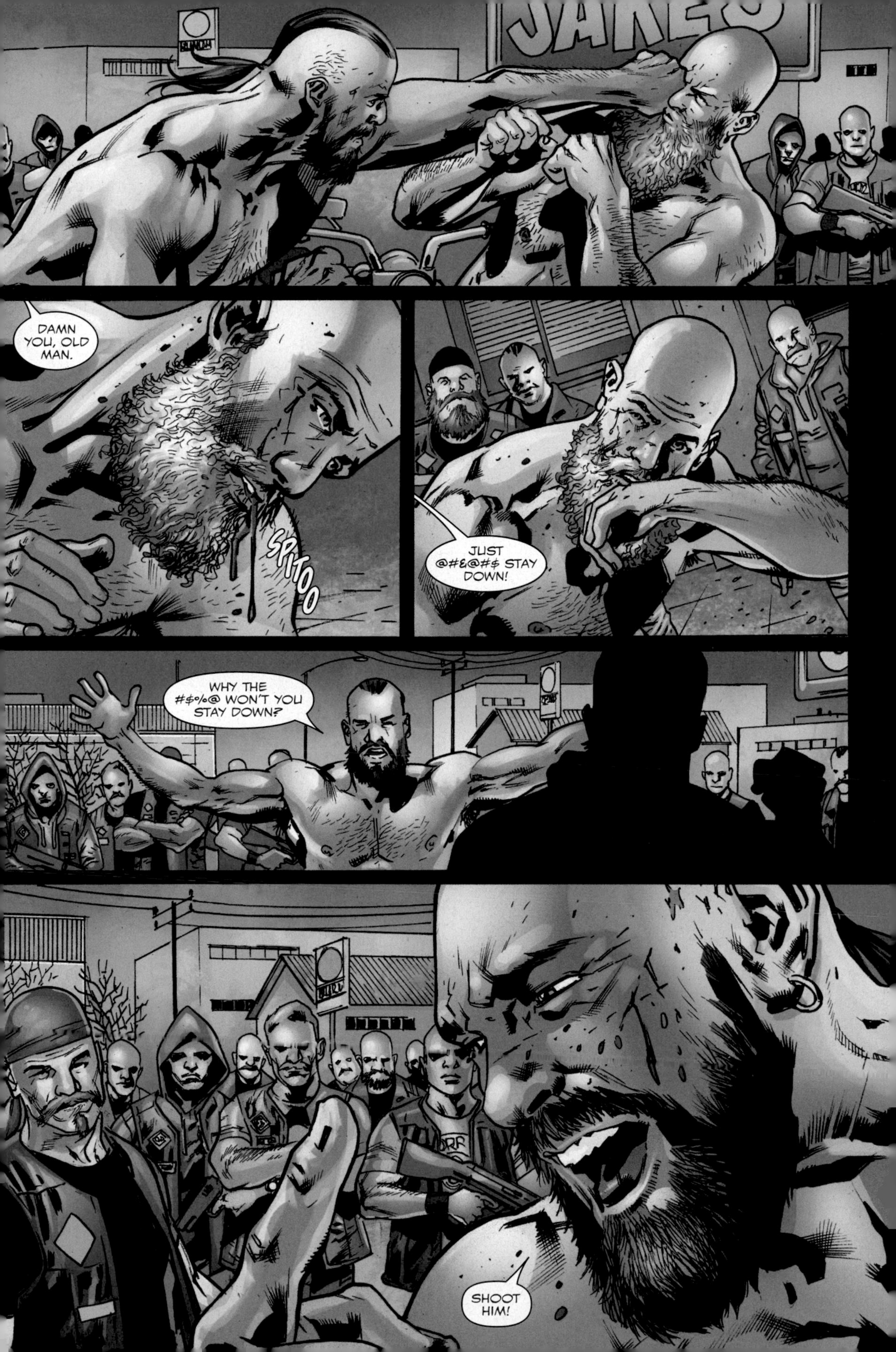
DAMN YOU, OLD MAN.
SPITOO
JUST @#&@#$ STAY DOWN!
WHY THE #$%@ WON'T YOU STAY DOWN?
SHOOT HIM!

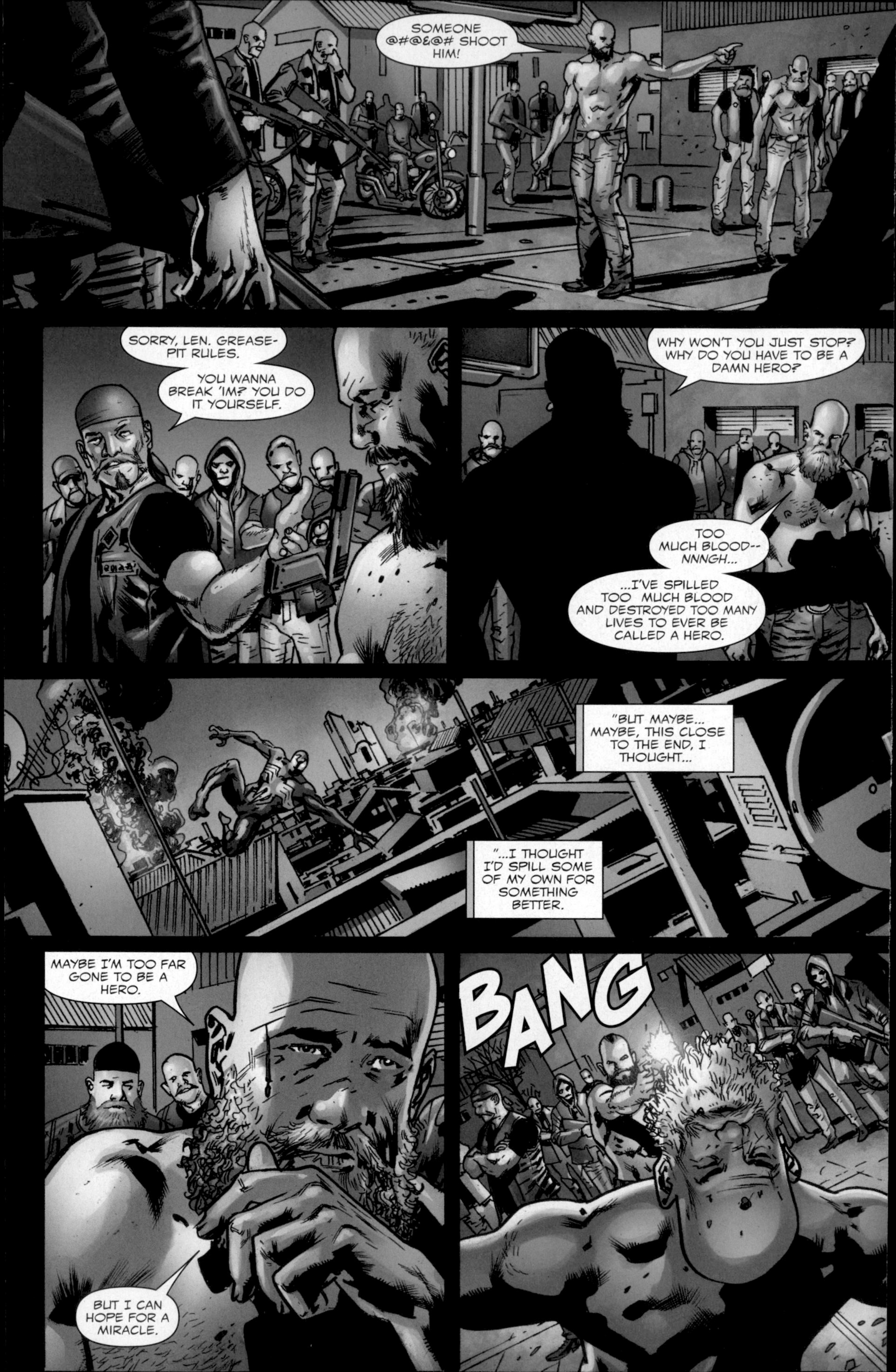
SOMEONE @#@&@# SHOOT HIM!
SORRY, LEN. GREASE-PIT RULES.
YOU WANNA BREAK 'IM? YOU DO IT YOURSELF.
WHY WON'T YOU JUST STOP? WHY DO YOU HAVE TO BE A DAMN HERO?
TOO MUCH BLOOD--NNNGH...
...I'VE SPILLED TOO MUCH BLOOD AND DESTROYED TOO MANY LIVES TO EVER BE CALLED A HERO.
"BUT MAYBE... MAYBE, THIS CLOSE TO THE END, I THOUGHT...
"...I THOUGHT I'D SPILL SOME OF MY OWN FOR SOMETHING BETTER.
MAYBE I'M TOO FAR GONE TO BE A HERO.
BUT I CAN HOPE FOR A MIRACLE.
BANG

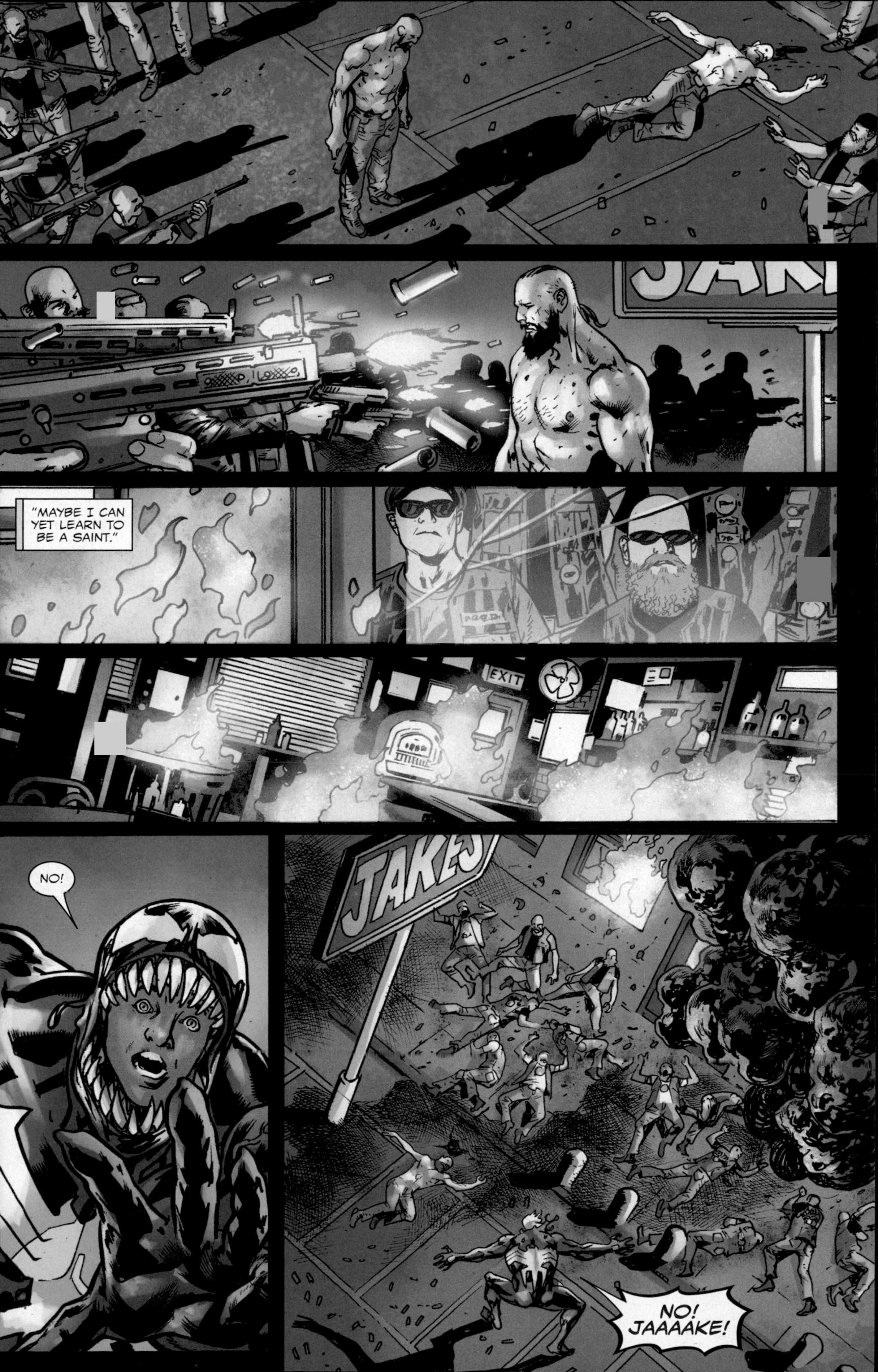
SAI
"MAYBE I CAN YET LEARN TO BE A SAINT."
EXIT
NO!
JAKES
NO! JAAAAKE!

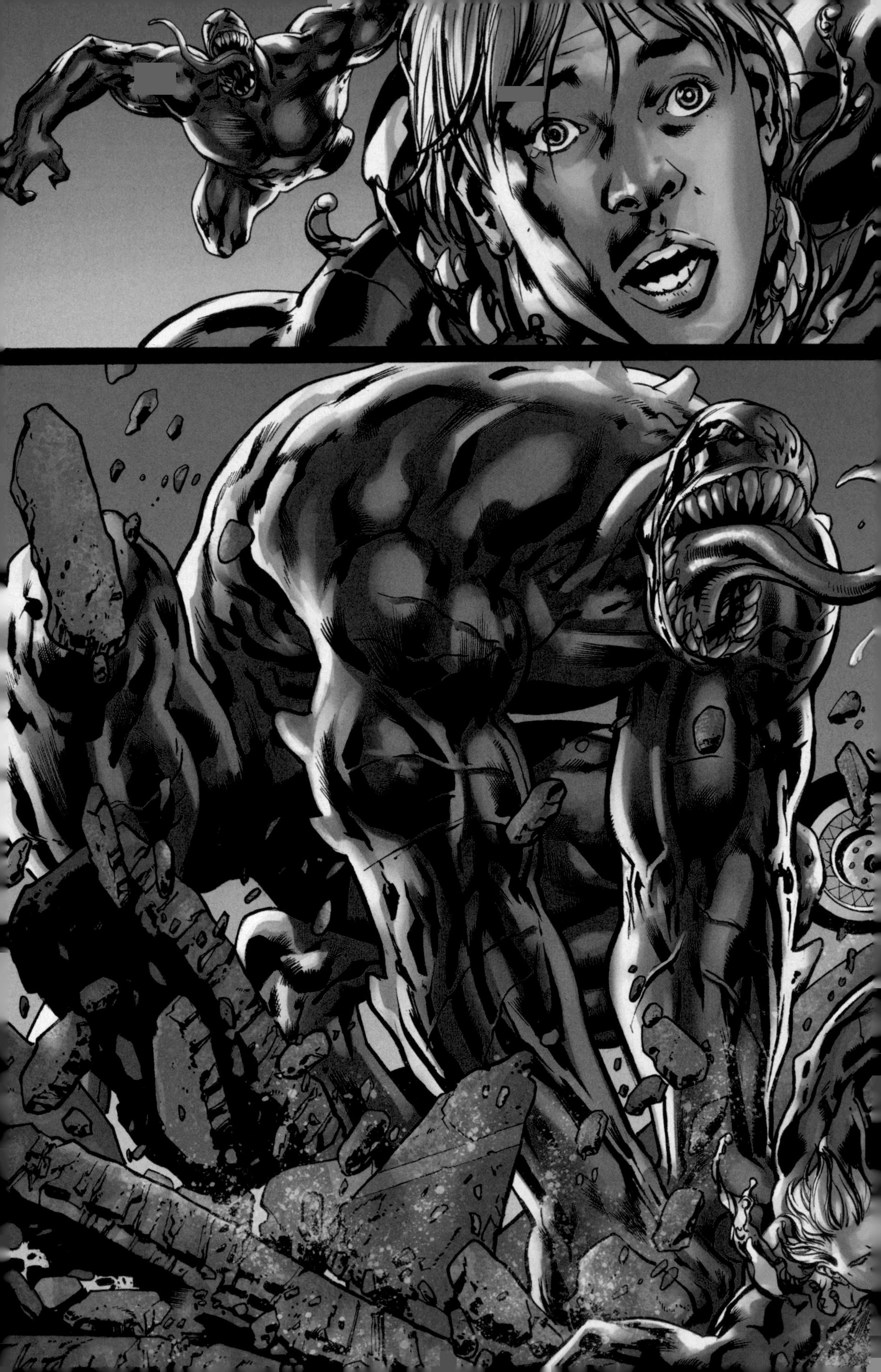

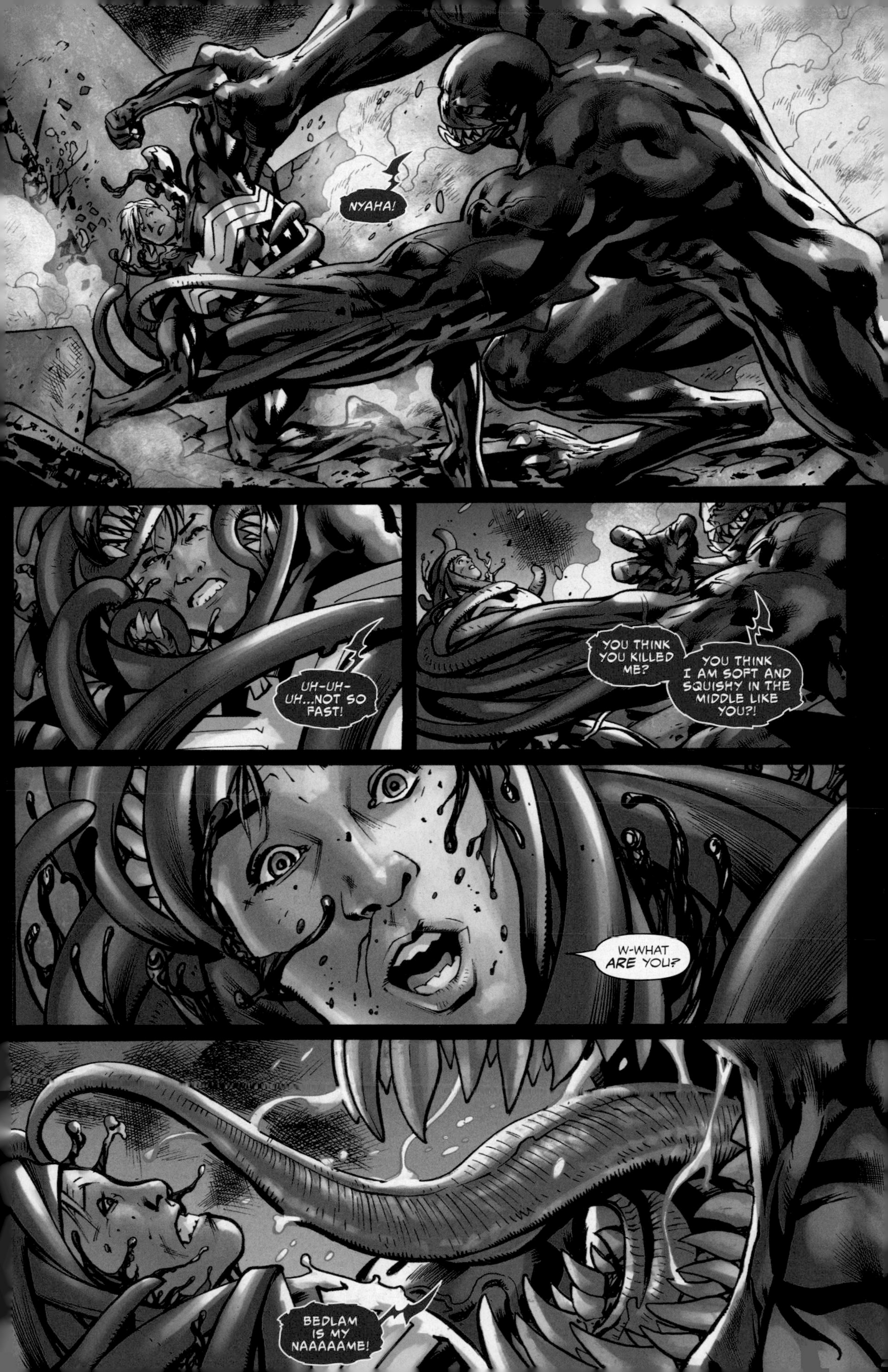
NYAHA!
UH-UH-UH...NOT SO FAST!
YOU THINK YOU KILLED ME?
YOU THINK I AM SOFT AND SQUISHY IN THE MIDDLE LIKE YOU?!
W-WHAT ARE YOU?
BEDLAM IS MY NAAAAAME!

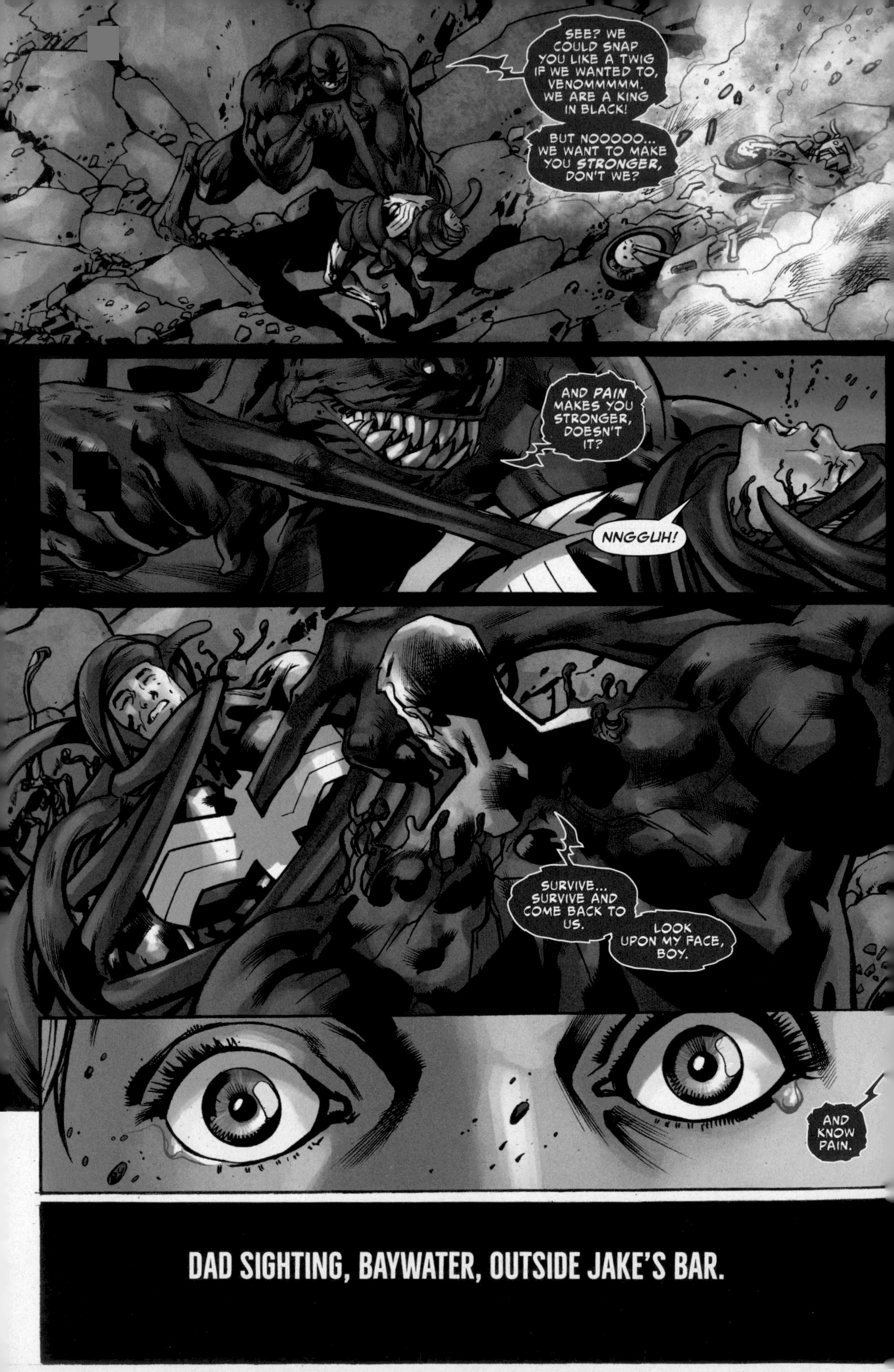

SEE? WE COULD SNAP YOU LIKE A TWIG IF WE WANTED TO, VENOMMMMM. WE ARE A KING IN BLACK!
BUT NOOOOO... WE WANT TO MAKE YOU STRONGER, DON'T WE?
AND PAIN MAKES YOU STRONGER, DOESN'T IT?
NNGGUH!
SURVIVE... SURVIVE AND COME BACK TO US.
LOOK UPON MY FACE, BOY.
AND KNOW PAIN.
DAD SIGHTING, BAYWATER, OUTSIDE JAKE'S BAR.

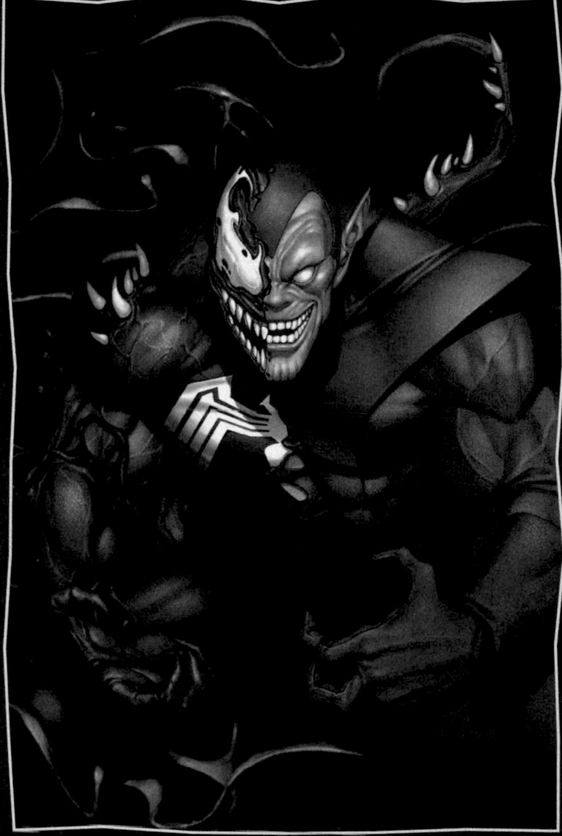

#8 Skrull variant by
INHYUK LEE

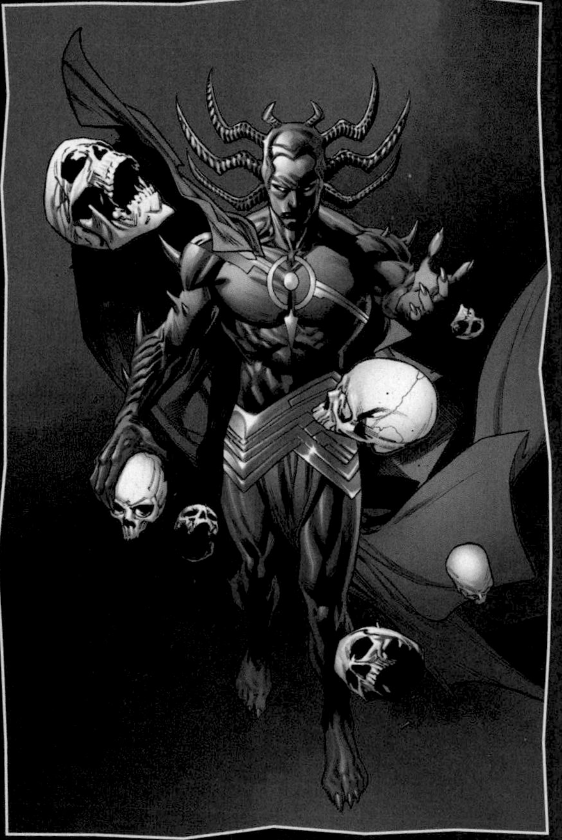

#8 variant by
STEPHEN SEGOVIA & RICHARD ISANOVE

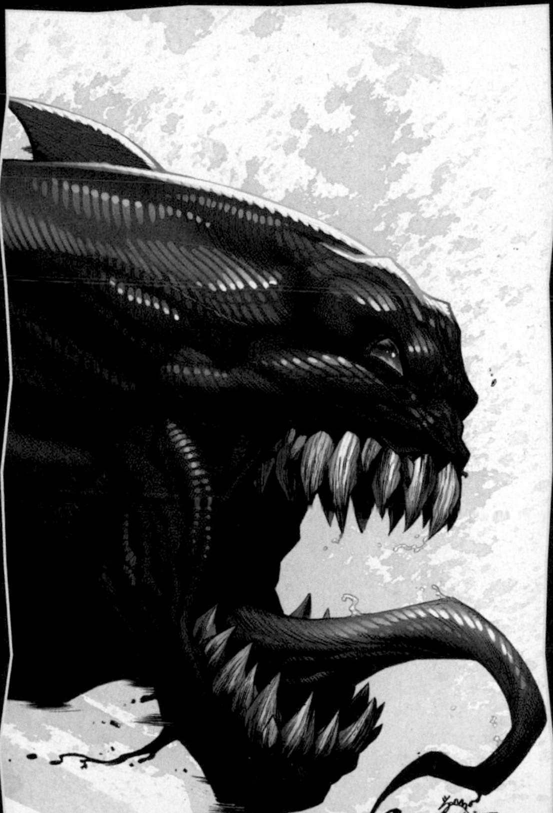

#9 variant by
RYAN STEGMAN & MARTE GRACIA

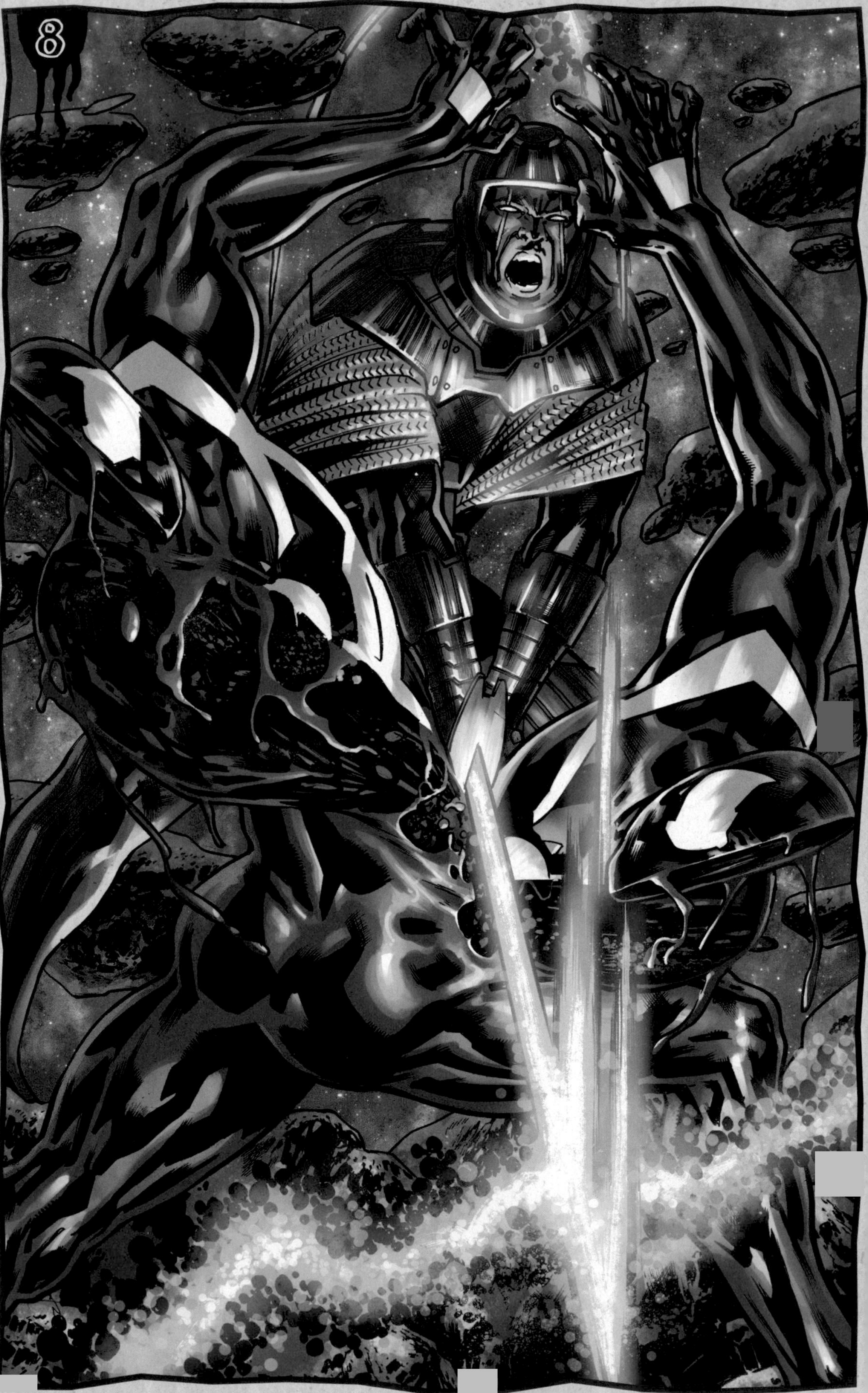
8

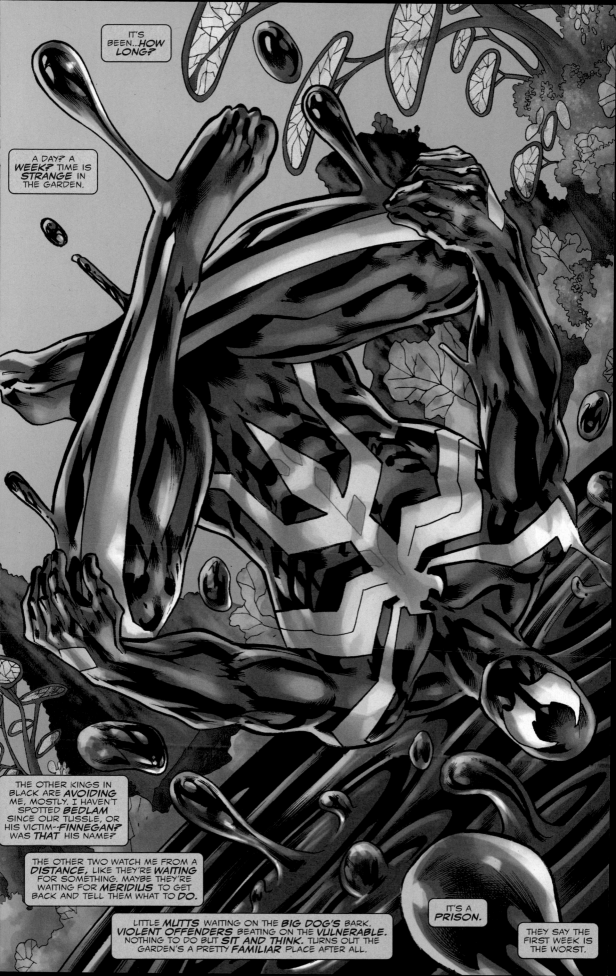

IT'S BEEN...HOW LONG?

A DAY? A WEEK? TIME IS STRANGE IN THE GARDEN.

THE OTHER KINGS IN BLACK ARE AVOIDING ME, MOSTLY. I HAVEN'T SPOTTED BEDLAM SINCE OUR TUSSLE, OR HIS VICTIM--FINNEGAN? WAS THAT HIS NAME?

THE OTHER TWO WATCH ME FROM A DISTANCE, LIKE THEY'RE WAITING FOR SOMETHING. MAYBE THEY'RE WAITING FOR MERIDIUS TO GET BACK AND TELL THEM WHAT TO DO.

LITTLE MUTTS WAITING ON THE BIG DOG'S BARK. VIOLENT OFFENDERS BEATING ON THE VULNERABLE. NOTHING TO DO BUT SIT AND THINK. TURNS OUT THE GARDEN'S A PRETTY FAMILIAR PLACE AFTER ALL.

IT'S A PRISON.

THEY SAY THE FIRST WEEK IS THE WORST.

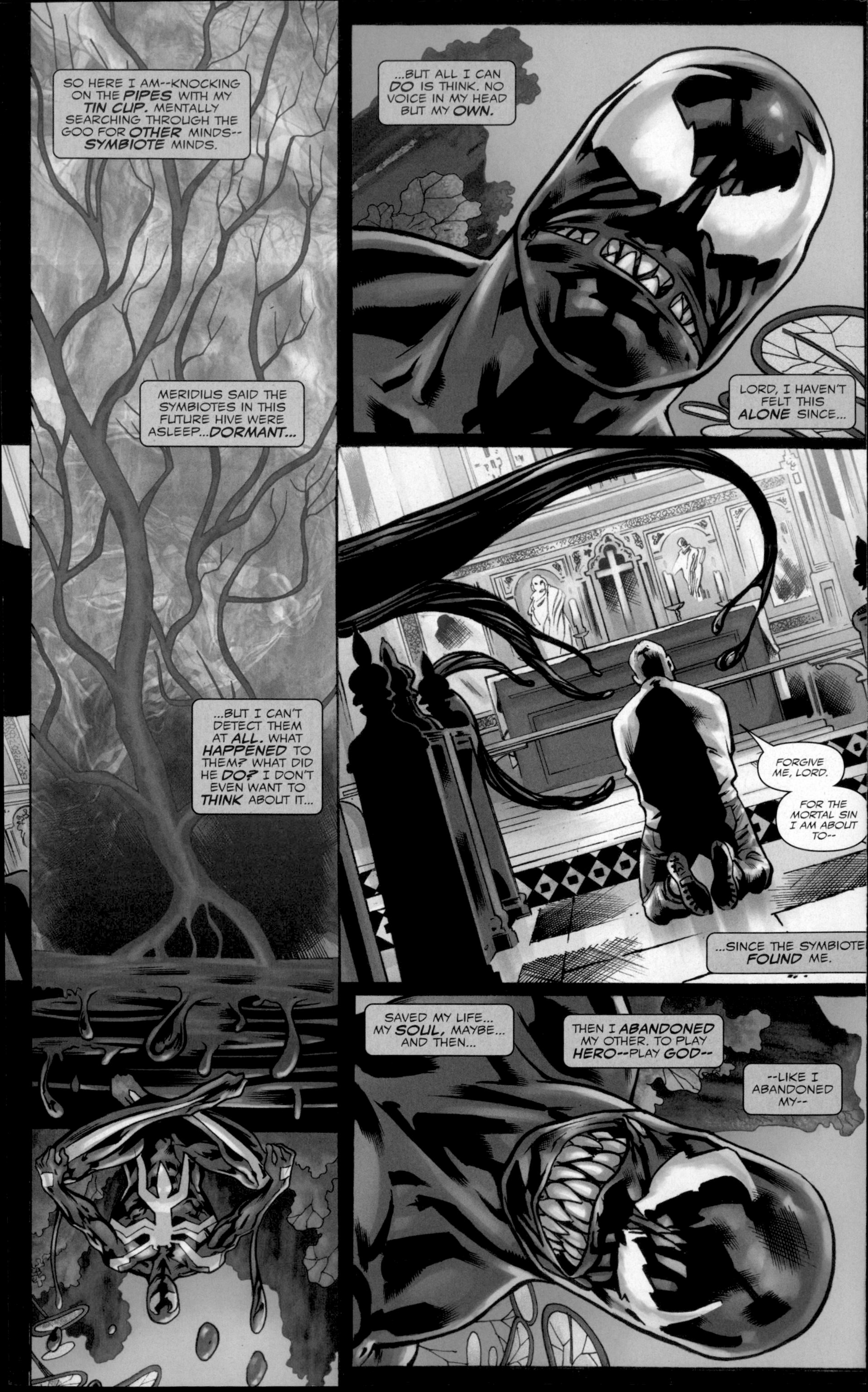

SO HERE I AM--KNOCKING ON THE PIPES WITH MY TIN CUP. MENTALLY SEARCHING THROUGH THE GOO FOR OTHER MINDS--SYMBIOTE MINDS.
...BUT ALL I CAN DO IS THINK. NO VOICE IN MY HEAD BUT MY OWN.
MERIDIUS SAID THE SYMBIOTES IN THIS FUTURE HIVE WERE ASLEEP...DORMANT...
LORD, I HAVEN'T FELT THIS ALONE SINCE...
...BUT I CAN'T DETECT THEM AT ALL. WHAT HAPPENED TO THEM? WHAT DID HE DO? I DON'T EVEN WANT TO THINK ABOUT IT...
FORGIVE ME, LORD.
FOR THE MORTAL SIN I AM ABOUT TO--
...SINCE THE SYMBIOTE FOUND ME.
SAVED MY LIFE... MY SOUL, MAYBE... AND THEN...
THEN I ABANDONED MY OTHER. TO PLAY HERO--PLAY GOD--
--LIKE I ABANDONED MY--

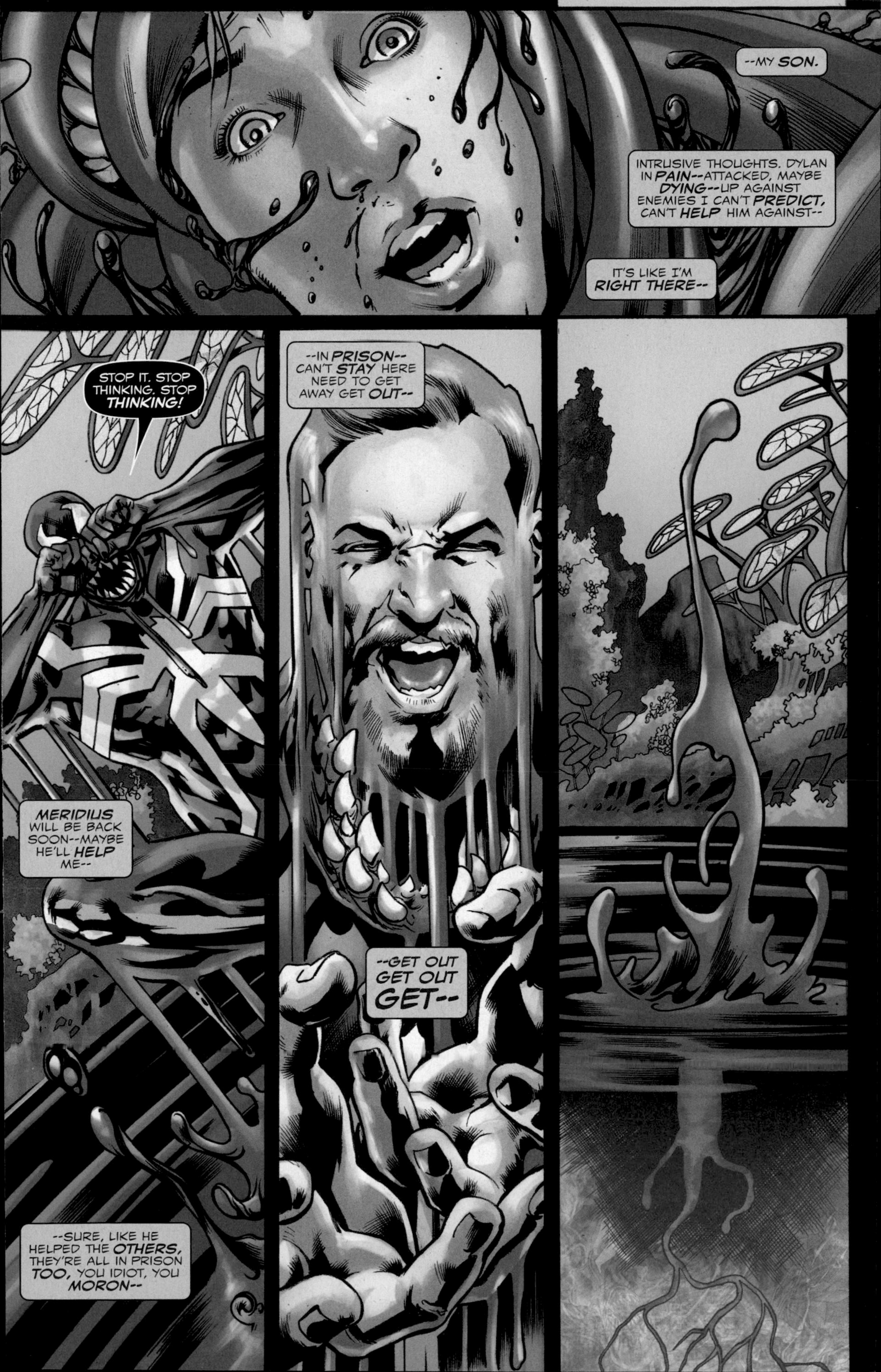
--MY SON.
INTRUSIVE THOUGHTS. DYLAN IN PAIN--ATTACKED, MAYBE DYING--UP AGAINST ENEMIES I CAN'T PREDICT, CAN'T HELP HIM AGAINST--
IT'S LIKE I'M RIGHT THERE--
STOP IT. STOP THINKING. STOP THINKING!
MERIDIUS WILL BE BACK SOON--MAYBE HE'LL HELP ME--
--SURE, LIKE HE HELPED THE OTHERS, THEY'RE ALL IN PRISON TOO, YOU IDIOT, YOU MORON--
--IN PRISON--CAN'T STAY HERE NEED TO GET AWAY GET OUT--
--GET OUT GET OUT GET--

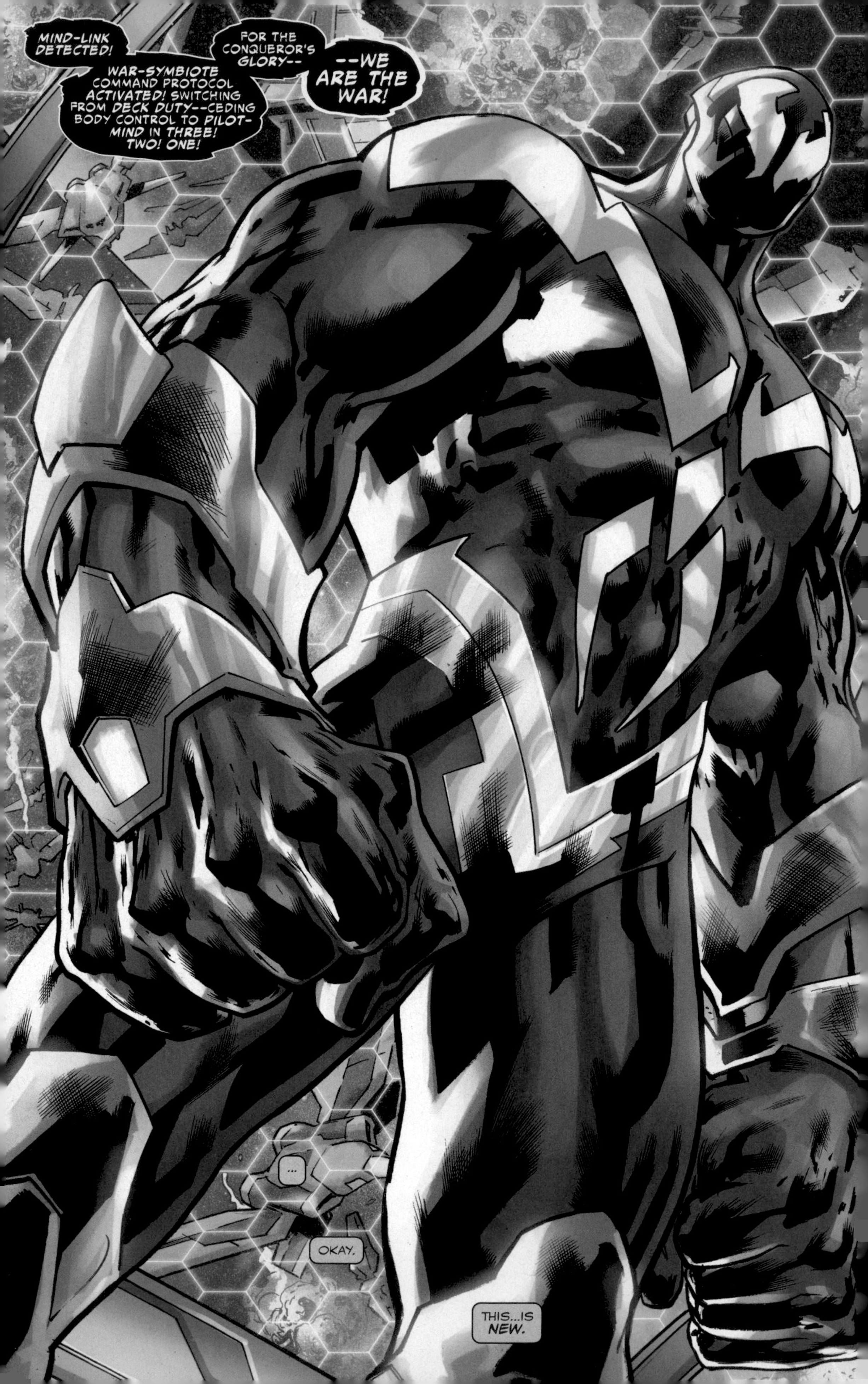
MIND-LINK DETECTED!
WAR-SYMBIOTE COMMAND PROTOCOL ACTIVATED! SWITCHING FROM DECK DUTY--CEDING BODY CONTROL TO PILOT-MIND IN THREE! TWO! ONE!
FOR THE CONQUEROR'S GLORY--
--WE ARE THE WAR!
...
OKAY.
THIS...IS NEW.

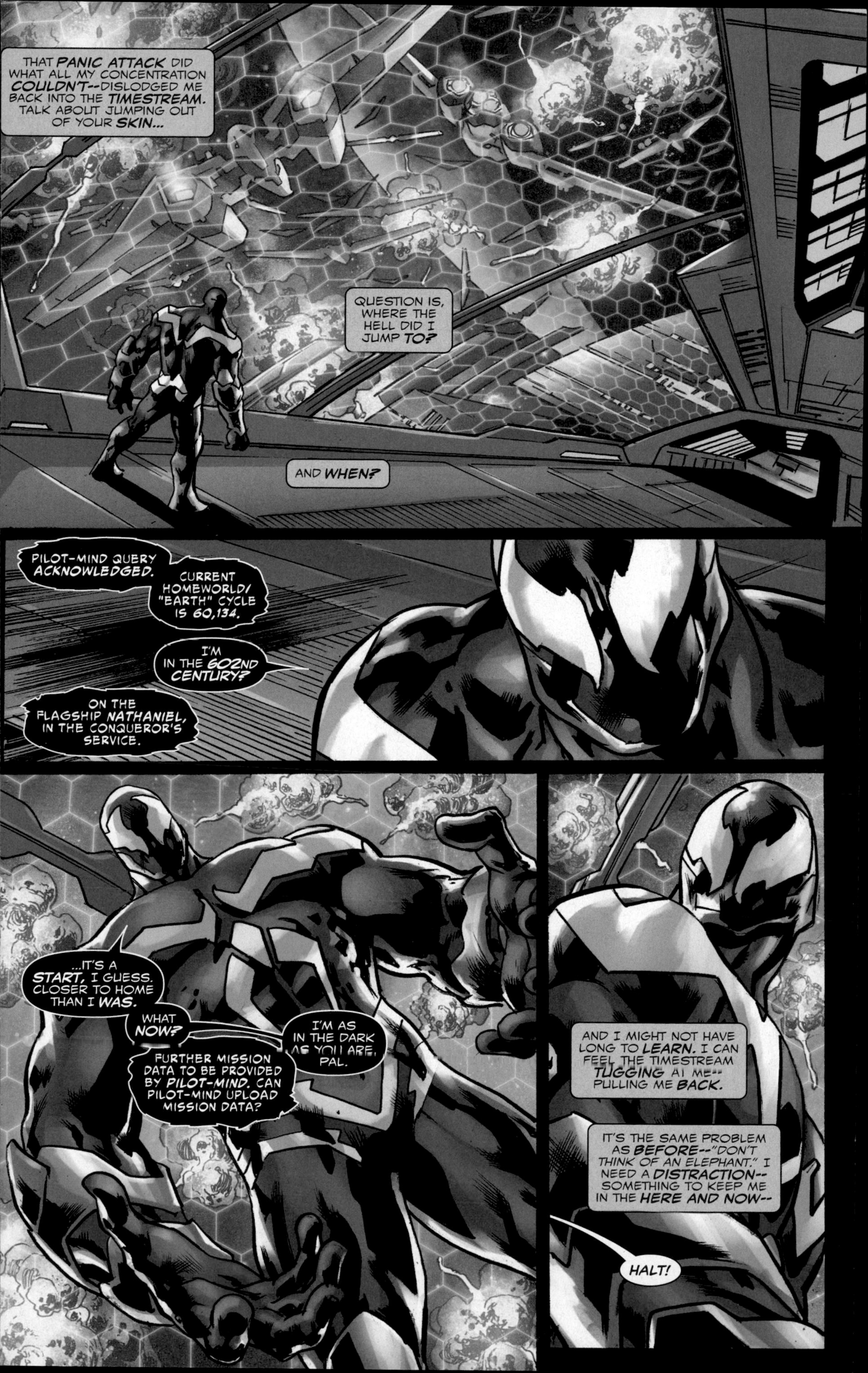
THAT PANIC ATTACK DID WHAT ALL MY CONCENTRATION COULDN'T--DISLODGED ME BACK INTO THE TIMESTREAM. TALK ABOUT JUMPING OUT OF YOUR SKIN...
QUESTION IS, WHERE THE HELL DID I JUMP TO?
AND WHEN?
PILOT-MIND QUERY ACKNOWLEDGED.
CURRENT HOMEWORLD/ "EARTH" CYCLE IS 60,134.
I'M IN THE 602ND CENTURY?
ON THE FLAGSHIP NATHANIEL, IN THE CONQUEROR'S SERVICE.
...IT'S A START, I GUESS. CLOSER TO HOME THAN I WAS.
WHAT NOW?
I'M AS IN THE DARK AS YOU ARE, PAL.
FURTHER MISSION DATA TO BE PROVIDED BY PILOT-MIND. CAN PILOT-MIND UPLOAD MISSION DATA?
AND I MIGHT NOT HAVE LONG TO LEARN. I CAN FEEL THE TIMESTREAM TUGGING AT ME-- PULLING ME BACK.
IT'S THE SAME PROBLEM AS BEFORE--"DON'T THINK OF AN ELEPHANT." I NEED A DISTRACTION-- SOMETHING TO KEEP ME IN THE HERE AND NOW--
HALT!

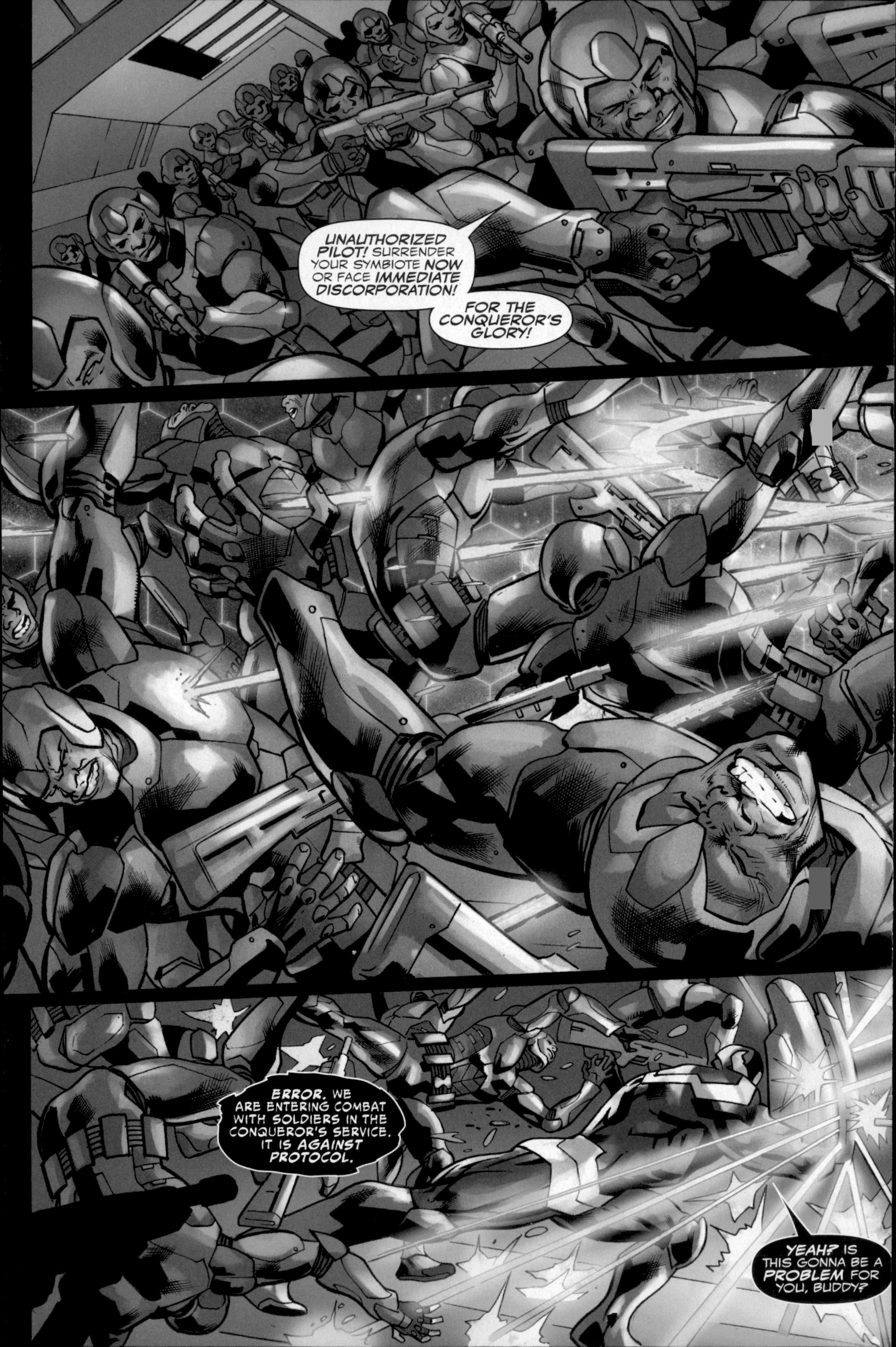
UNAUTHORIZED PILOT! SURRENDER YOUR SYMBIOTE NOW OR FACE IMMEDIATE DISCORPORATION!
FOR THE CONQUEROR'S GLORY!
ERROR. WE ARE ENTERING COMBAT WITH SOLDIERS IN THE CONQUEROR'S SERVICE. IT IS AGAINST PROTOCOL.
YEAH? IS THIS GONNA BE A PROBLEM FOR YOU, BUDDY?

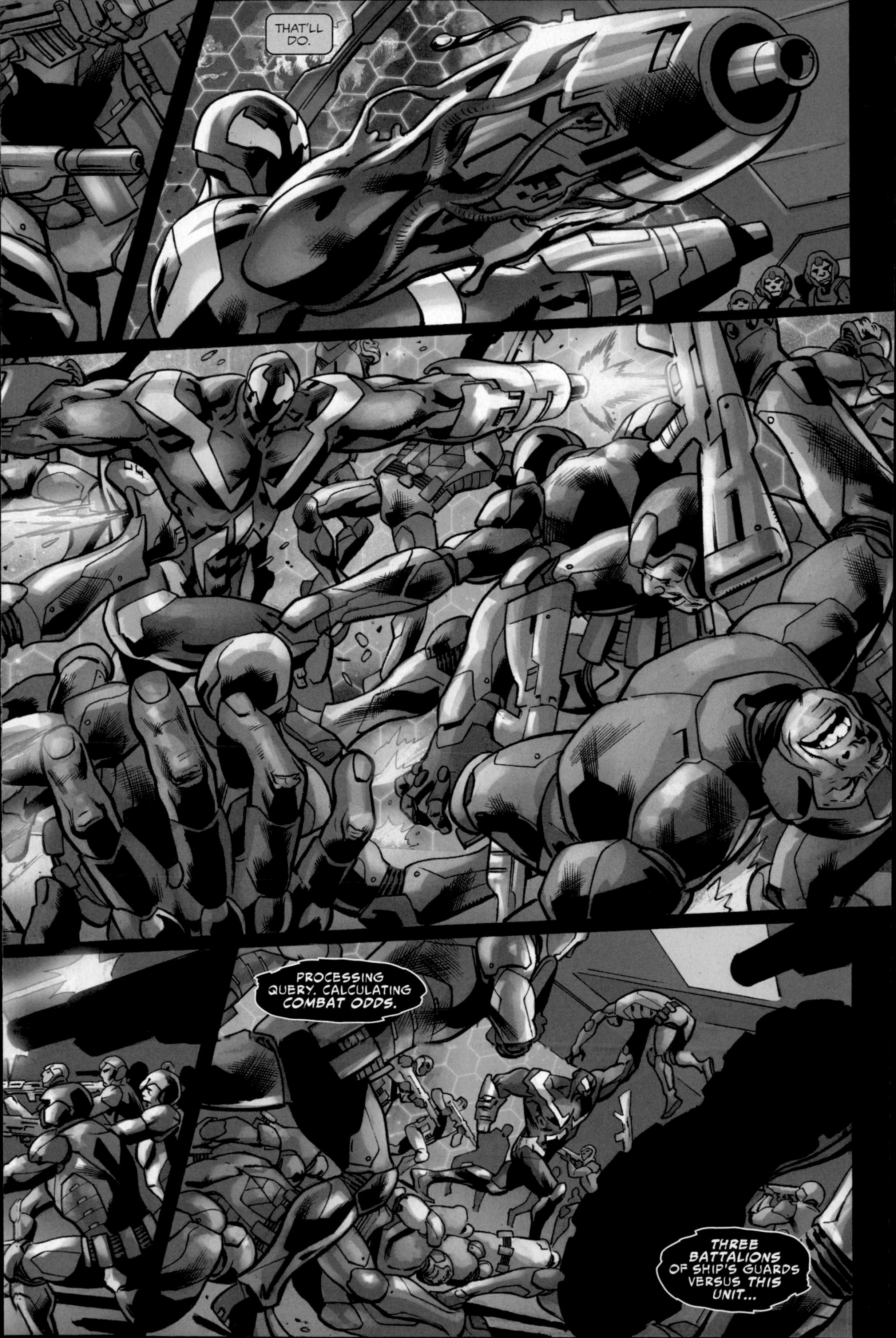
THAT'LL DO.
PROCESSING QUERY. CALCULATING COMBAT ODDS.
THREE BATTALIONS OF SHIP'S GUARDS VERSUS THIS UNIT...

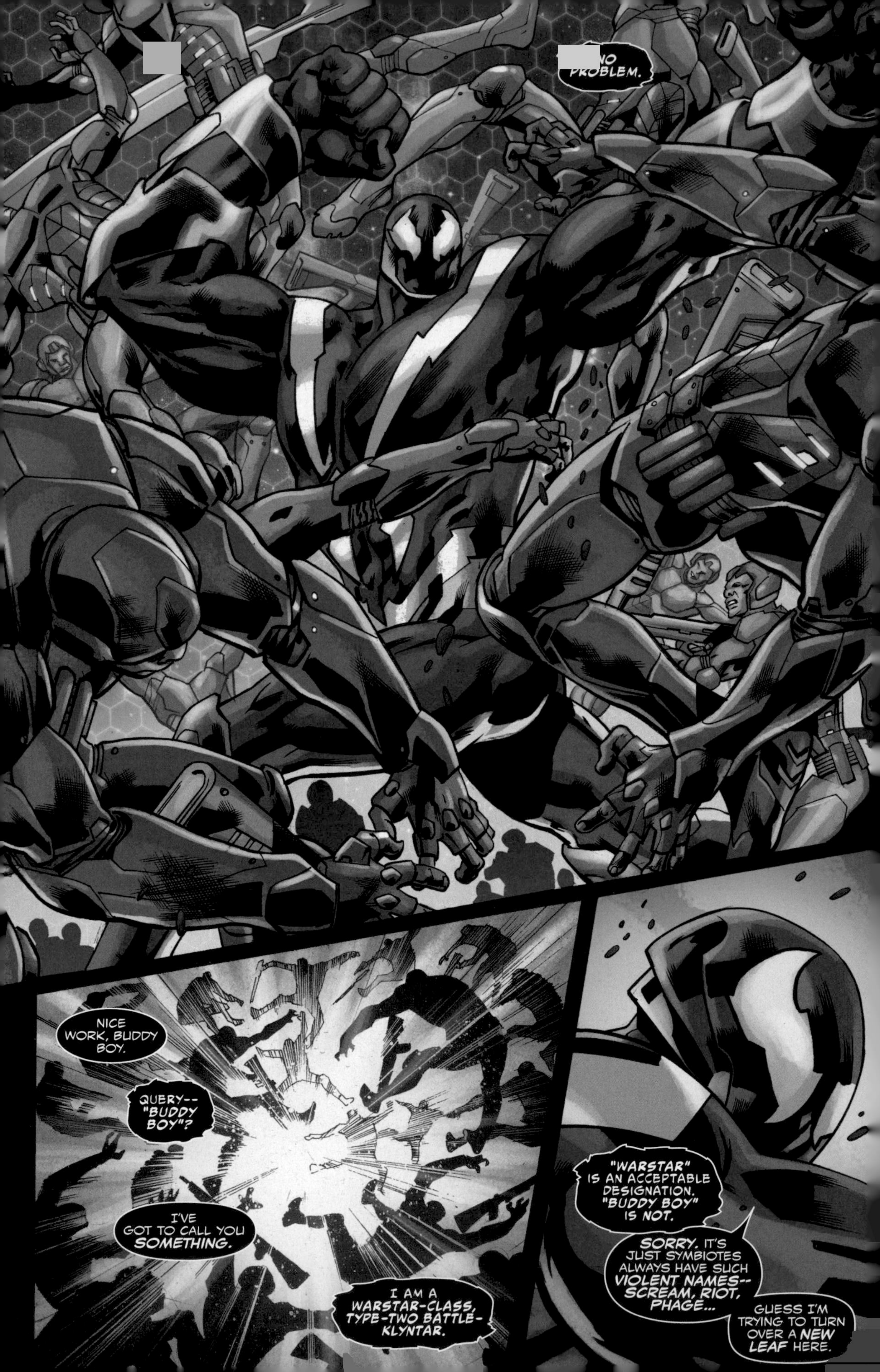
NO PROBLEM.
NICE WORK, BUDDY BOY.
QUERY-- "BUDDY BOY"?
I'VE GOT TO CALL YOU SOMETHING.
I AM A WARSTAR-CLASS, TYPE-TWO BATTLE-KLYNTAR.
"WARSTAR" IS AN ACCEPTABLE DESIGNATION. "BUDDY BOY" IS NOT.
SORRY. IT'S JUST SYMBIOTES ALWAYS HAVE SUCH VIOLENT NAMES-- SCREAM, RIOT, PHAGE...
GUESS I'M TRYING TO TURN OVER A NEW LEAF HERE.

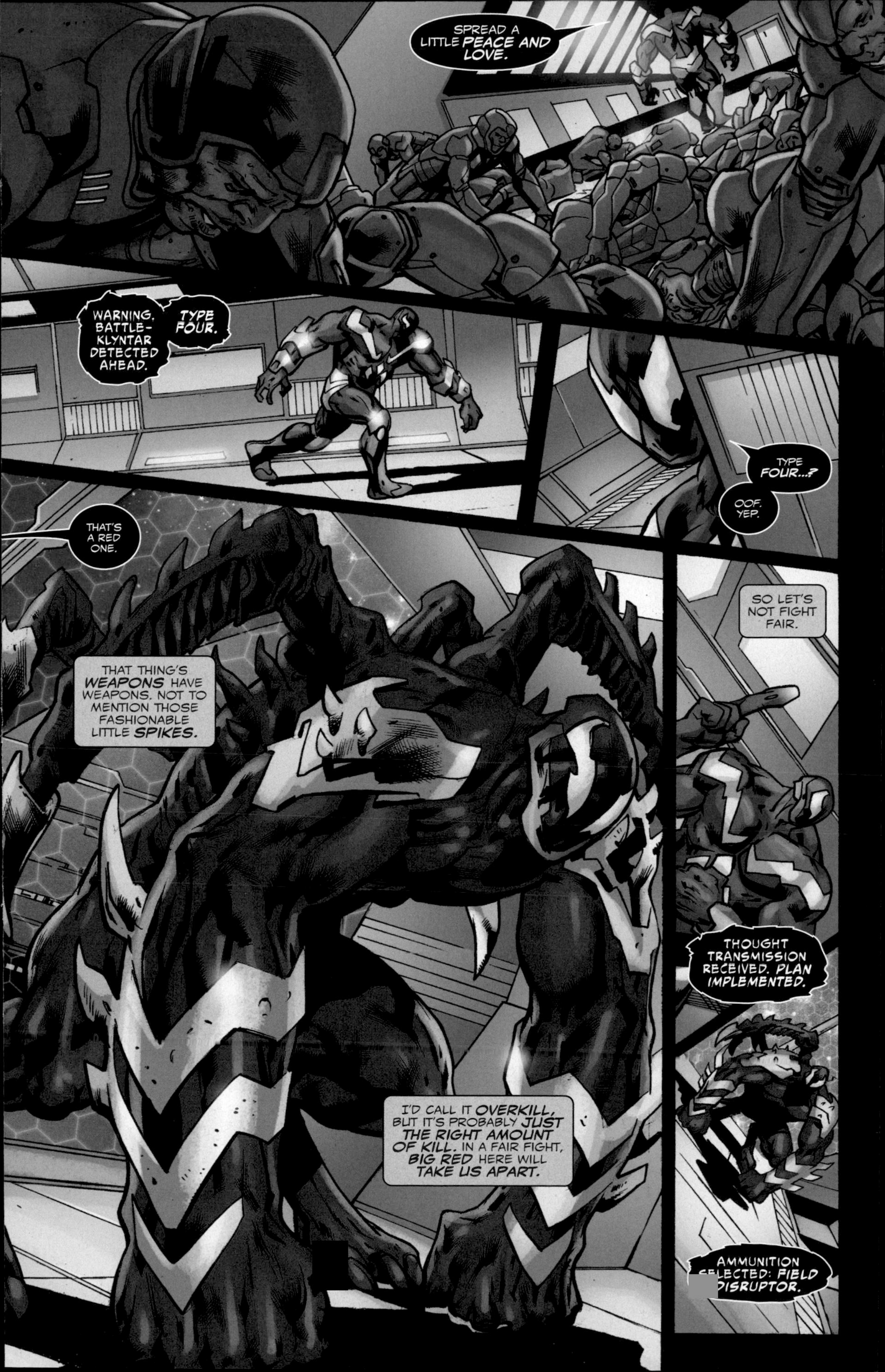
SPREAD A LITTLE PEACE AND LOVE.
WARNING. BATTLE-KLYNTAR DETECTED AHEAD.
TYPE FOUR.
TYPE FOUR...?
OOF. YEP.
THAT'S A RED ONE.
THAT THING'S WEAPONS HAVE WEAPONS. NOT TO MENTION THOSE FASHIONABLE LITTLE SPIKES.
I'D CALL IT OVERKILL, BUT IT'S PROBABLY JUST THE RIGHT AMOUNT OF KILL. IN A FAIR FIGHT, BIG RED HERE WILL TAKE US APART.
SO LET'S NOT FIGHT FAIR.
THOUGHT TRANSMISSION RECEIVED. PLAN IMPLEMENTED.
AMMUNITION SELECTED: FIELD DISRUPTOR.

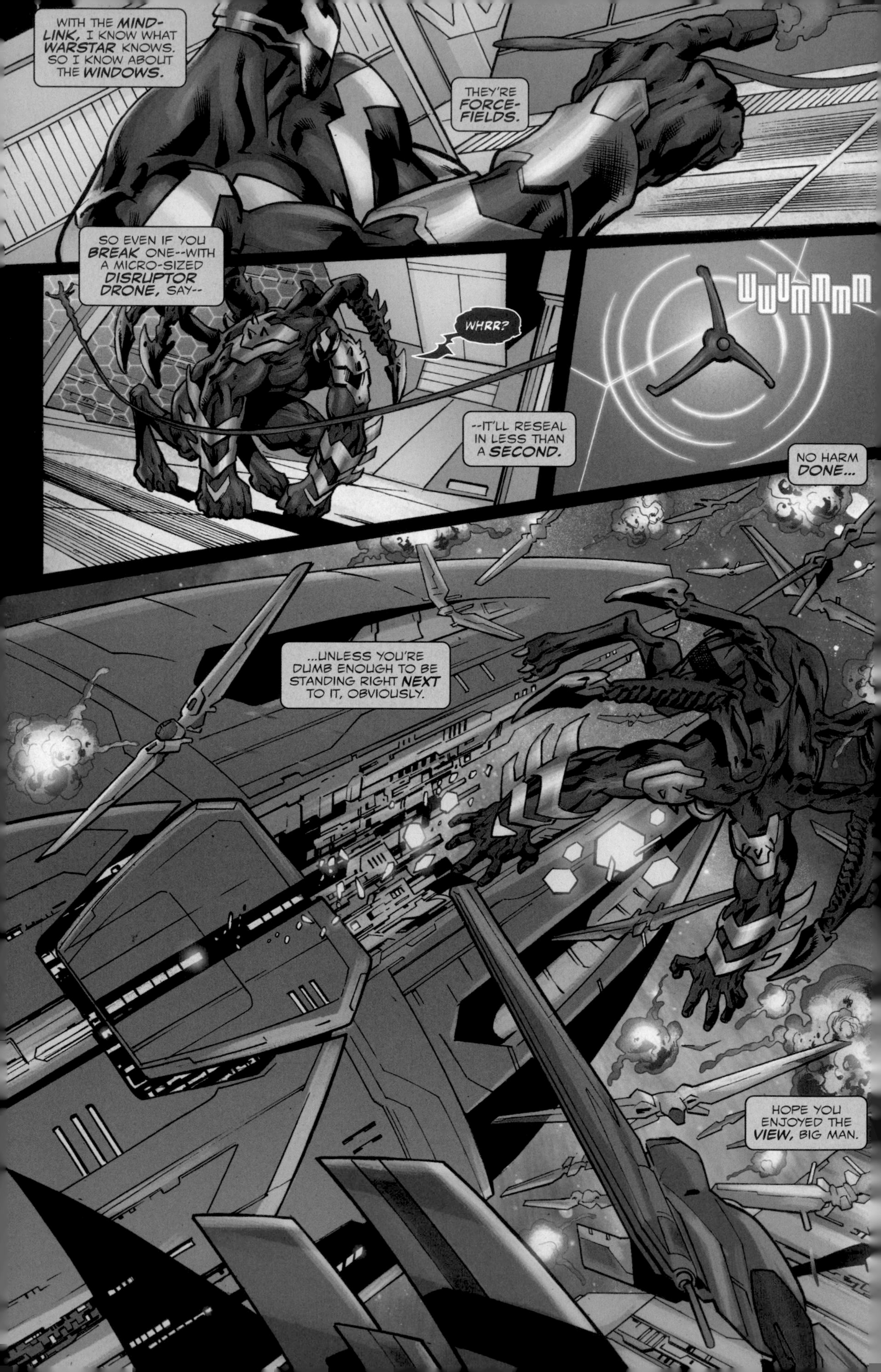
WITH THE MIND-LINK, I KNOW WHAT WARSTAR KNOWS. SO I KNOW ABOUT THE WINDOWS.
THEY'RE FORCE-FIELDS.
SO EVEN IF YOU BREAK ONE--WITH A MICRO-SIZED DISRUPTOR DRONE, SAY--
WHRR?
WWUMMMM
--IT'LL RESEAL IN LESS THAN A SECOND.
NO HARM DONE...
...UNLESS YOU'RE DUMB ENOUGH TO BE STANDING RIGHT NEXT TO IT, OBVIOUSLY.
HOPE YOU ENJOYED THE VIEW, BIG MAN.

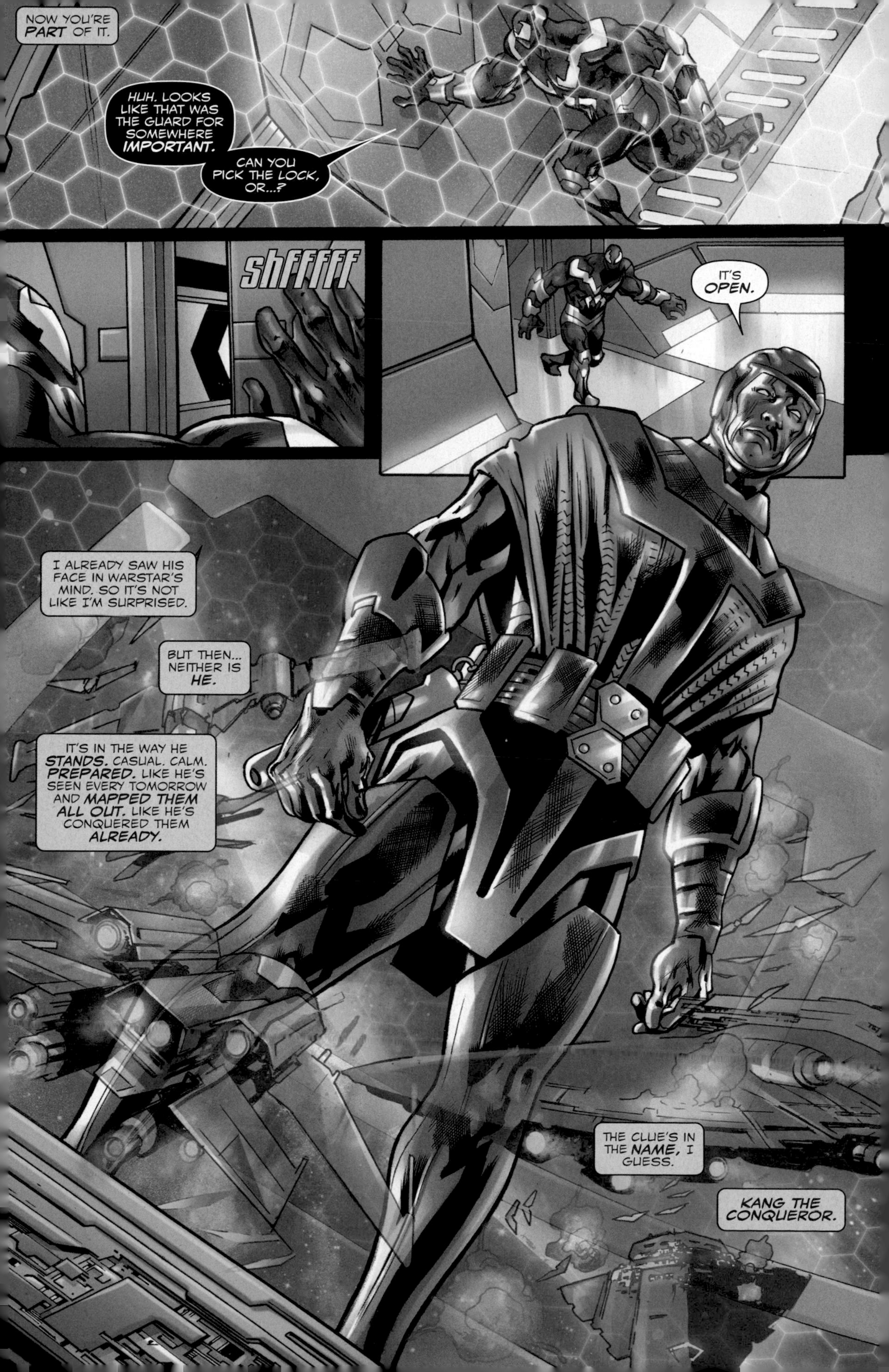

NOW YOU'RE PART OF IT.
HUH. LOOKS LIKE THAT WAS THE GUARD FOR SOMEWHERE IMPORTANT.
CAN YOU PICK THE LOCK, OR...?
shffffff
IT'S OPEN.
I ALREADY SAW HIS FACE IN WARSTAR'S MIND. SO IT'S NOT LIKE I'M SURPRISED.
BUT THEN... NEITHER IS HE.
IT'S IN THE WAY HE STANDS. CASUAL. CALM. PREPARED. LIKE HE'S SEEN EVERY TOMORROW AND MAPPED THEM ALL OUT. LIKE HE'S CONQUERED THEM ALREADY.
THE CLUE'S IN THE NAME, I GUESS.
KANG THE CONQUEROR.

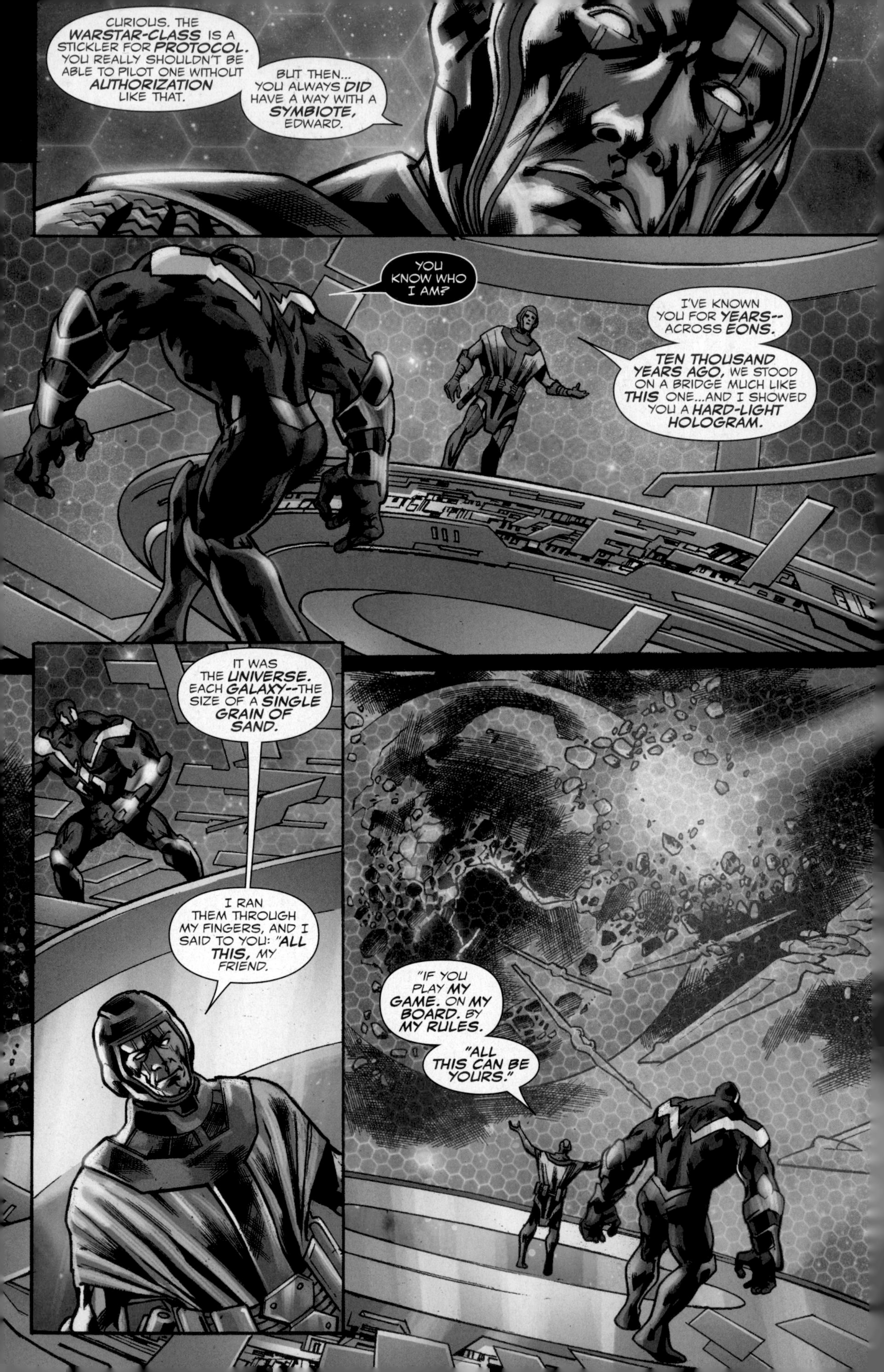
CURIOUS. THE WARSTAR-CLASS IS A STICKLER FOR PROTOCOL. YOU REALLY SHOULDN'T BE ABLE TO PILOT ONE WITHOUT AUTHORIZATION LIKE THAT.
BUT THEN... YOU ALWAYS DID HAVE A WAY WITH A SYMBIOTE, EDWARD.
YOU KNOW WHO I AM?
I'VE KNOWN YOU FOR YEARS-- ACROSS EONS.
TEN THOUSAND YEARS AGO, WE STOOD ON A BRIDGE MUCH LIKE THIS ONE...AND I SHOWED YOU A HARD-LIGHT HOLOGRAM.
IT WAS THE UNIVERSE. EACH GALAXY--THE SIZE OF A SINGLE GRAIN OF SAND.
I RAN THEM THROUGH MY FINGERS, AND I SAID TO YOU: "ALL THIS, MY FRIEND.
"IF YOU PLAY MY GAME. ON MY BOARD. BY MY RULES.
"ALL THIS CAN BE YOURS."

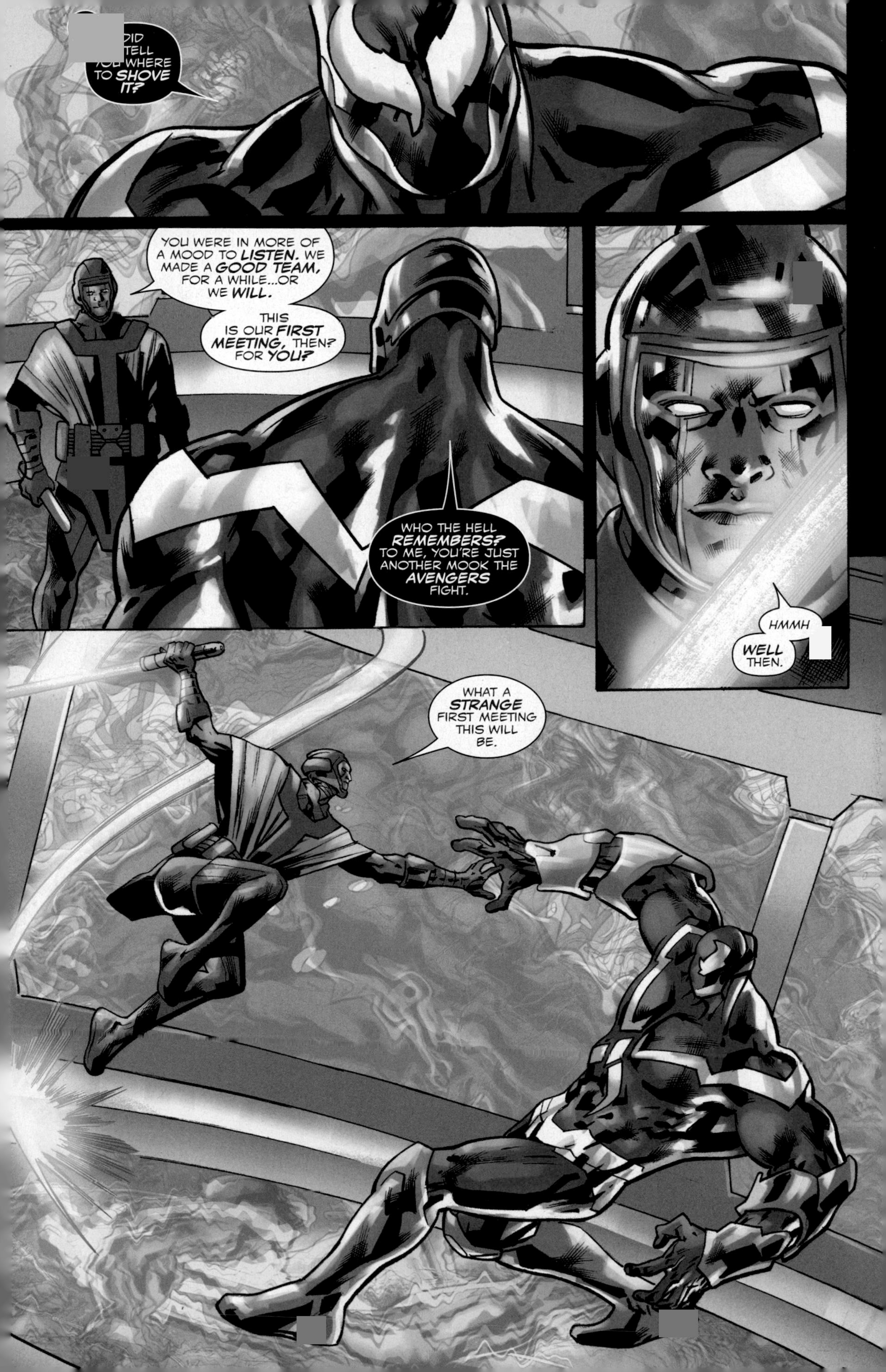

DID TELL YOU WHERE TO SHOVE IT?
YOU WERE IN MORE OF A MOOD TO LISTEN. WE MADE A GOOD TEAM, FOR A WHILE...OR WE WILL.
THIS IS OUR FIRST MEETING, THEN? FOR YOU?
WHO THE HELL REMEMBERS? TO ME, YOU'RE JUST ANOTHER MOOK THE AVENGERS FIGHT.
HMMH
WELL THEN.
WHAT A STRANGE FIRST MEETING THIS WILL BE.

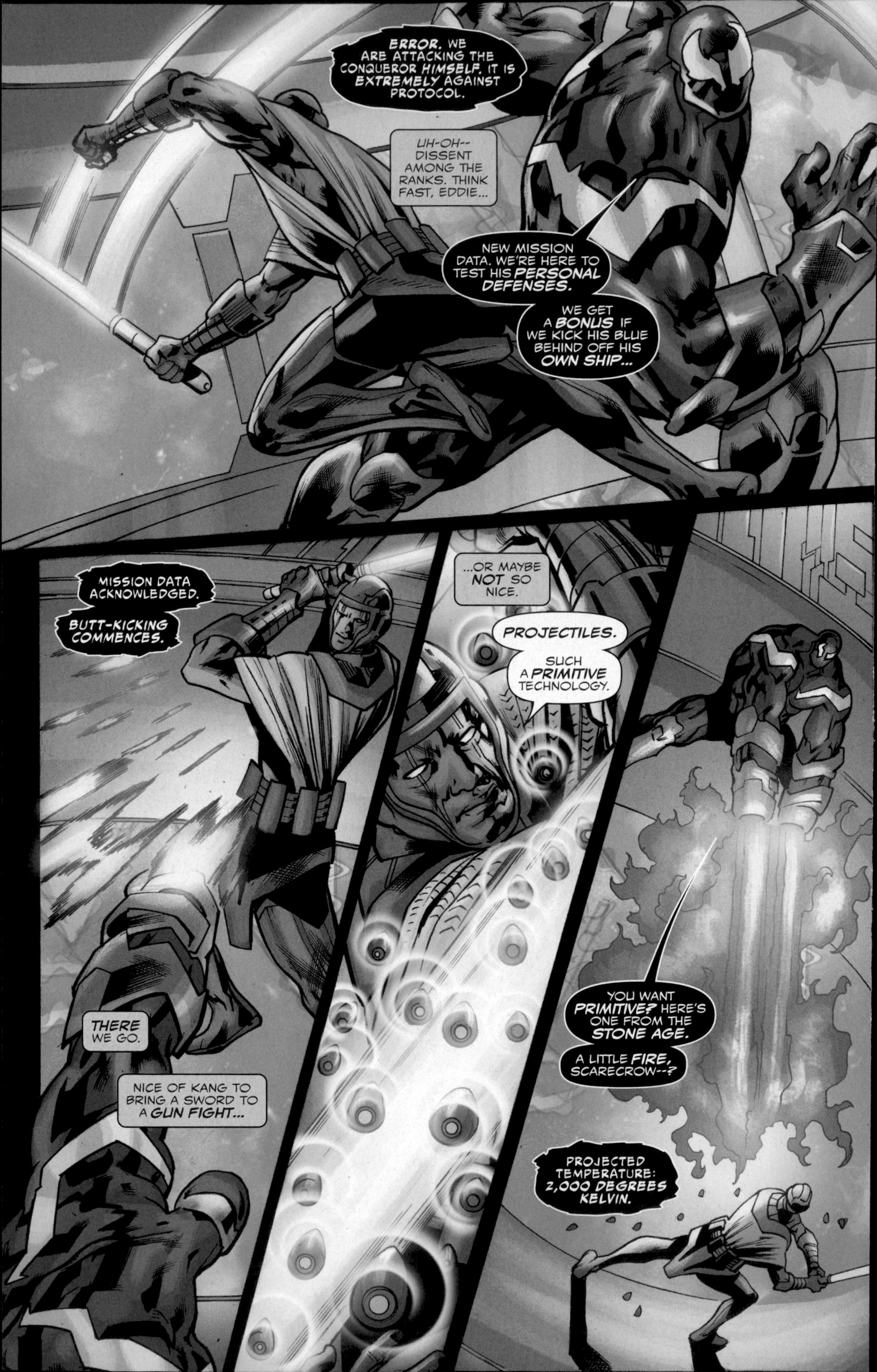
ERROR. WE ARE ATTACKING THE CONQUEROR HIMSELF. IT IS EXTREMELY AGAINST PROTOCOL.
UH-OH-- DISSENT AMONG THE RANKS. THINK FAST, EDDIE...
NEW MISSION DATA. WE'RE HERE TO TEST HIS PERSONAL DEFENSES.
WE GET A BONUS IF WE KICK HIS BLUE BEHIND OFF HIS OWN SHIP...
MISSION DATA ACKNOWLEDGED.
BUTT-KICKING COMMENCES.
THERE WE GO.
NICE OF KANG TO BRING A SWORD TO A GUN FIGHT...
...OR MAYBE NOT SO NICE.
PROJECTILES.
SUCH A PRIMITIVE TECHNOLOGY.
YOU WANT PRIMITIVE? HERE'S ONE FROM THE STONE AGE.
A LITTLE FIRE, SCARECROW--?
PROJECTED TEMPERATURE: 2,000 DEGREES KELVIN.

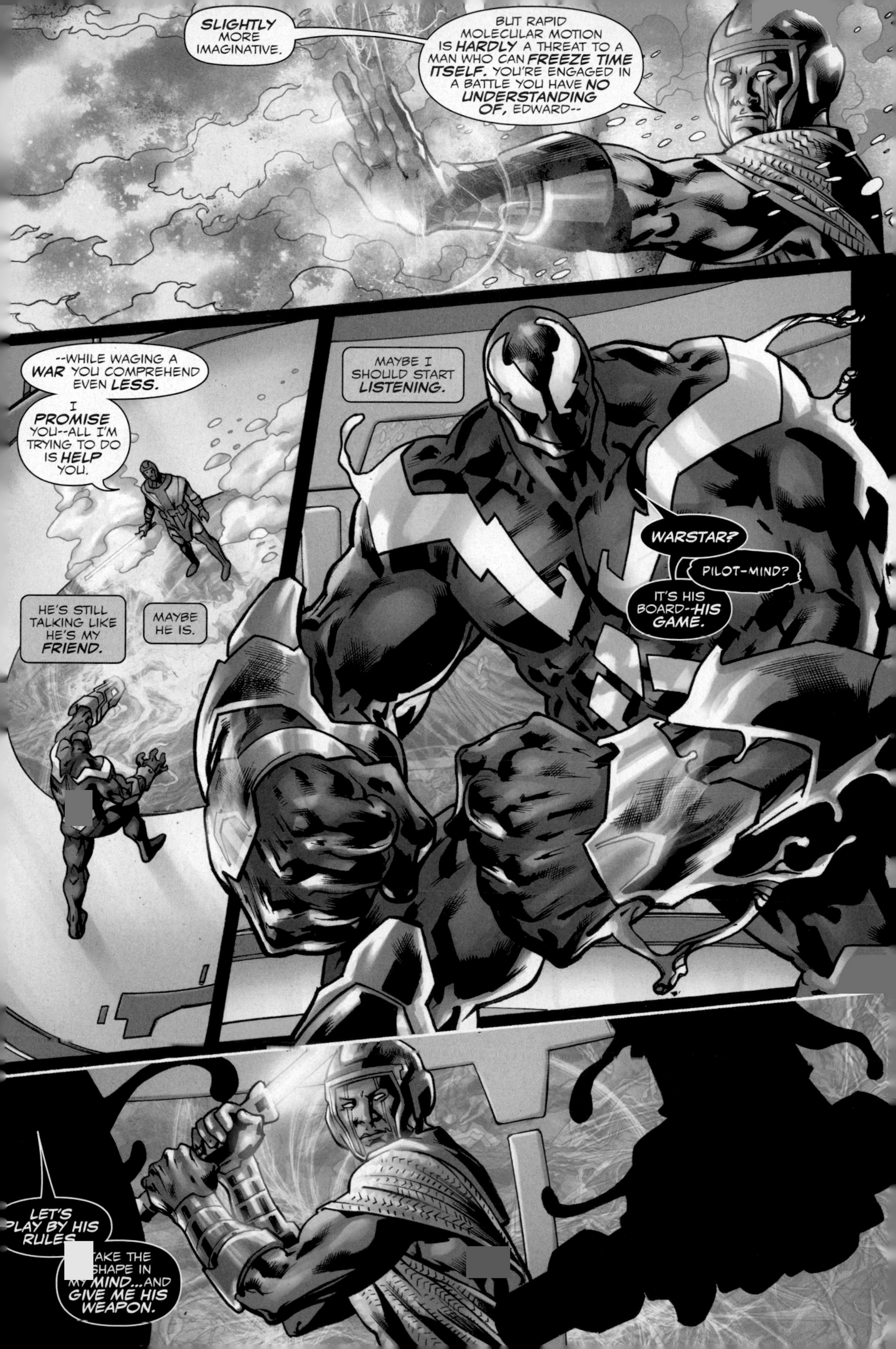
SLIGHTLY MORE IMAGINATIVE.
BUT RAPID MOLECULAR MOTION IS HARDLY A THREAT TO A MAN WHO CAN FREEZE TIME ITSELF. YOU'RE ENGAGED IN A BATTLE YOU HAVE NO UNDERSTANDING OF, EDWARD--
--WHILE WAGING A WAR YOU COMPREHEND EVEN LESS.
I PROMISE YOU--ALL I'M TRYING TO DO IS HELP YOU.
MAYBE I SHOULD START LISTENING.
HE'S STILL TALKING LIKE HE'S MY FRIEND.
MAYBE HE IS.
WARSTAR?
PILOT-MIND?
IT'S HIS BOARD--HIS GAME.
LET'S PLAY BY HIS RULES
TAKE THE SHAPE IN MY MIND...AND GIVE ME HIS WEAPON.

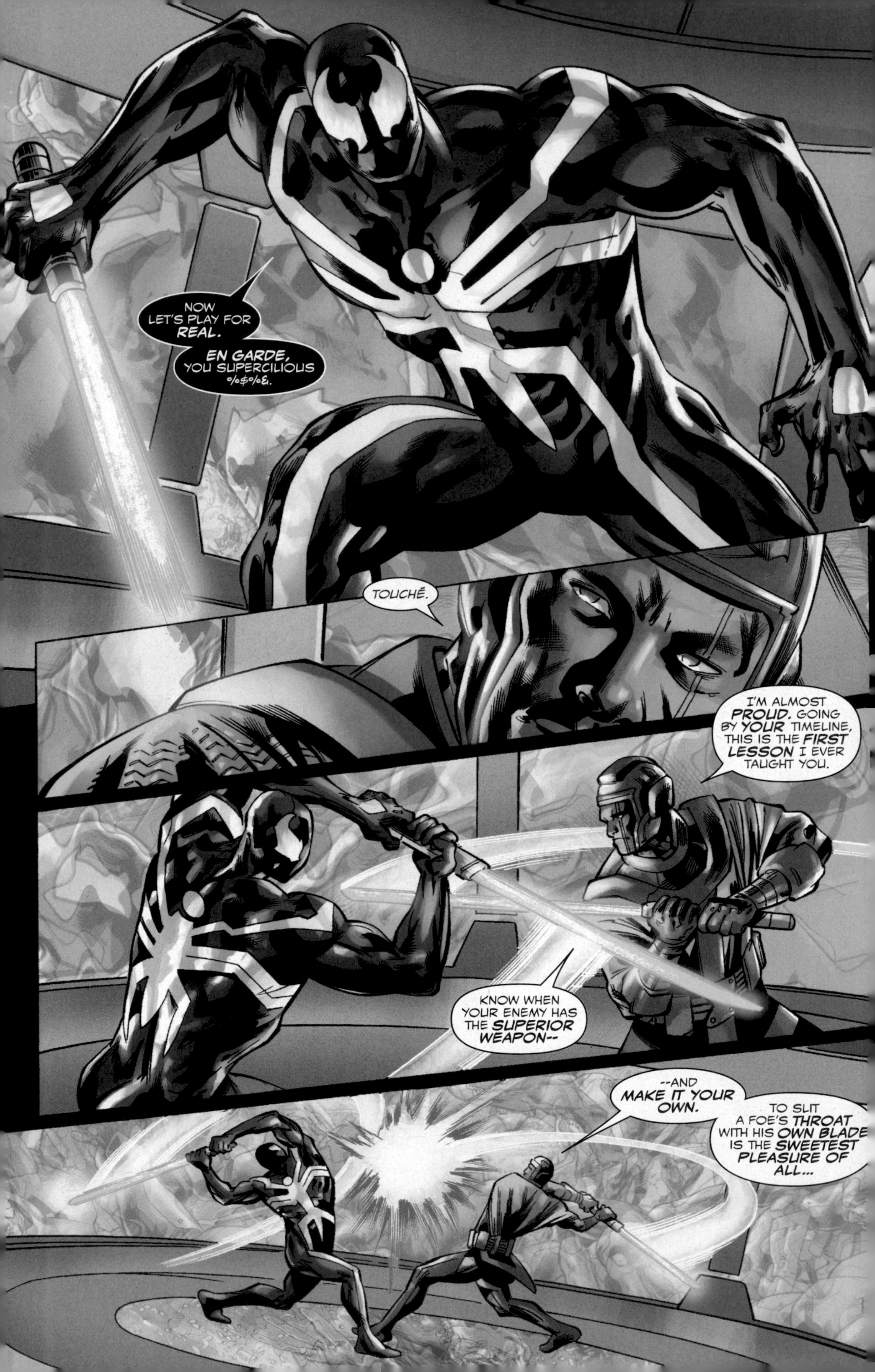
NOW LET'S PLAY FOR REAL.
EN GARDE, YOU SUPERCILIOUS %$%£.
TOUCHÉ.
I'M ALMOST PROUD. GOING BY YOUR TIMELINE, THIS IS THE FIRST LESSON I EVER TAUGHT YOU.
KNOW WHEN YOUR ENEMY HAS THE SUPERIOR WEAPON--
--AND MAKE IT YOUR OWN.
TO SLIT A FOE'S THROAT WITH HIS OWN BLADE IS THE SWEETEST PLEASURE OF ALL...

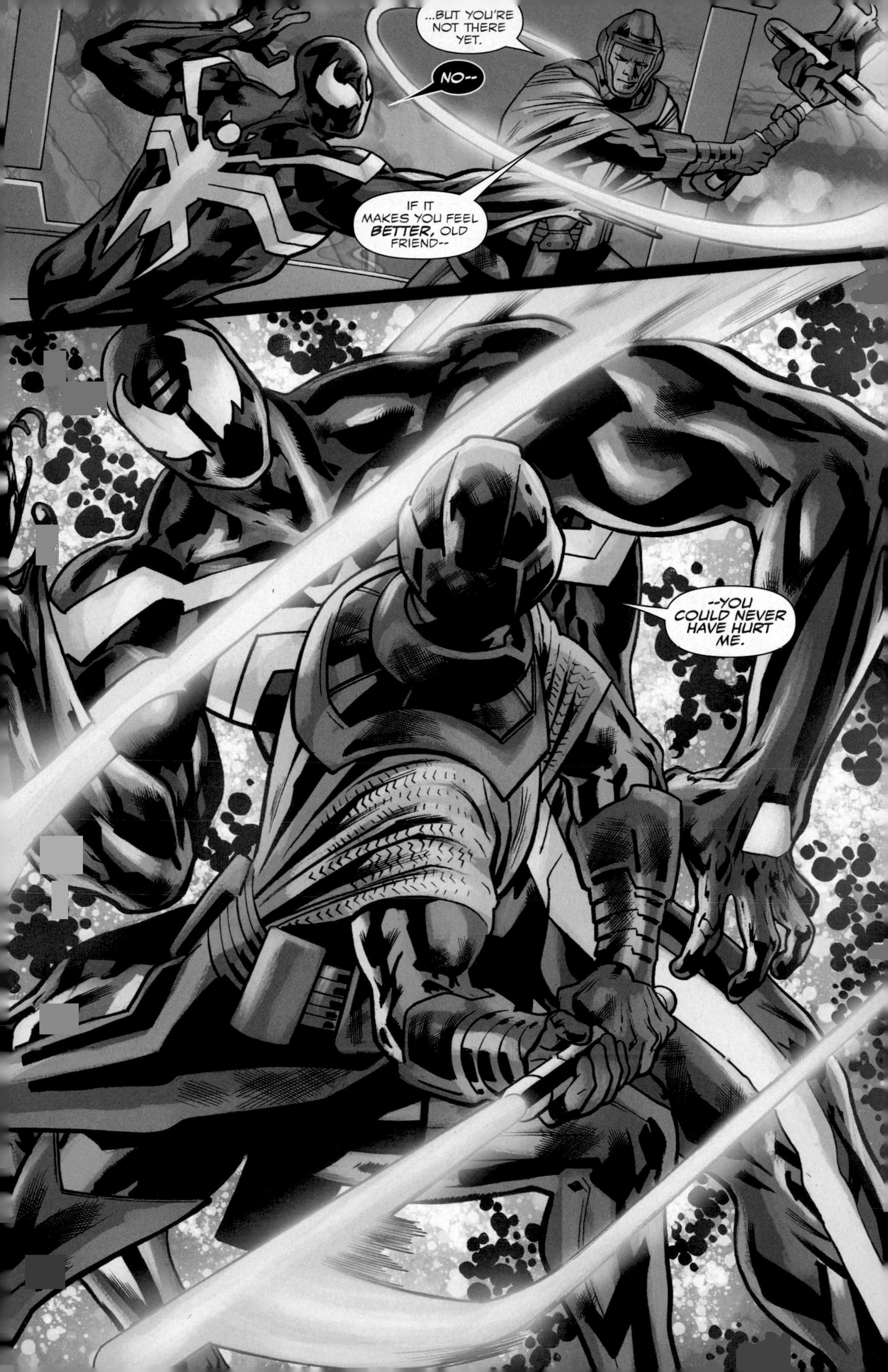
...BUT YOU'RE NOT THERE YET.
NO--
IF IT MAKES YOU FEEL BETTER, OLD FRIEND--
--YOU COULD NEVER HAVE HURT ME.

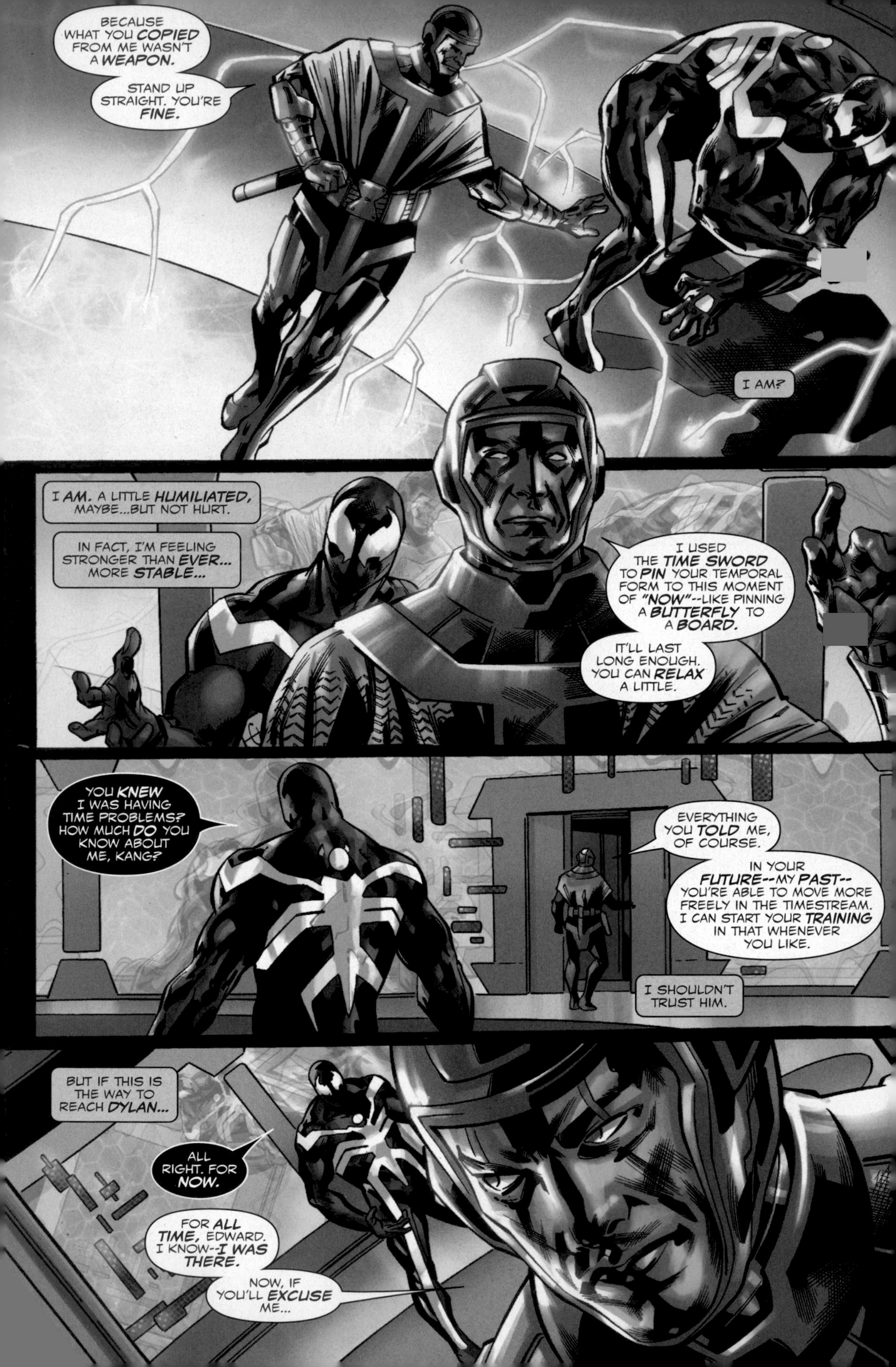
BECAUSE WHAT YOU COPIED FROM ME WASN'T A WEAPON.
STAND UP STRAIGHT. YOU'RE FINE.
I AM?
I AM. A LITTLE HUMILIATED, MAYBE...BUT NOT HURT.
IN FACT, I'M FEELING STRONGER THAN EVER... MORE STABLE...
I USED THE TIME SWORD TO PIN YOUR TEMPORAL FORM TO THIS MOMENT OF "NOW"--LIKE PINNING A BUTTERFLY TO A BOARD.
IT'LL LAST LONG ENOUGH. YOU CAN RELAX A LITTLE.
YOU KNEW I WAS HAVING TIME PROBLEMS? HOW MUCH DO YOU KNOW ABOUT ME, KANG?
EVERYTHING YOU TOLD ME, OF COURSE.
IN YOUR FUTURE--MY PAST--YOU'RE ABLE TO MOVE MORE FREELY IN THE TIMESTREAM. I CAN START YOUR TRAINING IN THAT WHENEVER YOU LIKE.
I SHOULDN'T TRUST HIM.
BUT IF THIS IS THE WAY TO REACH DYLAN...
ALL RIGHT. FOR NOW.
FOR ALL TIME, EDWARD. I KNOW--I WAS THERE.
NOW, IF YOU'LL EXCUSE ME...

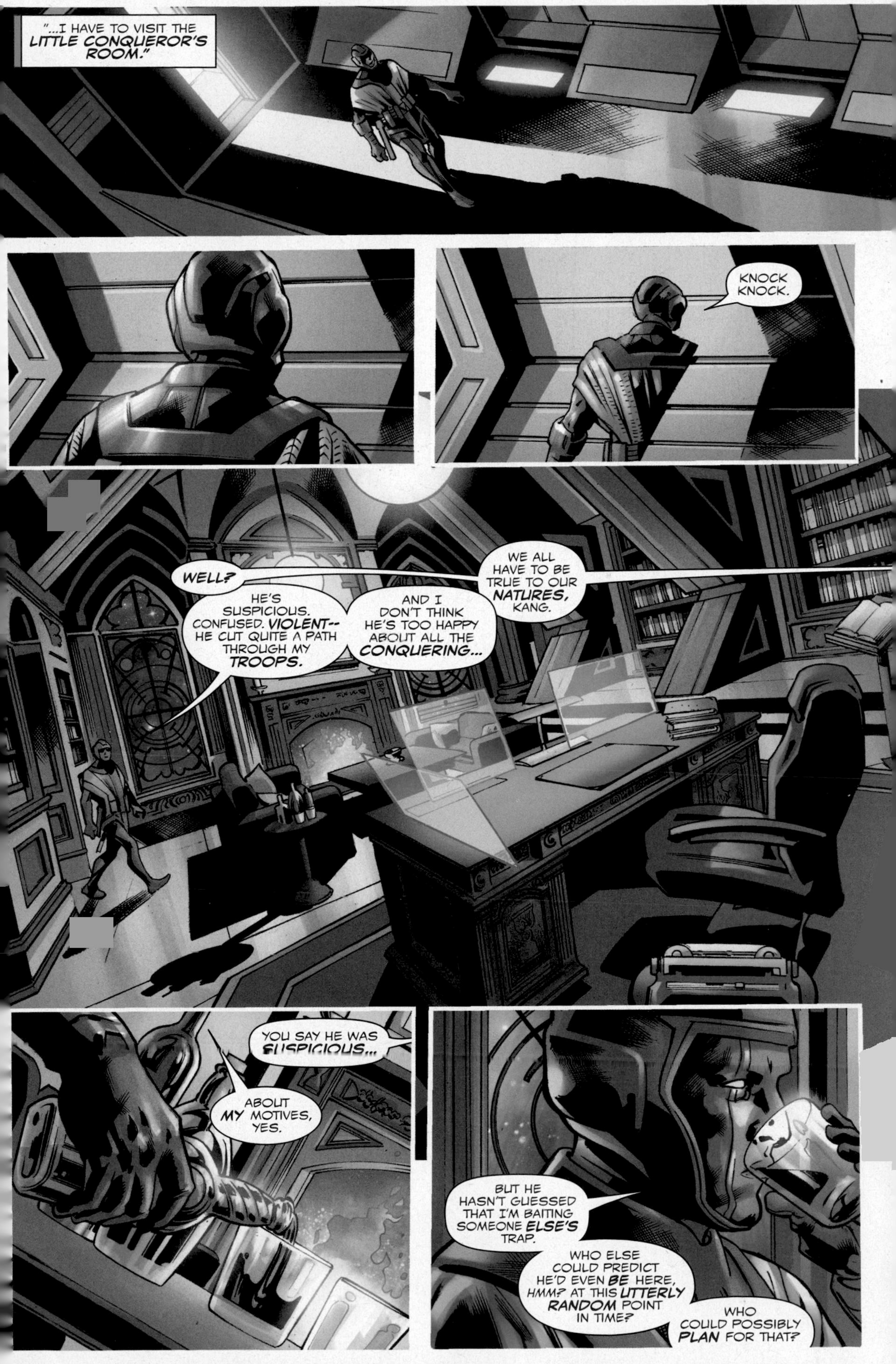
"...I HAVE TO VISIT THE LITTLE CONQUEROR'S ROOM."
KNOCK KNOCK.
WELL?
HE'S SUSPICIOUS. CONFUSED. VIOLENT-- HE CUT QUITE A PATH THROUGH MY TROOPS.
AND I DON'T THINK HE'S TOO HAPPY ABOUT ALL THE CONQUERING...
WE ALL HAVE TO BE TRUE TO OUR NATURES, KANG.
YOU SAY HE WAS SUSPICIOUS...
ABOUT MY MOTIVES, YES.
BUT HE HASN'T GUESSED THAT I'M BAITING SOMEONE ELSE'S TRAP.
WHO ELSE COULD PREDICT HE'D EVEN BE HERE, HMM? AT THIS UTTERLY RANDOM POINT IN TIME?
WHO COULD POSSIBLY PLAN FOR THAT?

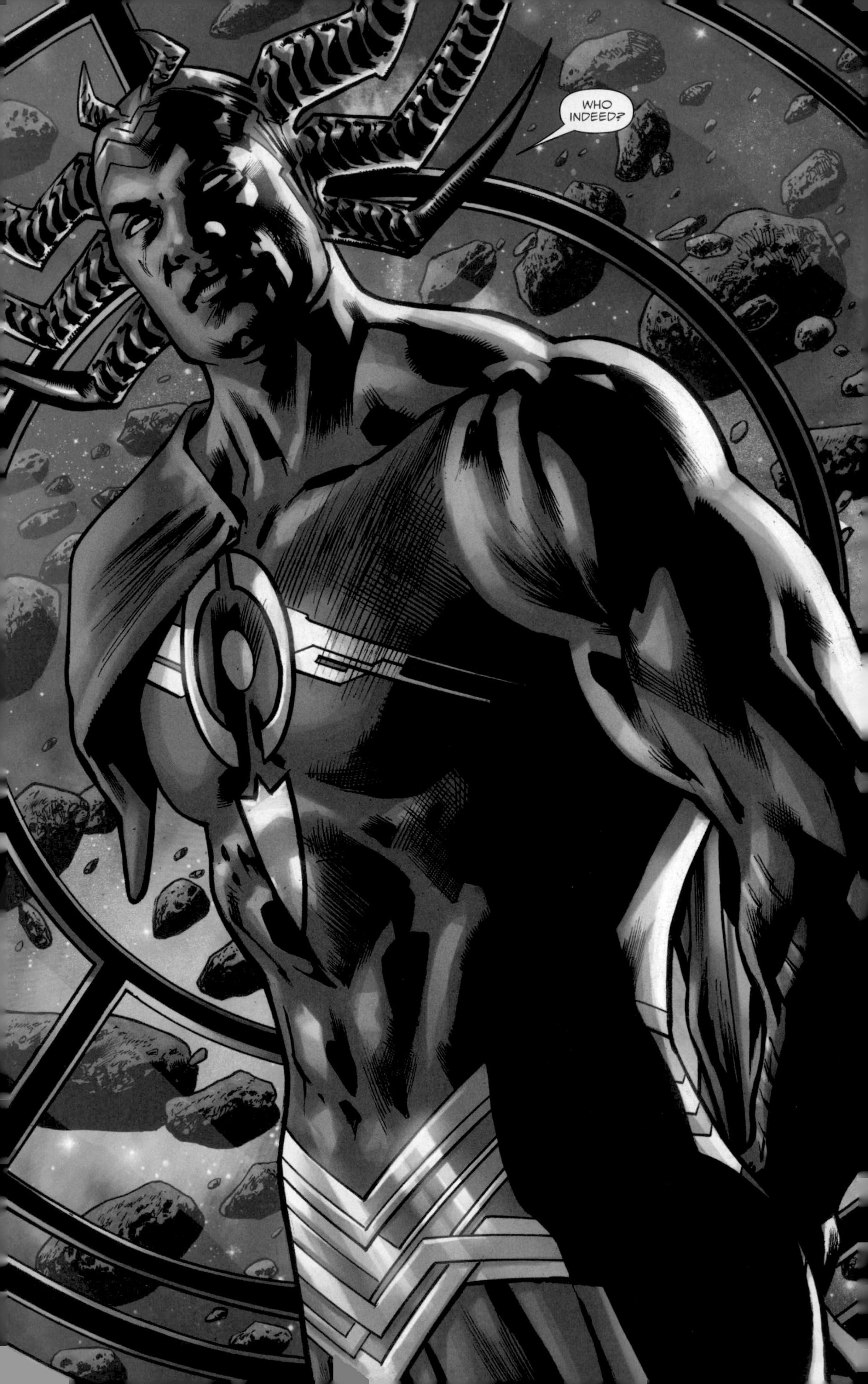
WHO INDEED?

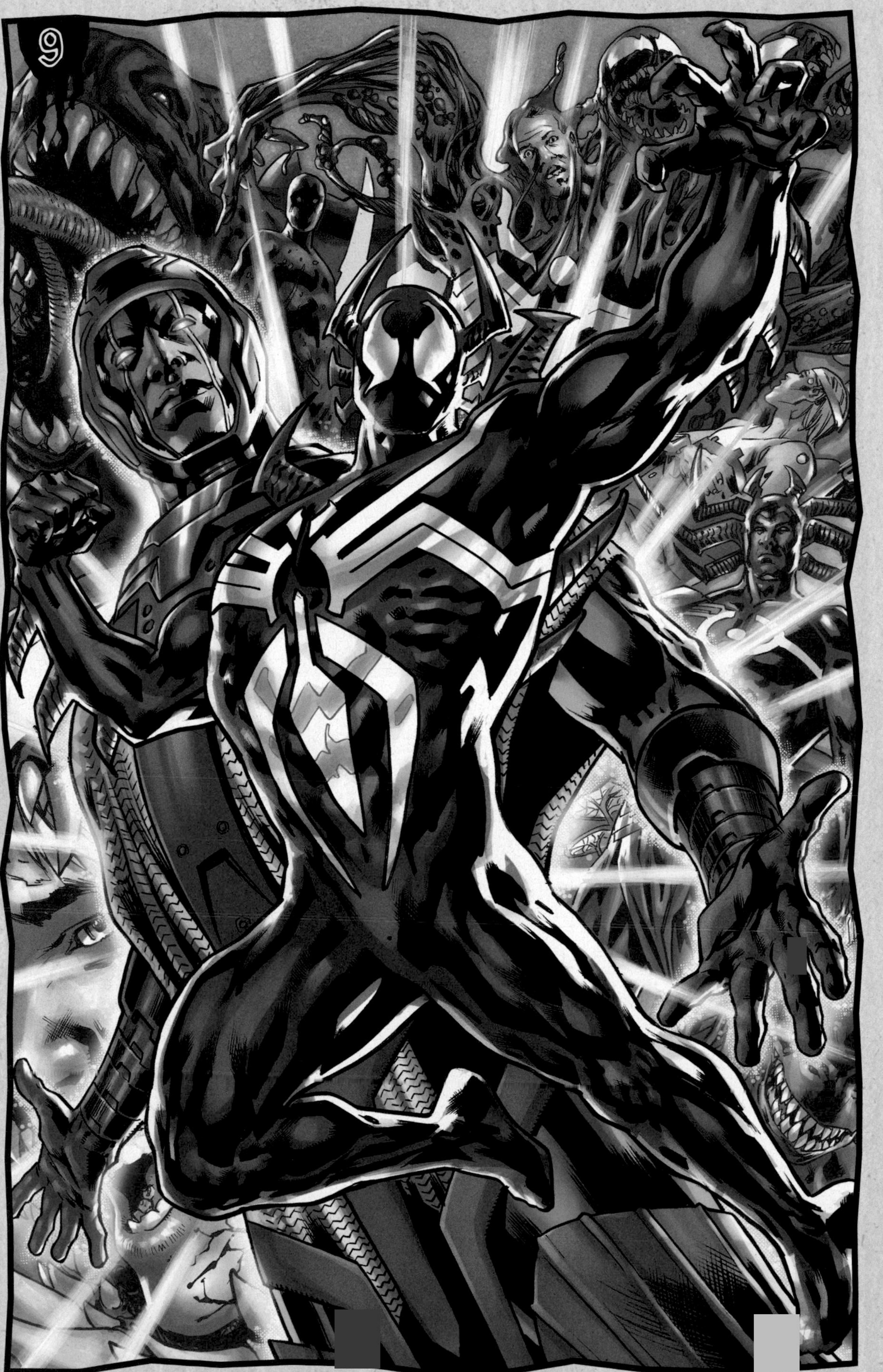
9

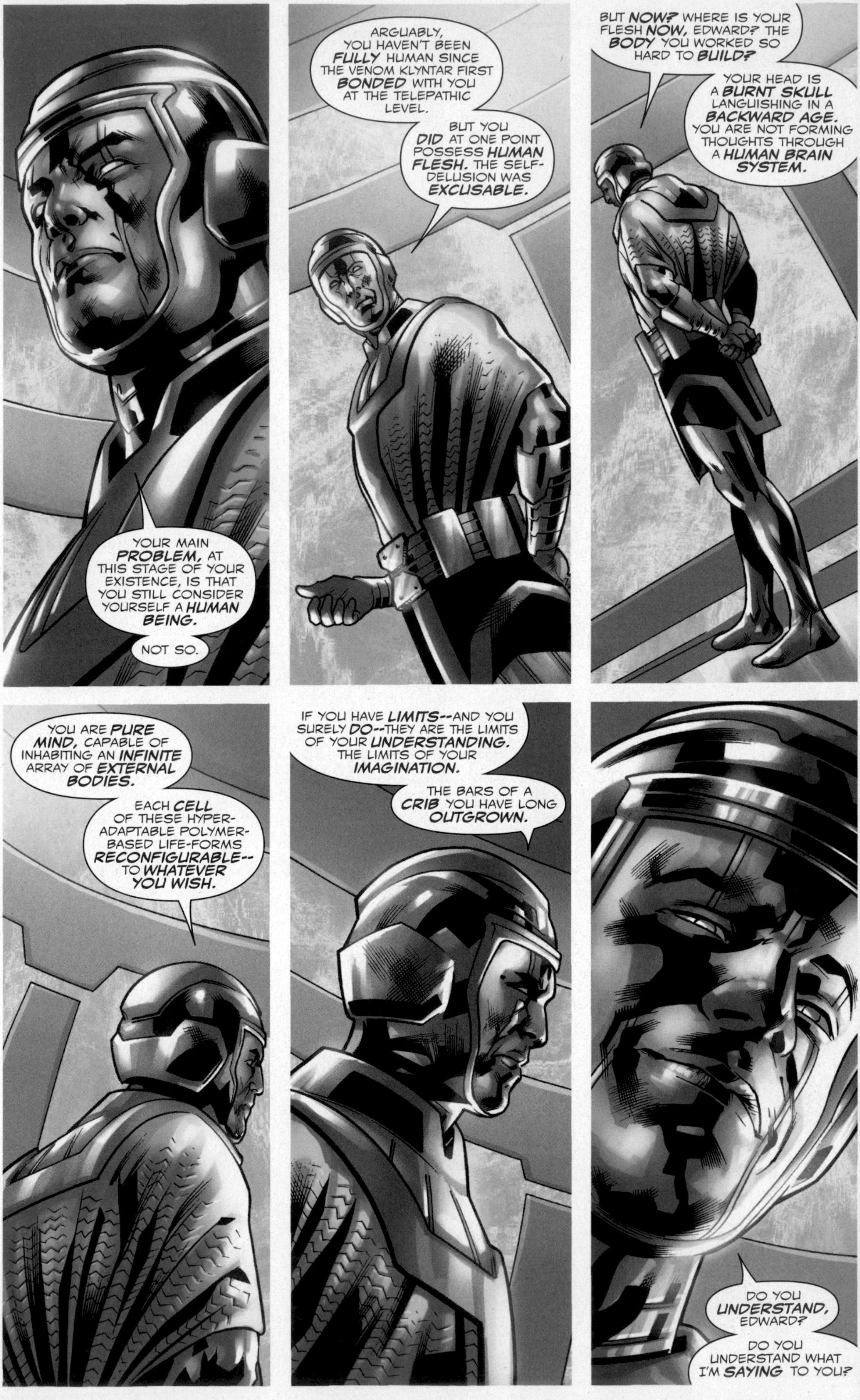
YOUR MAIN PROBLEM, AT THIS STAGE OF YOUR EXISTENCE, IS THAT YOU STILL CONSIDER YOURSELF A HUMAN BEING.
NOT SO.
ARGUABLY, YOU HAVEN'T BEEN FULLY HUMAN SINCE THE VENOM KLYNTAR FIRST BONDED WITH YOU AT THE TELEPATHIC LEVEL.
BUT YOU DID AT ONE POINT POSSESS HUMAN FLESH. THE SELF-DELUSION WAS EXCUSABLE.
BUT NOW? WHERE IS YOUR FLESH NOW, EDWARD? THE BODY YOU WORKED SO HARD TO BUILD?
YOUR HEAD IS A BURNT SKULL LANGUISHING IN A BACKWARD AGE. YOU ARE NOT FORMING THOUGHTS THROUGH A HUMAN BRAIN SYSTEM.
YOU ARE PURE MIND, CAPABLE OF INHABITING AN INFINITE ARRAY OF EXTERNAL BODIES.
EACH CELL OF THESE HYPER-ADAPTABLE POLYMER-BASED LIFE-FORMS RECONFIGURABLE-- TO WHATEVER YOU WISH.
IF YOU HAVE LIMITS--AND YOU SURELY DO--THEY ARE THE LIMITS OF YOUR UNDERSTANDING. THE LIMITS OF YOUR IMAGINATION.
THE BARS OF A CRIB YOU HAVE LONG OUTGROWN.
DO YOU UNDERSTAND, EDWARD?
DO YOU UNDERSTAND WHAT I'M SAYING TO YOU?

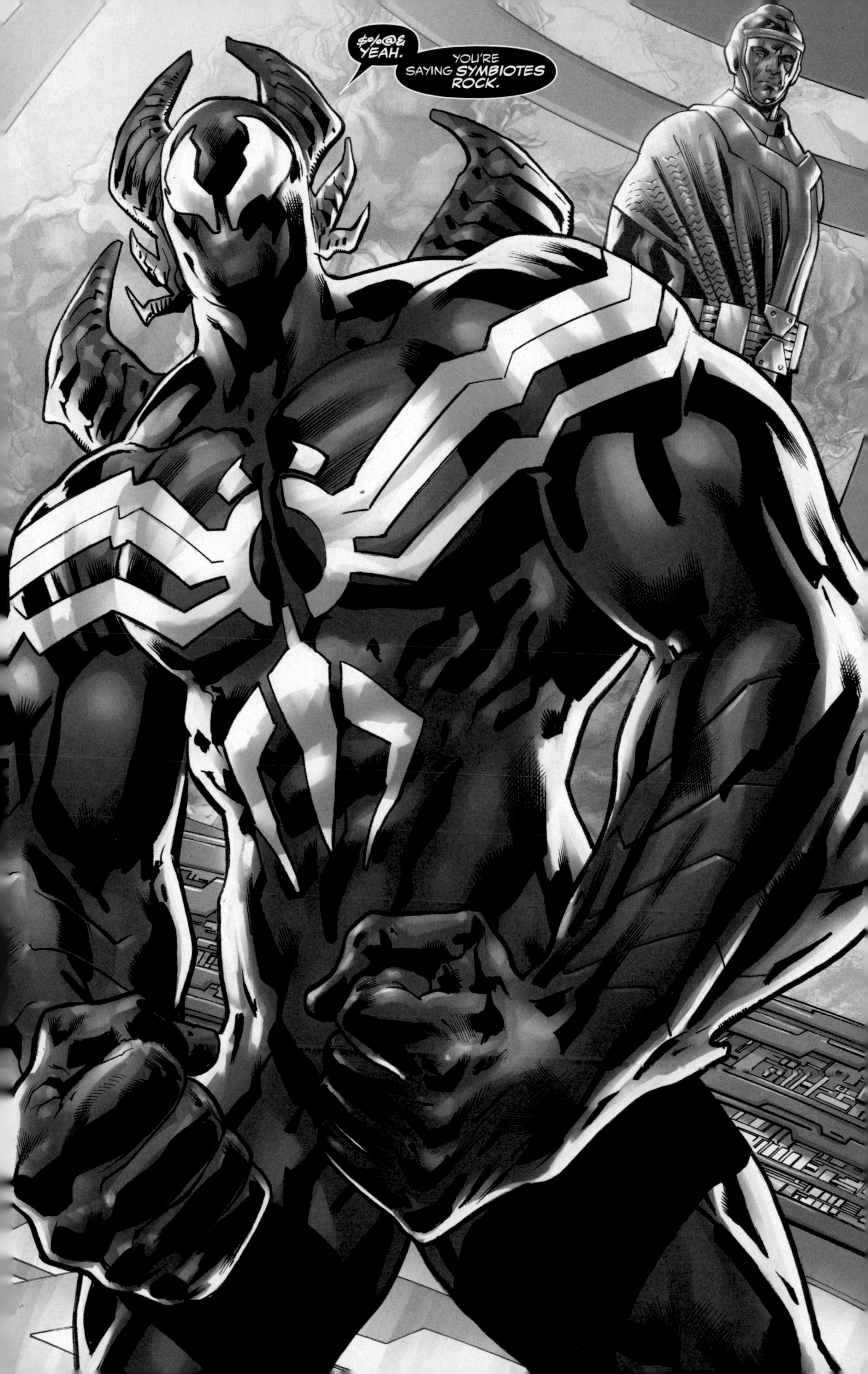
$%@& YEAH.
YOU'RE SAYING SYMBIOTES ROCK.

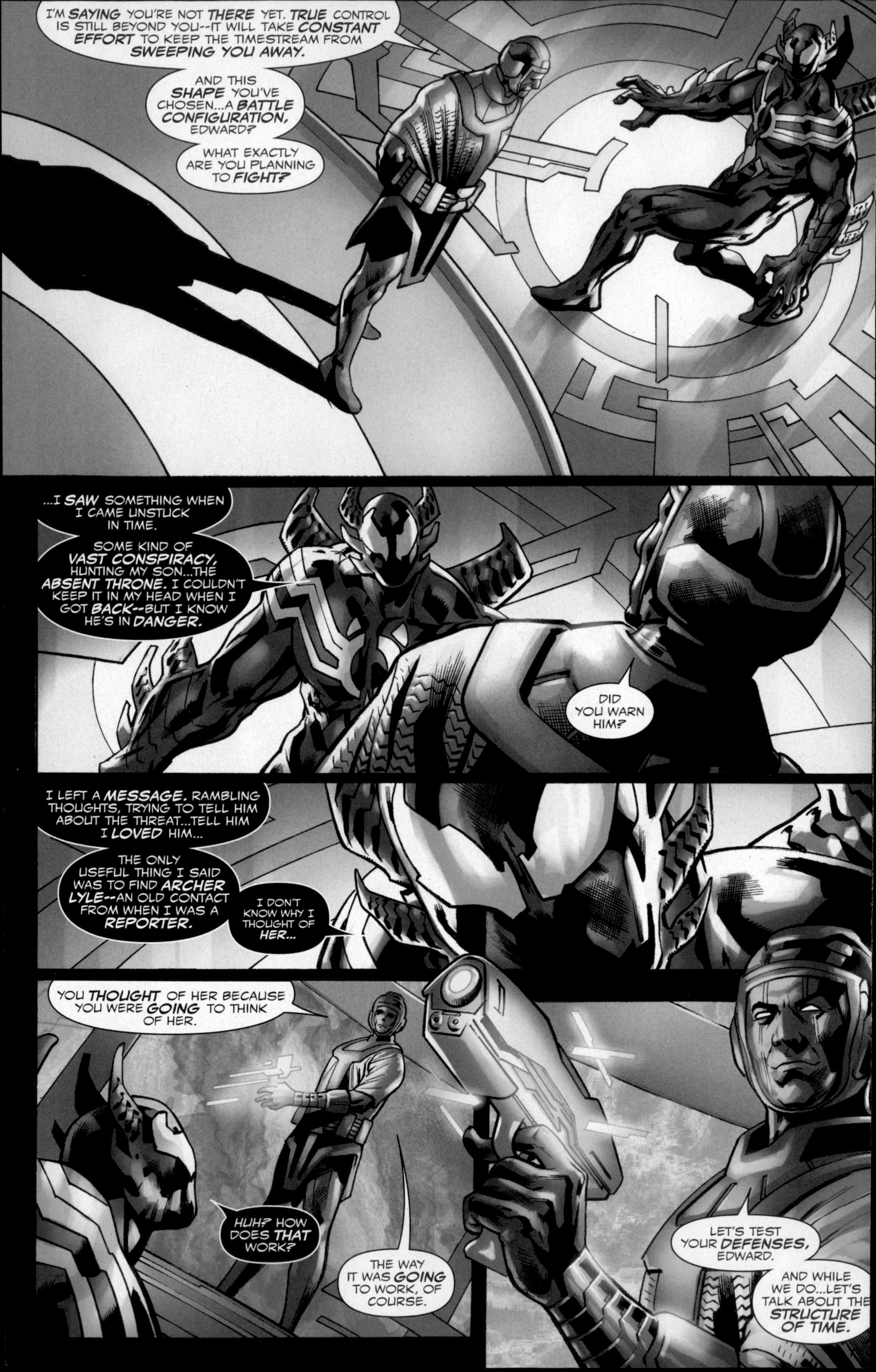
I'M SAYING YOU'RE NOT THERE YET. TRUE CONTROL IS STILL BEYOND YOU--IT WILL TAKE CONSTANT EFFORT TO KEEP THE TIMESTREAM FROM SWEEPING YOU AWAY.
AND THIS SHAPE YOU'VE CHOSEN...A BATTLE CONFIGURATION, EDWARD?
WHAT EXACTLY ARE YOU PLANNING TO FIGHT?
...I SAW SOMETHING WHEN I CAME UNSTUCK IN TIME.
SOME KIND OF VAST CONSPIRACY, HUNTING MY SON...THE ABSENT THRONE. I COULDN'T KEEP IT IN MY HEAD WHEN I GOT BACK--BUT I KNOW HE'S IN DANGER.
DID YOU WARN HIM?
I LEFT A MESSAGE. RAMBLING THOUGHTS, TRYING TO TELL HIM ABOUT THE THREAT...TELL HIM I LOVED HIM...
THE ONLY USEFUL THING I SAID WAS TO FIND ARCHER LYLE--AN OLD CONTACT FROM WHEN I WAS A REPORTER.
I DON'T KNOW WHY I THOUGHT OF HER...
YOU THOUGHT OF HER BECAUSE YOU WERE GOING TO THINK OF HER.
HUH? HOW DOES THAT WORK?
THE WAY IT WAS GOING TO WORK, OF COURSE.
LET'S TEST YOUR DEFENSES, EDWARD.
AND WHILE WE DO...LET'S TALK ABOUT THE STRUCTURE OF TIME.

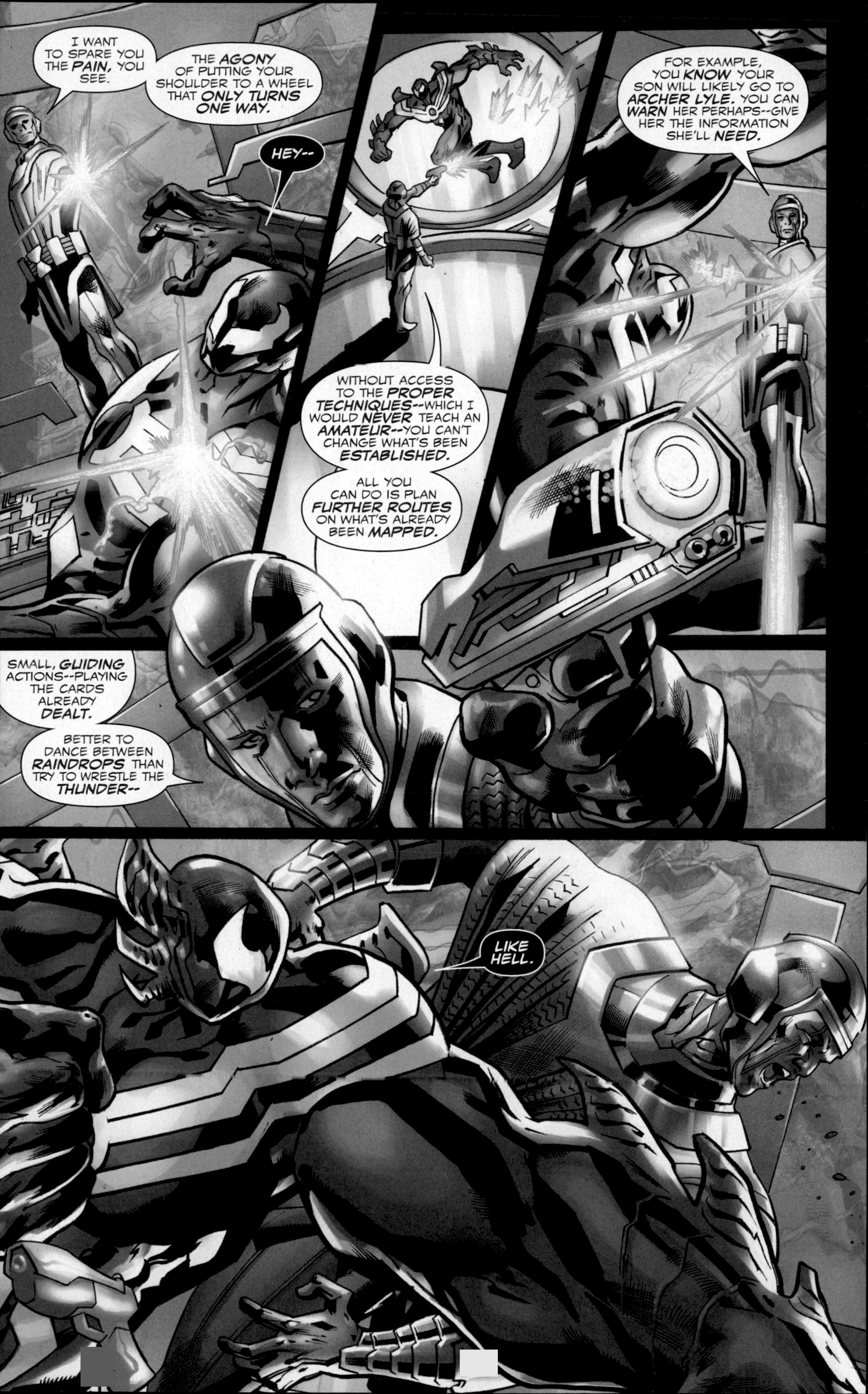
I WANT TO SPARE YOU THE PAIN, YOU SEE.
THE AGONY OF PUTTING YOUR SHOULDER TO A WHEEL THAT ONLY TURNS ONE WAY.
HEY--
WITHOUT ACCESS TO THE PROPER TECHNIQUES--WHICH I WOULD NEVER TEACH AN AMATEUR--YOU CAN'T CHANGE WHAT'S BEEN ESTABLISHED.
ALL YOU CAN DO IS PLAN FURTHER ROUTES ON WHAT'S ALREADY BEEN MAPPED.
FOR EXAMPLE, YOU KNOW YOUR SON WILL LIKELY GO TO ARCHER LYLE. YOU CAN WARN HER PERHAPS--GIVE HER THE INFORMATION SHE'LL NEED.
SMALL, GUIDING ACTIONS--PLAYING THE CARDS ALREADY DEALT.
BETTER TO DANCE BETWEEN RAINDROPS THAN TRY TO WRESTLE THE THUNDER--
LIKE HELL.

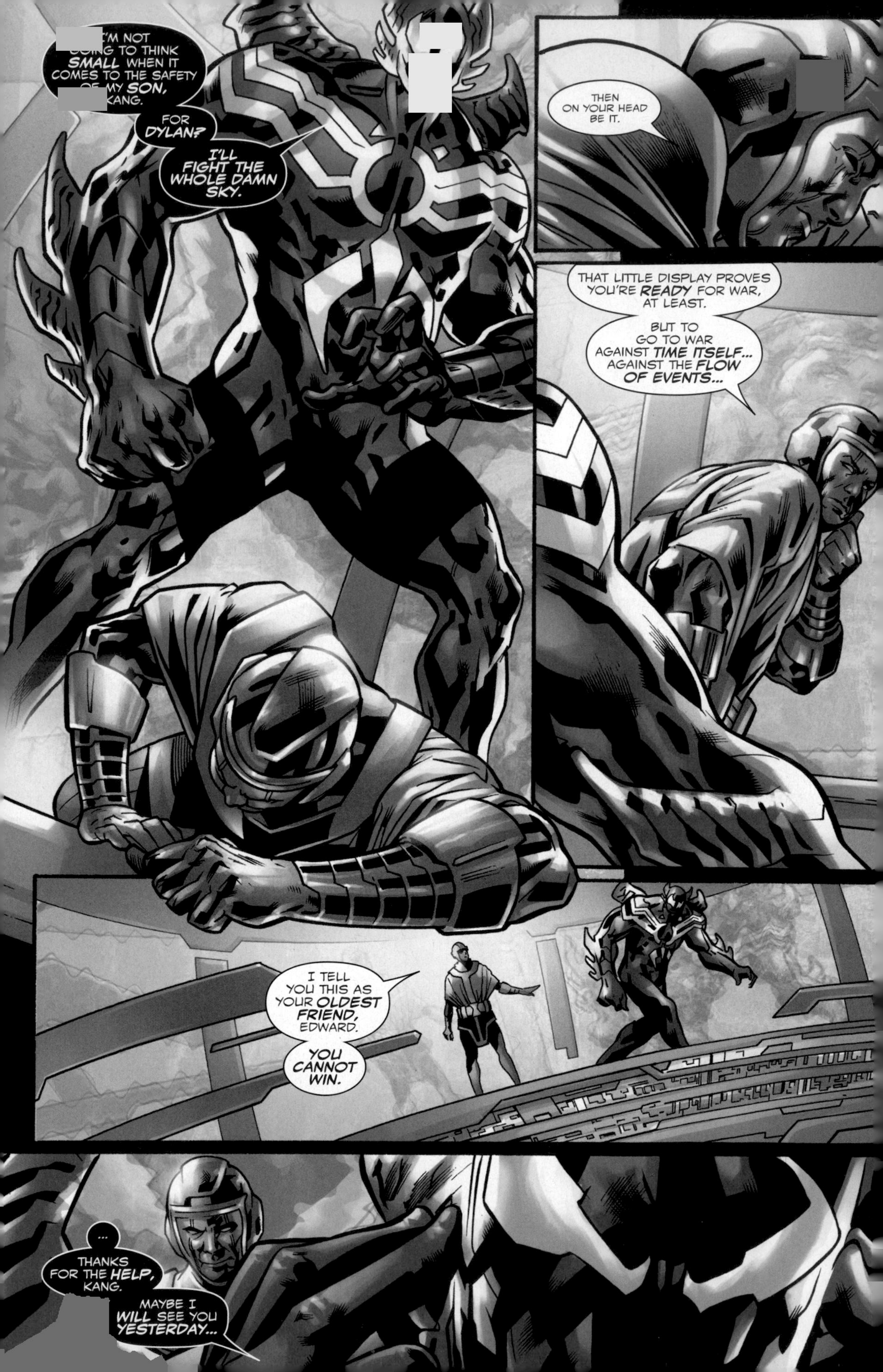
I'M NOT GOING TO THINK SMALL WHEN IT COMES TO THE SAFETY OF MY SON, KANG.
FOR DYLAN?
I'LL FIGHT THE WHOLE DAMN SKY.
THEN ON YOUR HEAD BE IT.
THAT LITTLE DISPLAY PROVES YOU'RE READY FOR WAR, AT LEAST.
BUT TO GO TO WAR AGAINST TIME ITSELF... AGAINST THE FLOW OF EVENTS...
I TELL YOU THIS AS YOUR OLDEST FRIEND, EDWARD.
YOU CANNOT WIN.
...
THANKS FOR THE HELP, KANG.
MAYBE I WILL SEE YOU YESTERDAY...

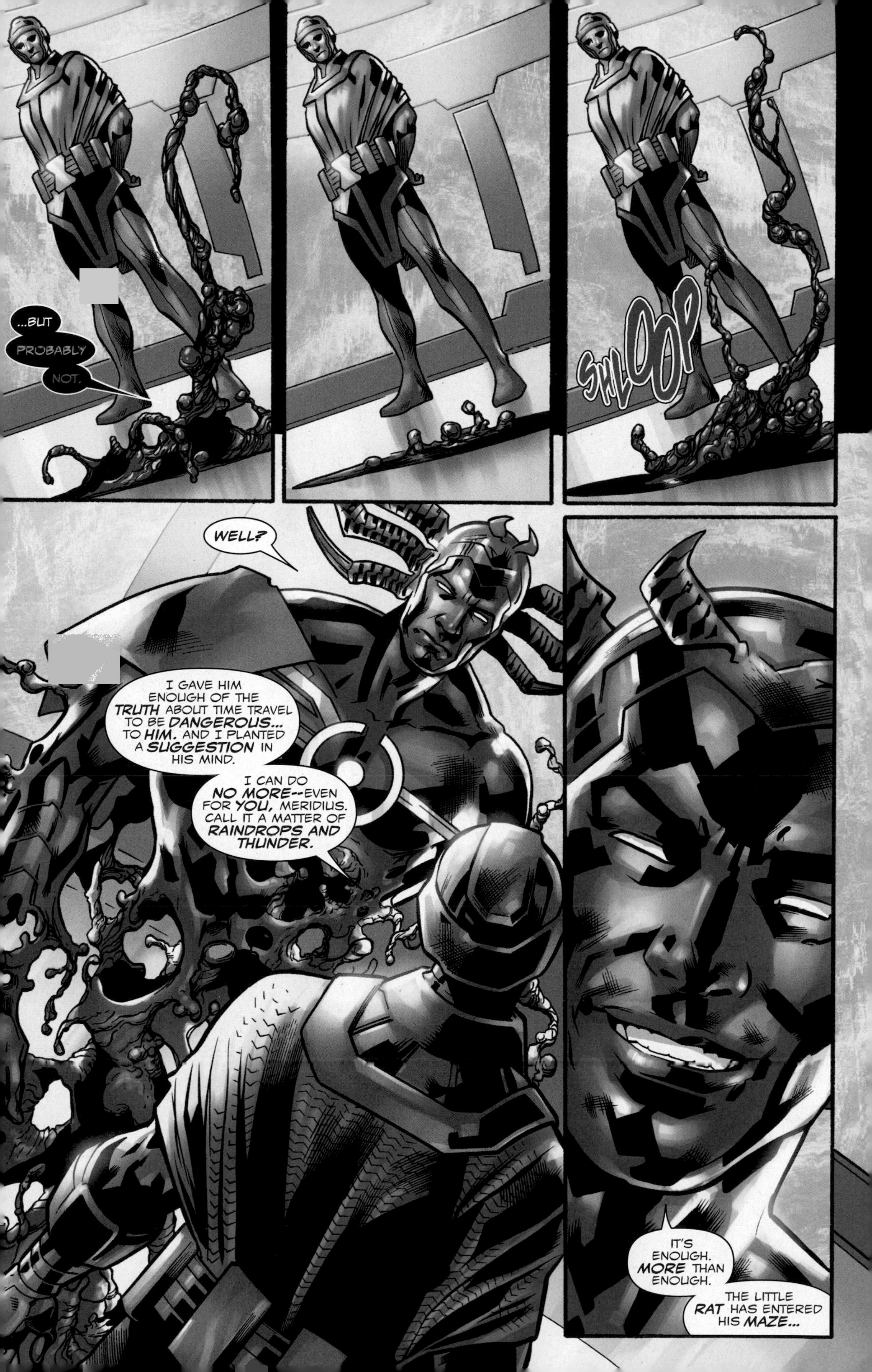

...BUT PROBABLY NOT.
SPHLOOP
WELL?
I GAVE HIM ENOUGH OF THE TRUTH ABOUT TIME TRAVEL TO BE DANGEROUS... TO HIM. AND I PLANTED A SUGGESTION IN HIS MIND.
I CAN DO NO MORE--EVEN FOR YOU, MERIDIUS. CALL IT A MATTER OF RAINDROPS AND THUNDER.
IT'S ENOUGH. MORE THAN ENOUGH.
THE LITTLE RAT HAS ENTERED HIS MAZE...

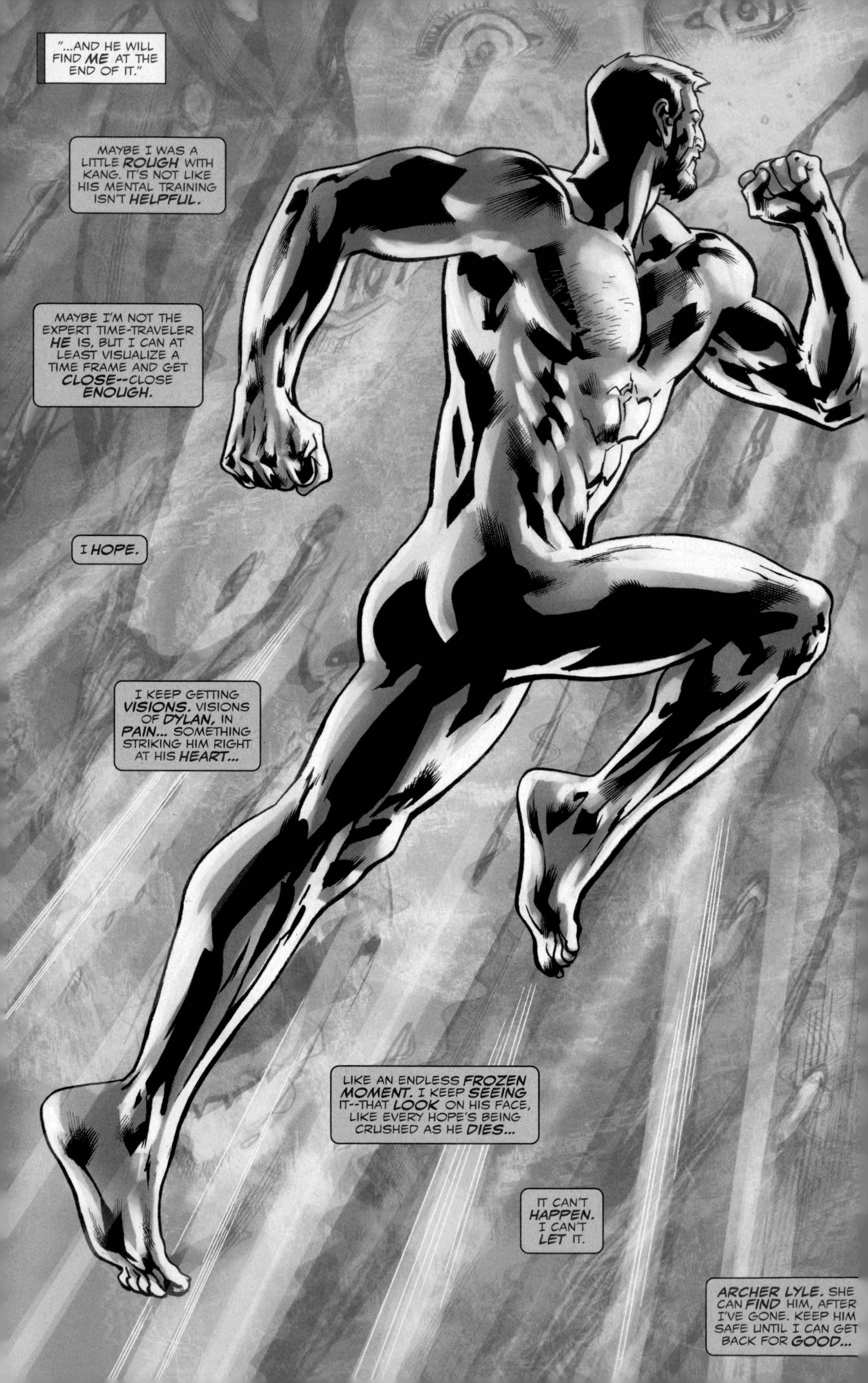
"...AND HE WILL FIND ME AT THE END OF IT."
MAYBE I WAS A LITTLE ROUGH WITH KANG. IT'S NOT LIKE HIS MENTAL TRAINING ISN'T HELPFUL.
MAYBE I'M NOT THE EXPERT TIME-TRAVELER HE IS, BUT I CAN AT LEAST VISUALIZE A TIME FRAME AND GET CLOSE--CLOSE ENOUGH.
I HOPE.
I KEEP GETTING VISIONS. VISIONS OF DYLAN, IN PAIN... SOMETHING STRIKING HIM RIGHT AT HIS HEART...
LIKE AN ENDLESS FROZEN MOMENT. I KEEP SEEING IT--THAT LOOK ON HIS FACE, LIKE EVERY HOPE'S BEING CRUSHED AS HE DIES...
IT CAN'T HAPPEN. I CAN'T LET IT.
ARCHER LYLE. SHE CAN FIND HIM, AFTER I'VE GONE. KEEP HIM SAFE UNTIL I CAN GET BACK FOR GOOD...

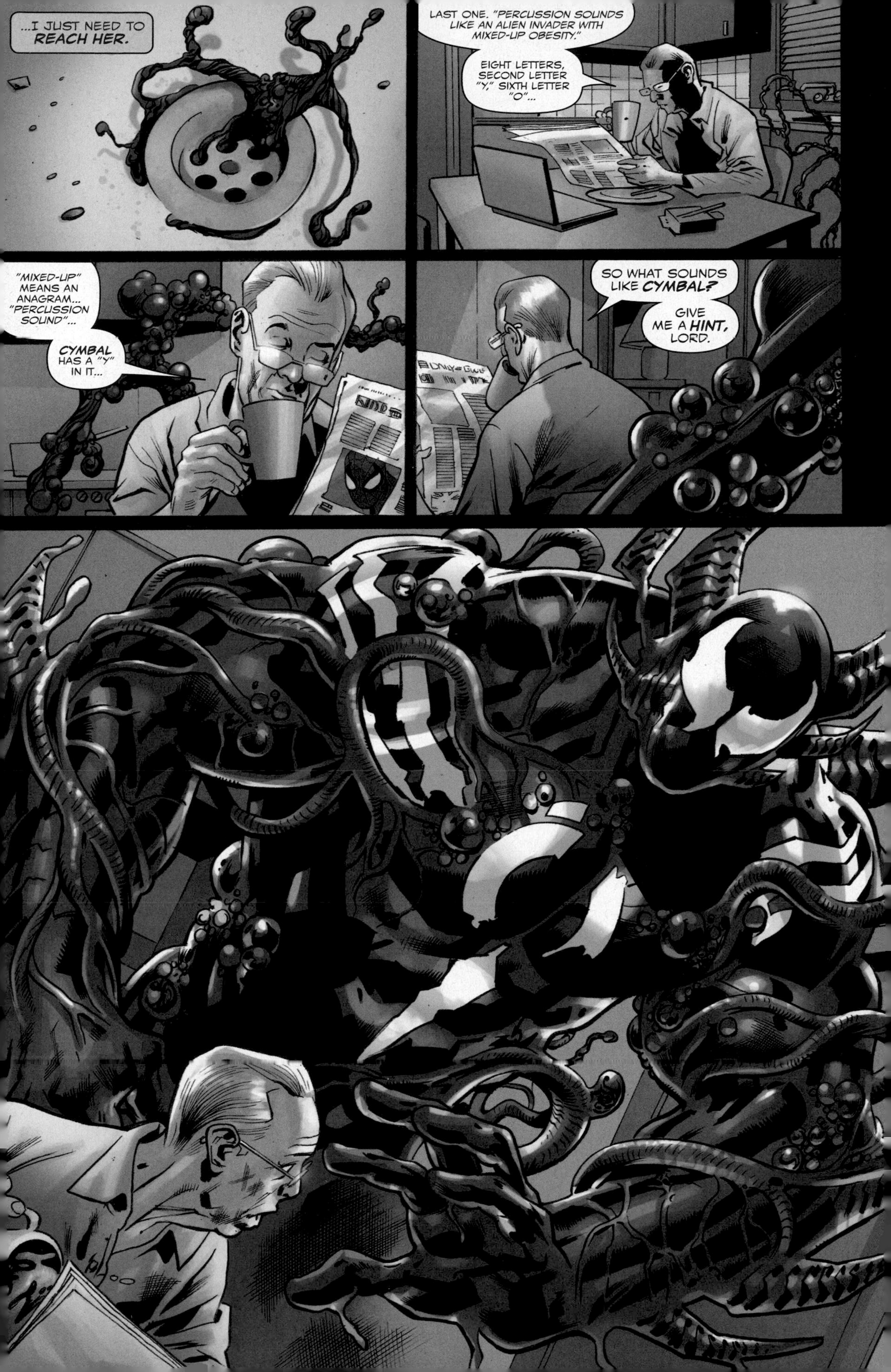
...I JUST NEED TO REACH HER.
LAST ONE. "PERCUSSION SOUNDS LIKE AN ALIEN INVADER WITH MIXED-UP OBESITY."
EIGHT LETTERS, SECOND LETTER "Y," SIXTH LETTER "O"...
"MIXED-UP" MEANS AN ANAGRAM... "PERCUSSION SOUND"...
CYMBAL HAS A "Y" IN IT...
SO WHAT SOUNDS LIKE CYMBAL?
GIVE ME A HINT, LORD.

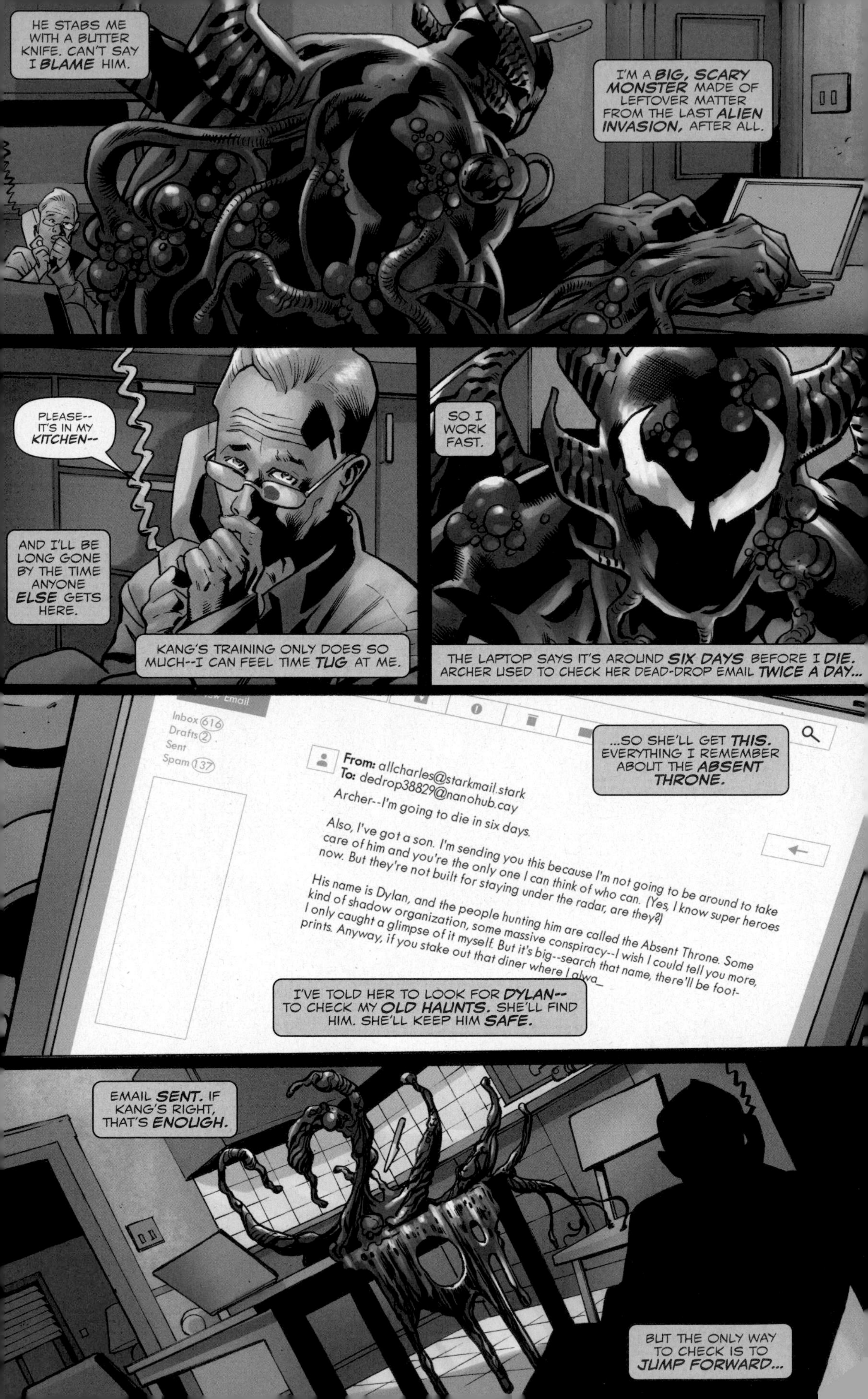
HE STABS ME WITH A BUTTER KNIFE. CAN'T SAY I BLAME HIM.
I'M A BIG, SCARY MONSTER MADE OF LEFTOVER MATTER FROM THE LAST ALIEN INVASION, AFTER ALL.
PLEASE-- IT'S IN MY KITCHEN--
AND I'LL BE LONG GONE BY THE TIME ANYONE ELSE GETS HERE.
KANG'S TRAINING ONLY DOES SO MUCH--I CAN FEEL TIME TUG AT ME.
SO I WORK FAST.
THE LAPTOP SAYS IT'S AROUND SIX DAYS BEFORE I DIE. ARCHER USED TO CHECK HER DEAD-DROP EMAIL TWICE A DAY...
Inbox 616
Drafts 2
Sent
Spam 137
From: allcharles@starkmail.stark
To: dedrop38829@nanohub.cay
Archer--I'm going to die in six days.
Also, I've got a son. I'm sending you this because I'm not going to be around to take care of him and you're the only one I can think of who can. (Yes, I know super heroes now. But they're not built for staying under the radar, are they?)
His name is Dylan, and the people hunting him are called the Absent Throne. Some kind of shadow organization, some massive conspiracy--I wish I could tell you more, I only caught a glimpse of it myself. But it's big--search that name, there'll be foot-prints. Anyway, if you stake out that diner where I alwa_
...SO SHE'LL GET THIS. EVERYTHING I REMEMBER ABOUT THE ABSENT THRONE.
I'VE TOLD HER TO LOOK FOR DYLAN-- TO CHECK MY OLD HAUNTS. SHE'LL FIND HIM. SHE'LL KEEP HIM SAFE.
EMAIL SENT. IF KANG'S RIGHT, THAT'S ENOUGH.
BUT THE ONLY WAY TO CHECK IS TO JUMP FORWARD...

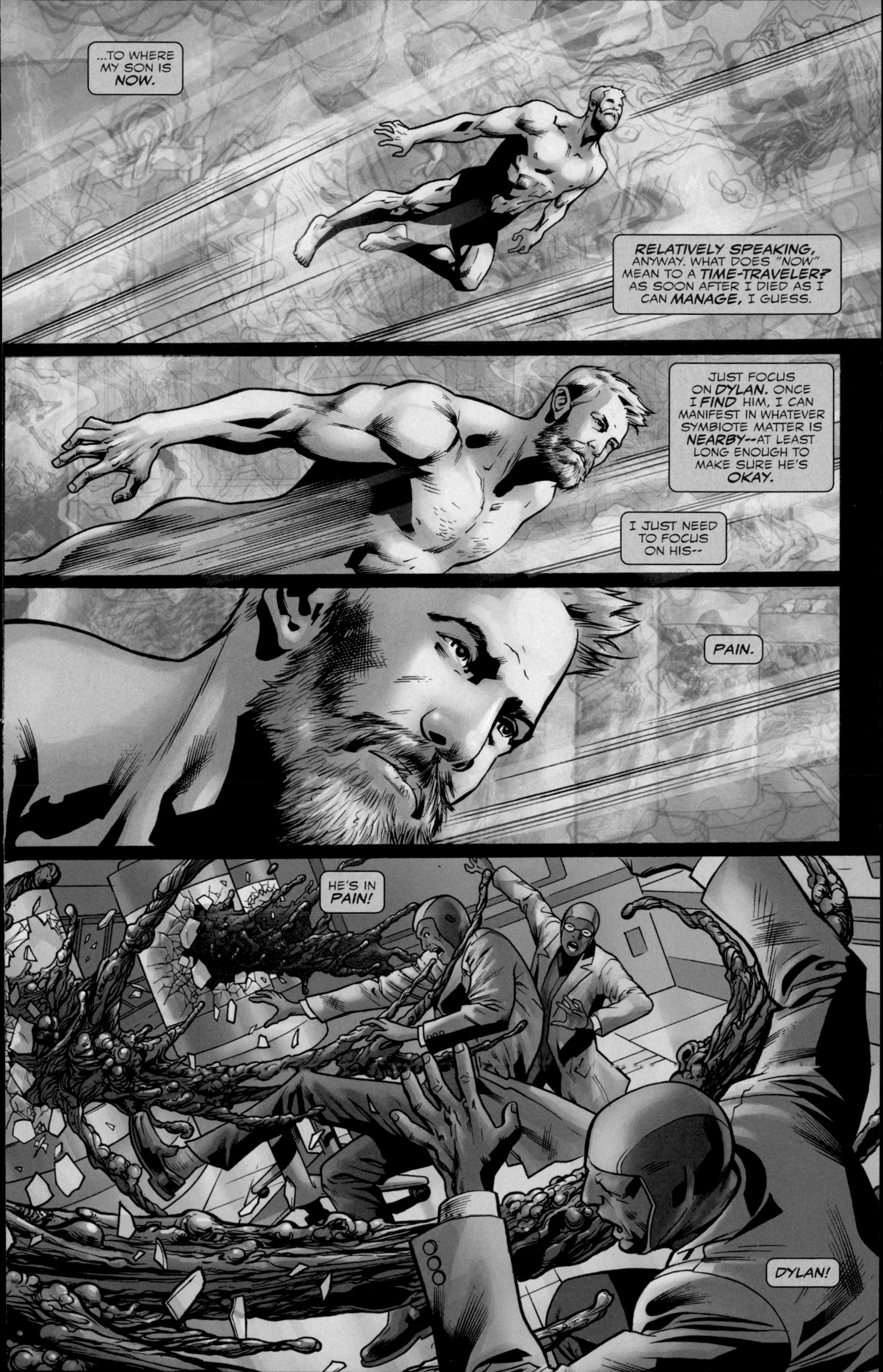
...TO WHERE MY SON IS NOW.
RELATIVELY SPEAKING, ANYWAY. WHAT DOES "NOW" MEAN TO A TIME-TRAVELER? AS SOON AFTER I DIED AS I CAN MANAGE, I GUESS.
JUST FOCUS ON DYLAN. ONCE I FIND HIM, I CAN MANIFEST IN WHATEVER SYMBIOTE MATTER IS NEARBY--AT LEAST LONG ENOUGH TO MAKE SURE HE'S OKAY.
I JUST NEED TO FOCUS ON HIS--
PAIN.
HE'S IN PAIN!
DYLAN!

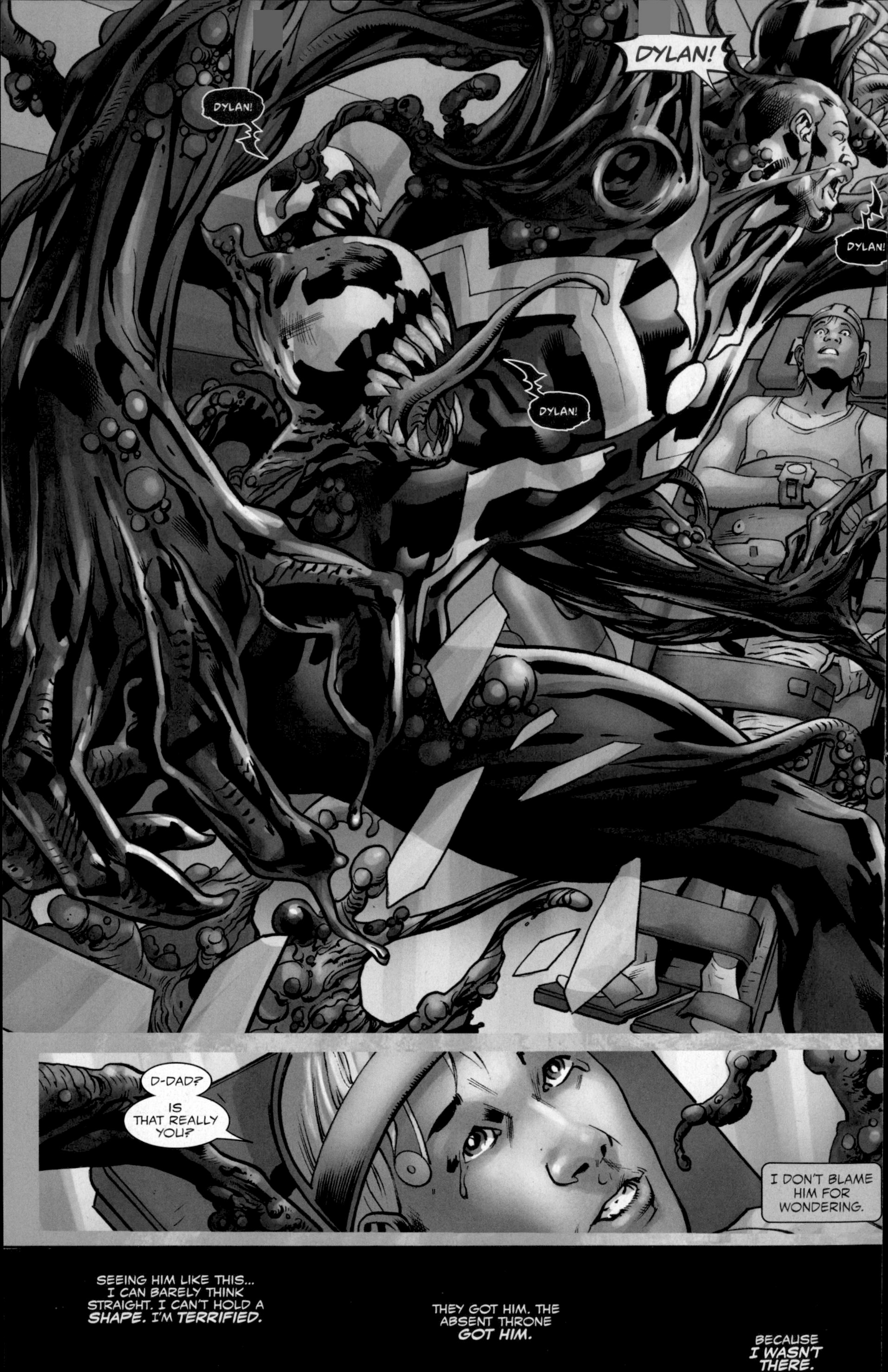
DYLAN!
DYLAN!
DYLAN!
DYLAN!
D-DAD? IS THAT REALLY YOU?
I DON'T BLAME HIM FOR WONDERING.
SEEING HIM LIKE THIS... I CAN BARELY THINK STRAIGHT. I CAN'T HOLD A SHAPE. I'M TERRIFIED.
THEY GOT HIM. THE ABSENT THRONE GOT HIM.
BECAUSE I WASN'T THERE.

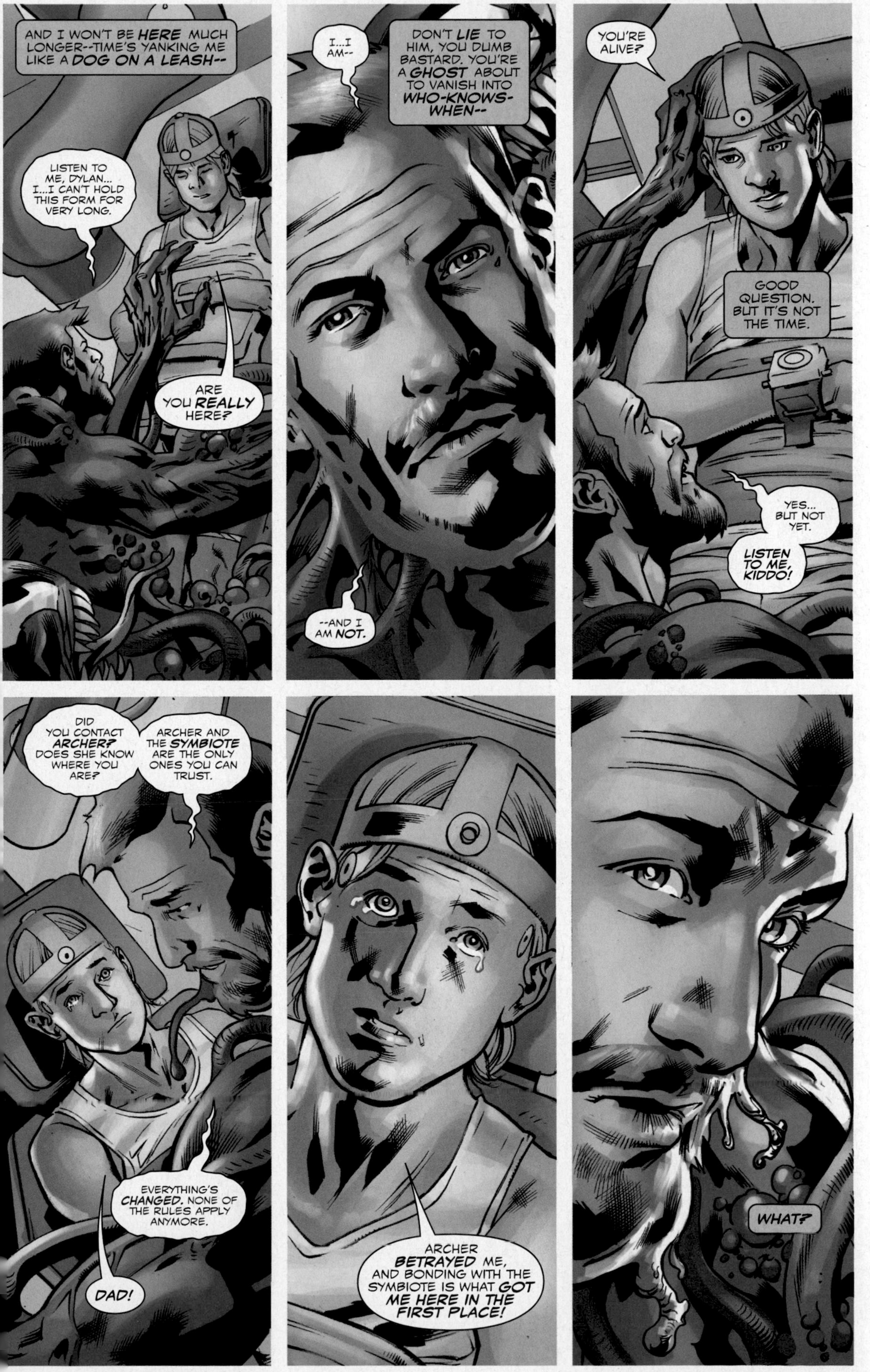

AND I WON'T BE HERE MUCH LONGER--TIME'S YANKING ME LIKE A DOG ON A LEASH--
LISTEN TO ME, DYLAN... I...I CAN'T HOLD THIS FORM FOR VERY LONG.
ARE YOU REALLY HERE?
I...I AM--
DON'T LIE TO HIM, YOU DUMB BASTARD. YOU'RE A GHOST ABOUT TO VANISH INTO WHO-KNOWS-WHEN--
--AND I AM NOT.
YOU'RE ALIVE?
GOOD QUESTION. BUT IT'S NOT THE TIME.
YES... BUT NOT YET.
LISTEN TO ME, KIDDO!
DID YOU CONTACT ARCHER? DOES SHE KNOW WHERE YOU ARE?
ARCHER AND THE SYMBIOTE ARE THE ONLY ONES YOU CAN TRUST.
EVERYTHING'S CHANGED. NONE OF THE RULES APPLY ANYMORE.
DAD!
ARCHER BETRAYED ME, AND BONDING WITH THE SYMBIOTE IS WHAT GOT ME HERE IN THE FIRST PLACE!
WHAT?

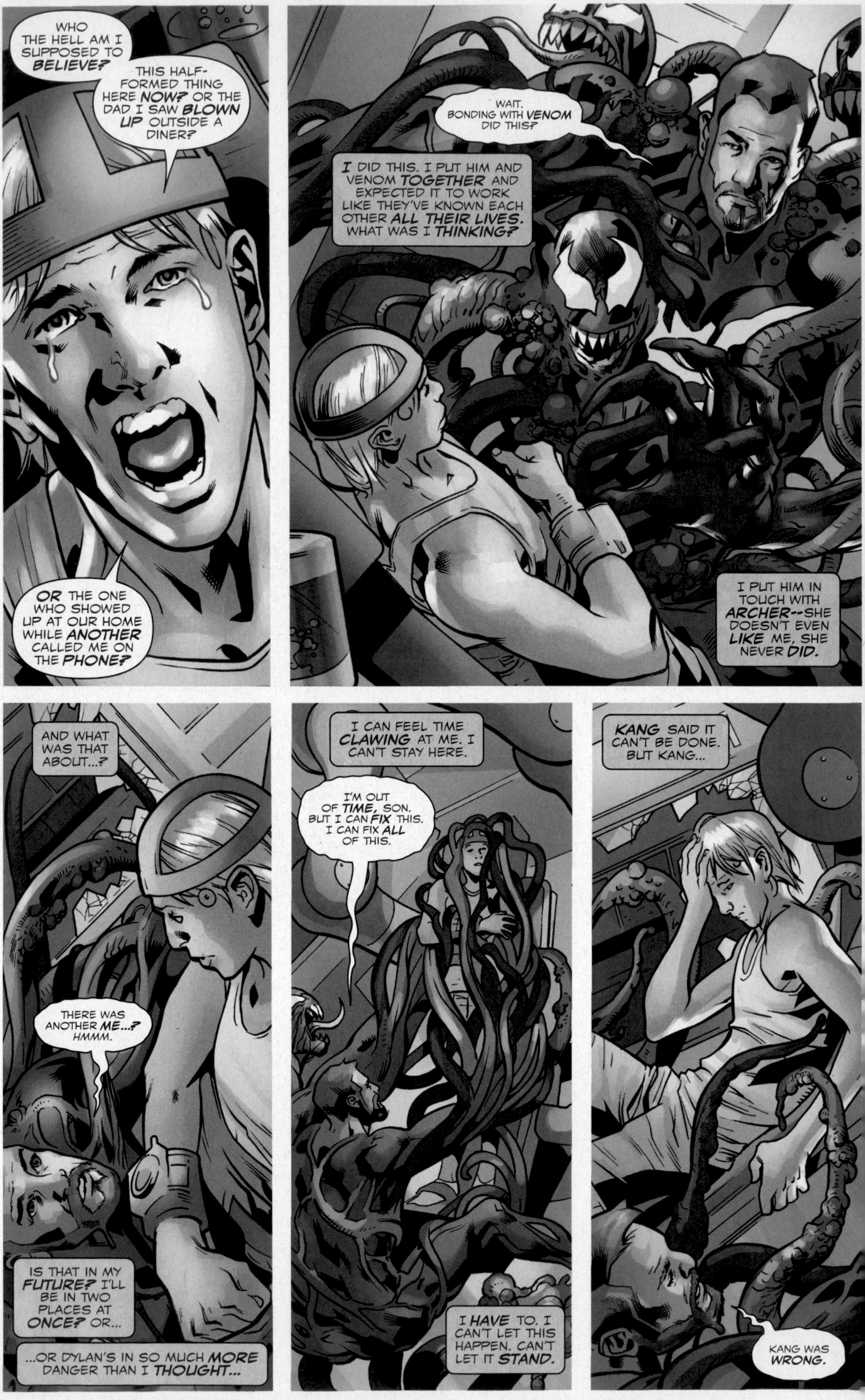
WHO THE HELL AM I SUPPOSED TO BELIEVE?
THIS HALF-FORMED THING HERE NOW? OR THE DAD I SAW BLOWN UP OUTSIDE A DINER?
OR THE ONE WHO SHOWED UP AT OUR HOME WHILE ANOTHER CALLED ME ON THE PHONE?
WAIT. BONDING WITH VENOM DID THIS?
I DID THIS. I PUT HIM AND VENOM TOGETHER AND EXPECTED IT TO WORK LIKE THEY'VE KNOWN EACH OTHER ALL THEIR LIVES. WHAT WAS I THINKING?
I PUT HIM IN TOUCH WITH ARCHER--SHE DOESN'T EVEN LIKE ME, SHE NEVER DID.
AND WHAT WAS THAT ABOUT...?
THERE WAS ANOTHER ME...? HMMM.
IS THAT IN MY FUTURE? I'LL BE IN TWO PLACES AT ONCE? OR...
...OR DYLAN'S IN SO MUCH MORE DANGER THAN I THOUGHT...
I CAN FEEL TIME CLAWING AT ME. I CAN'T STAY HERE.
I'M OUT OF TIME, SON. BUT I CAN FIX THIS. I CAN FIX ALL OF THIS.
I HAVE TO. I CAN'T LET THIS HAPPEN. CAN'T LET IT STAND.
KANG SAID IT CAN'T BE DONE. BUT KANG...
KANG WAS WRONG.

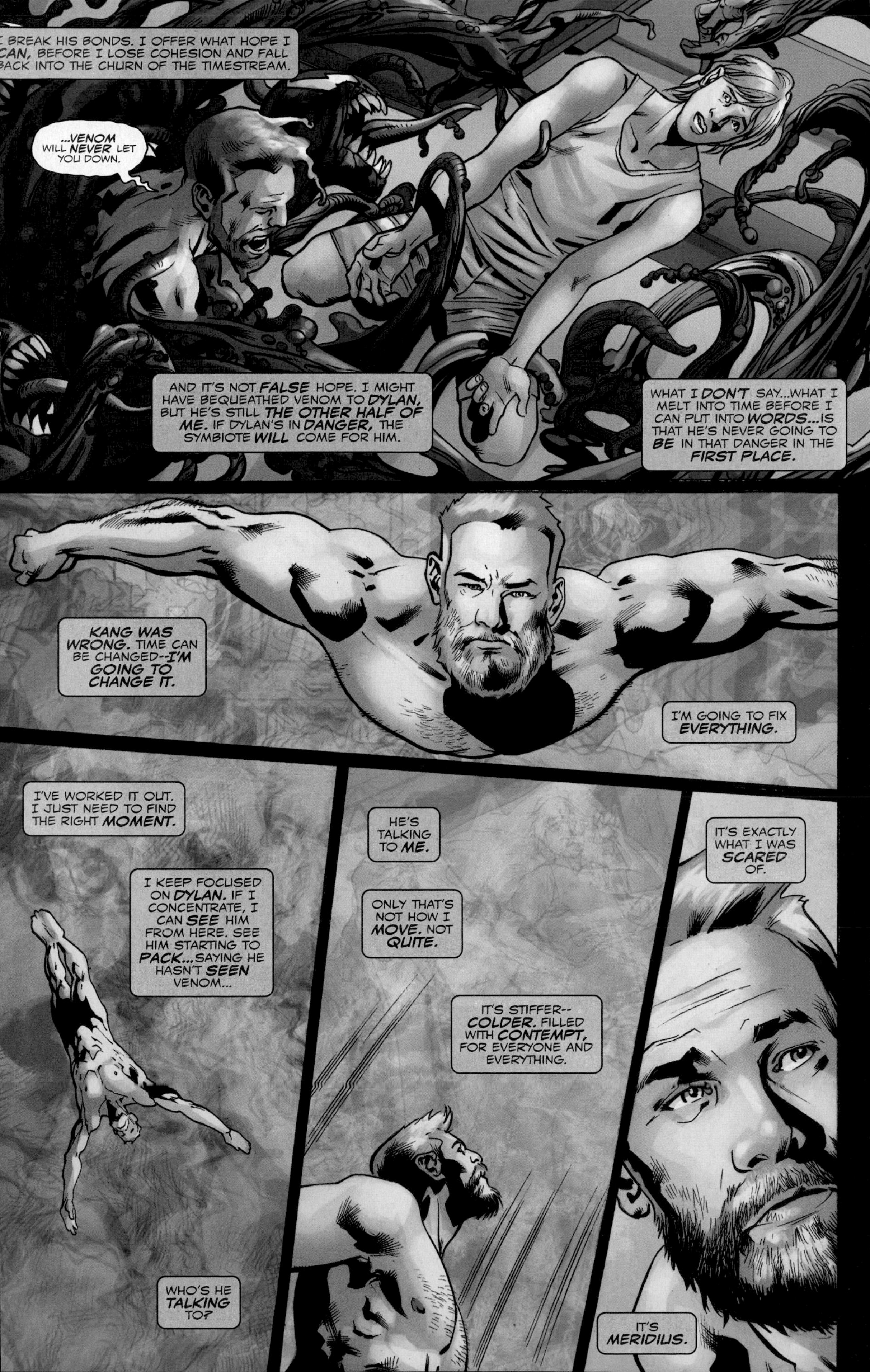

I BREAK HIS BONDS. I OFFER WHAT HOPE I CAN, BEFORE I LOSE COHESION AND FALL BACK INTO THE CHURN OF THE TIMESTREAM.
...VENOM WILL NEVER LET YOU DOWN.
AND IT'S NOT FALSE HOPE. I MIGHT HAVE BEQUEATHED VENOM TO DYLAN, BUT HE'S STILL THE OTHER HALF OF ME. IF DYLAN'S IN DANGER, THE SYMBIOTE WILL COME FOR HIM.
WHAT I DON'T SAY...WHAT I MELT INTO TIME BEFORE I CAN PUT INTO WORDS...IS THAT HE'S NEVER GOING TO BE IN THAT DANGER IN THE FIRST PLACE.
KANG WAS WRONG. TIME CAN BE CHANGED--I'M GOING TO CHANGE IT.
I'M GOING TO FIX EVERYTHING.
I'VE WORKED IT OUT. I JUST NEED TO FIND THE RIGHT MOMENT.
I KEEP FOCUSED ON DYLAN. IF I CONCENTRATE, I CAN SEE HIM FROM HERE. SEE HIM STARTING TO PACK...SAYING HE HASN'T SEEN VENOM...
WHO'S HE TALKING TO?
HE'S TALKING TO ME.
ONLY THAT'S NOT HOW I MOVE. NOT QUITE.
IT'S STIFFER--COLDER. FILLED WITH CONTEMPT, FOR EVERYONE AND EVERYTHING.
IT'S EXACTLY WHAT I WAS SCARED OF.
IT'S MERIDIUS.

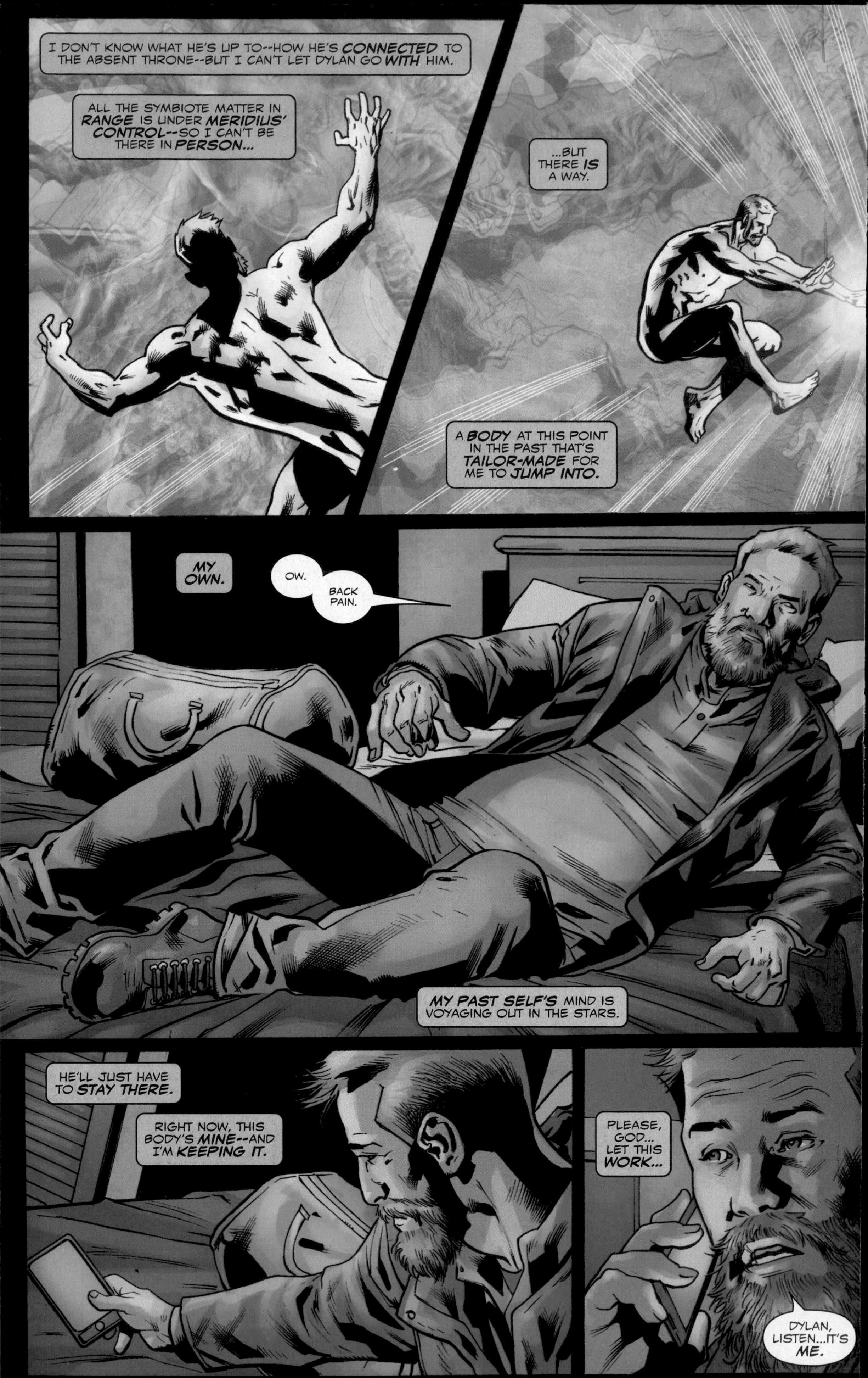
I DON'T KNOW WHAT HE'S UP TO--HOW HE'S CONNECTED TO THE ABSENT THRONE--BUT I CAN'T LET DYLAN GO WITH HIM.
ALL THE SYMBIOTE MATTER IN RANGE IS UNDER MERIDIUS' CONTROL--SO I CAN'T BE THERE IN PERSON...
...BUT THERE IS A WAY.
A BODY AT THIS POINT IN THE PAST THAT'S TAILOR-MADE FOR ME TO JUMP INTO.
MY OWN.
OW.
BACK PAIN.
MY PAST SELF'S MIND IS VOYAGING OUT IN THE STARS.
HE'LL JUST HAVE TO STAY THERE.
RIGHT NOW, THIS BODY'S MINE--AND I'M KEEPING IT.
PLEASE, GOD... LET THIS WORK...
DYLAN, LISTEN...IT'S ME.

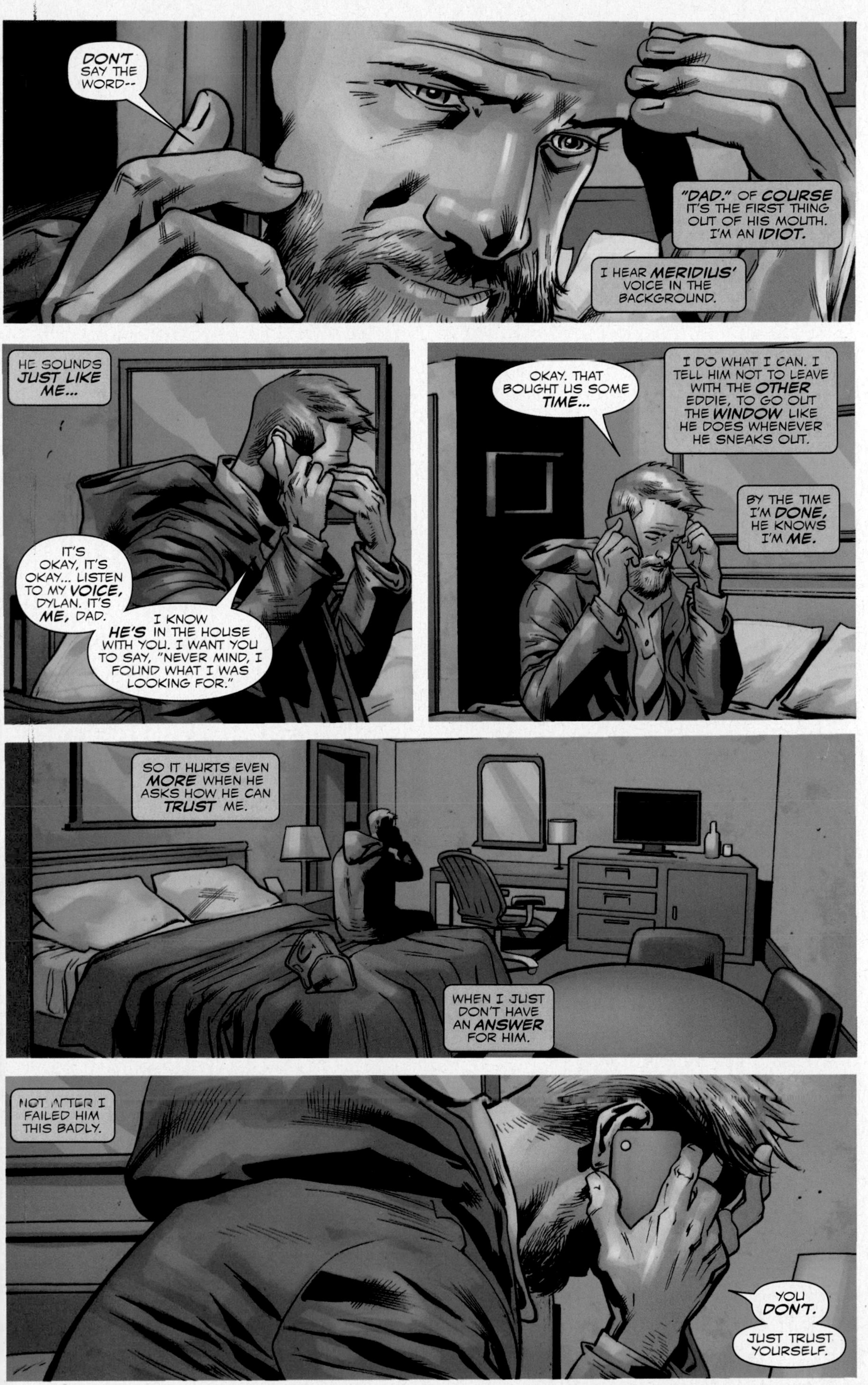
DON'T SAY THE WORD--
"DAD." OF COURSE IT'S THE FIRST THING OUT OF HIS MOUTH. I'M AN IDIOT.
I HEAR MERIDIUS' VOICE IN THE BACKGROUND.
HE SOUNDS JUST LIKE ME...
IT'S OKAY, IT'S OKAY... LISTEN TO MY VOICE, DYLAN. IT'S ME, DAD.
I KNOW HE'S IN THE HOUSE WITH YOU. I WANT YOU TO SAY, "NEVER MIND, I FOUND WHAT I WAS LOOKING FOR."
OKAY. THAT BOUGHT US SOME TIME...
I DO WHAT I CAN. I TELL HIM NOT TO LEAVE WITH THE OTHER EDDIE, TO GO OUT THE WINDOW LIKE HE DOES WHENEVER HE SNEAKS OUT.
BY THE TIME I'M DONE, HE KNOWS I'M ME.
SO IT HURTS EVEN MORE WHEN HE ASKS HOW HE CAN TRUST ME.
WHEN I JUST DON'T HAVE AN ANSWER FOR HIM.
NOT AFTER I FAILED HIM THIS BADLY.
YOU DON'T.
JUST TRUST YOURSELF.

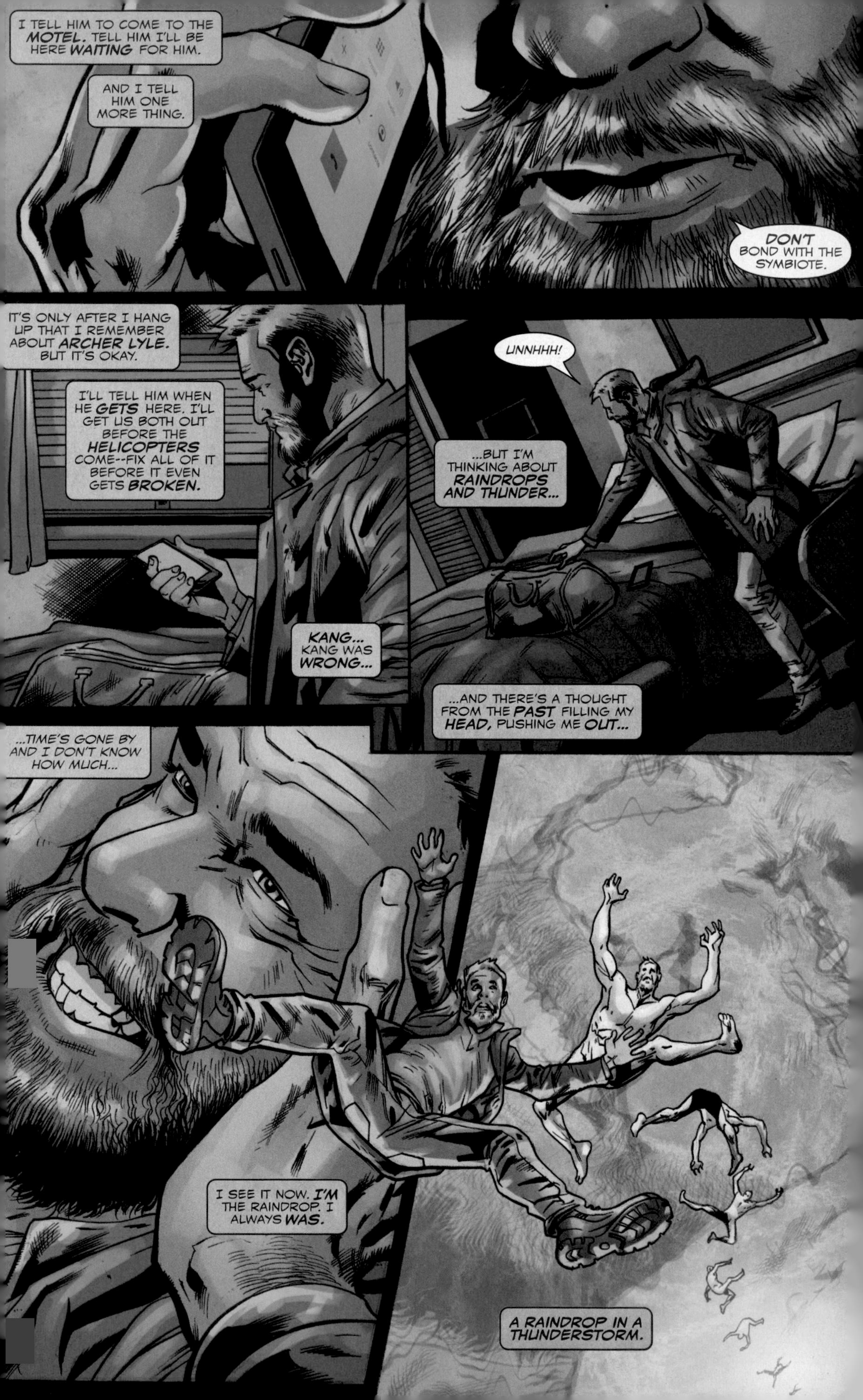

I TELL HIM TO COME TO THE MOTEL. TELL HIM I'LL BE HERE WAITING FOR HIM.
AND I TELL HIM ONE MORE THING.
DON'T BOND WITH THE SYMBIOTE.
IT'S ONLY AFTER I HANG UP THAT I REMEMBER ABOUT ARCHER LYLE. BUT IT'S OKAY.
I'LL TELL HIM WHEN HE GETS HERE. I'LL GET US BOTH OUT BEFORE THE HELICOPTERS COME--FIX ALL OF IT BEFORE IT EVEN GETS BROKEN.
KANG... KANG WAS WRONG...
UNNHHH!
...BUT I'M THINKING ABOUT RAINDROPS AND THUNDER...
...AND THERE'S A THOUGHT FROM THE PAST FILLING MY HEAD, PUSHING ME OUT...
...TIME'S GONE BY AND I DON'T KNOW HOW MUCH...
I SEE IT NOW. I'M THE RAINDROP. I ALWAYS WAS.
A RAINDROP IN A THUNDERSTORM.

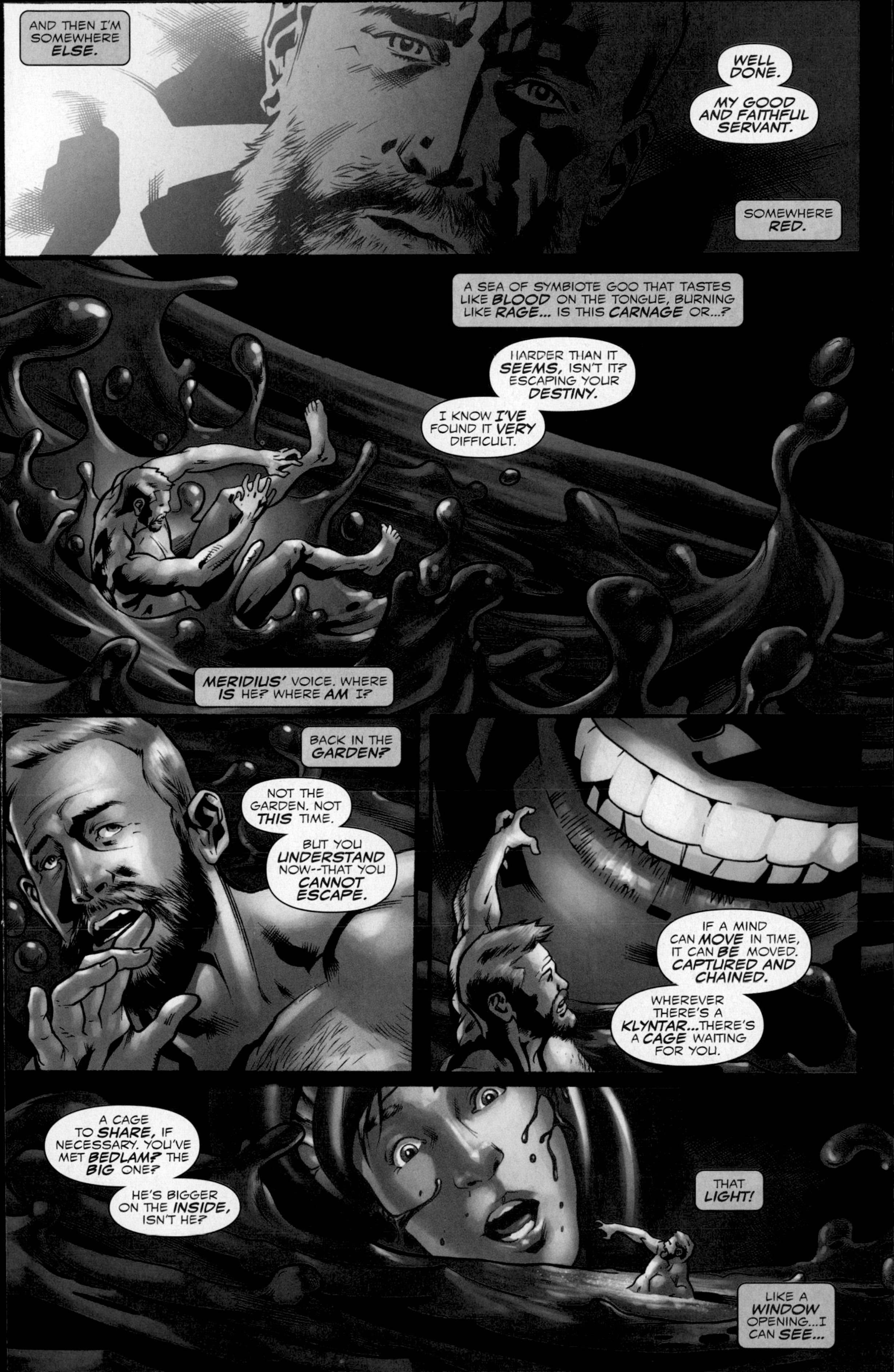
AND THEN I'M SOMEWHERE ELSE.
WELL DONE.
MY GOOD AND FAITHFUL SERVANT.
SOMEWHERE RED.
A SEA OF SYMBIOTE GOO THAT TASTES LIKE BLOOD ON THE TONGUE, BURNING LIKE RAGE... IS THIS CARNAGE OR...?
HARDER THAN IT SEEMS, ISN'T IT? ESCAPING YOUR DESTINY.
I KNOW I'VE FOUND IT VERY DIFFICULT.
MERIDIUS' VOICE. WHERE IS HE? WHERE AM I?
BACK IN THE GARDEN?
NOT THE GARDEN. NOT THIS TIME.
BUT YOU UNDERSTAND NOW--THAT YOU CANNOT ESCAPE.
IF A MIND CAN MOVE IN TIME, IT CAN BE MOVED. CAPTURED AND CHAINED.
WHEREVER THERE'S A KLYNTAR...THERE'S A CAGE WAITING FOR YOU.
A CAGE TO SHARE, IF NECESSARY. YOU'VE MET BEDLAM? THE BIG ONE?
HE'S BIGGER ON THE INSIDE, ISN'T HE?
THAT LIGHT!
LIKE A WINDOW OPENING...I CAN SEE...

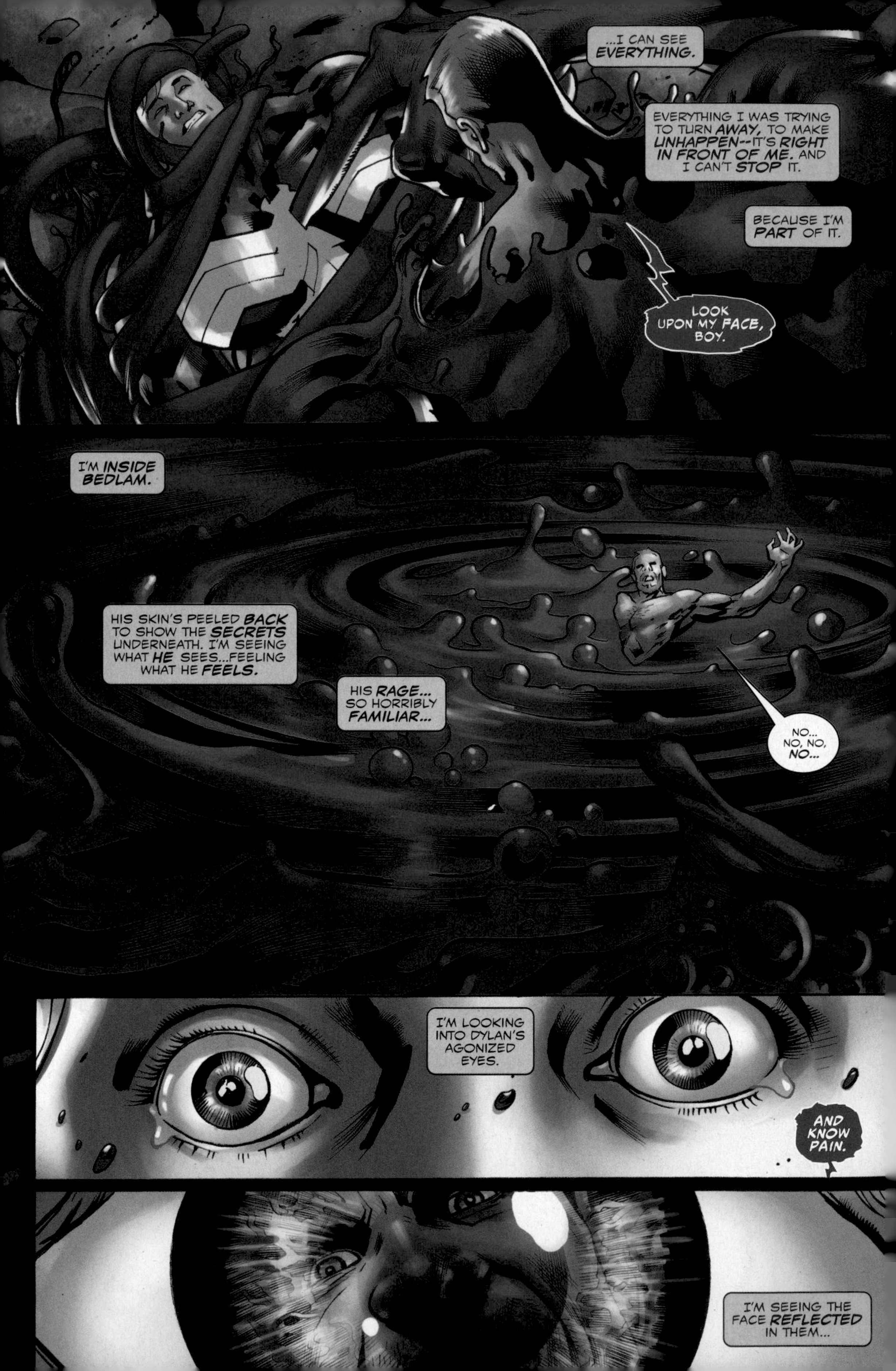

...I CAN SEE EVERYTHING.
EVERYTHING I WAS TRYING TO TURN AWAY, TO MAKE UNHAPPEN--IT'S RIGHT IN FRONT OF ME. AND I CAN'T STOP IT.
BECAUSE I'M PART OF IT.
LOOK UPON MY FACE, BOY.
I'M INSIDE BEDLAM.
HIS SKIN'S PEELED BACK TO SHOW THE SECRETS UNDERNEATH. I'M SEEING WHAT HE SEES...FEELING WHAT HE FEELS.
HIS RAGE... SO HORRIBLY FAMILIAR...
NO... NO, NO, NO...
I'M LOOKING INTO DYLAN'S AGONIZED EYES.
AND KNOW PAIN.
I'M SEEING THE FACE REFLECTED IN THEM...

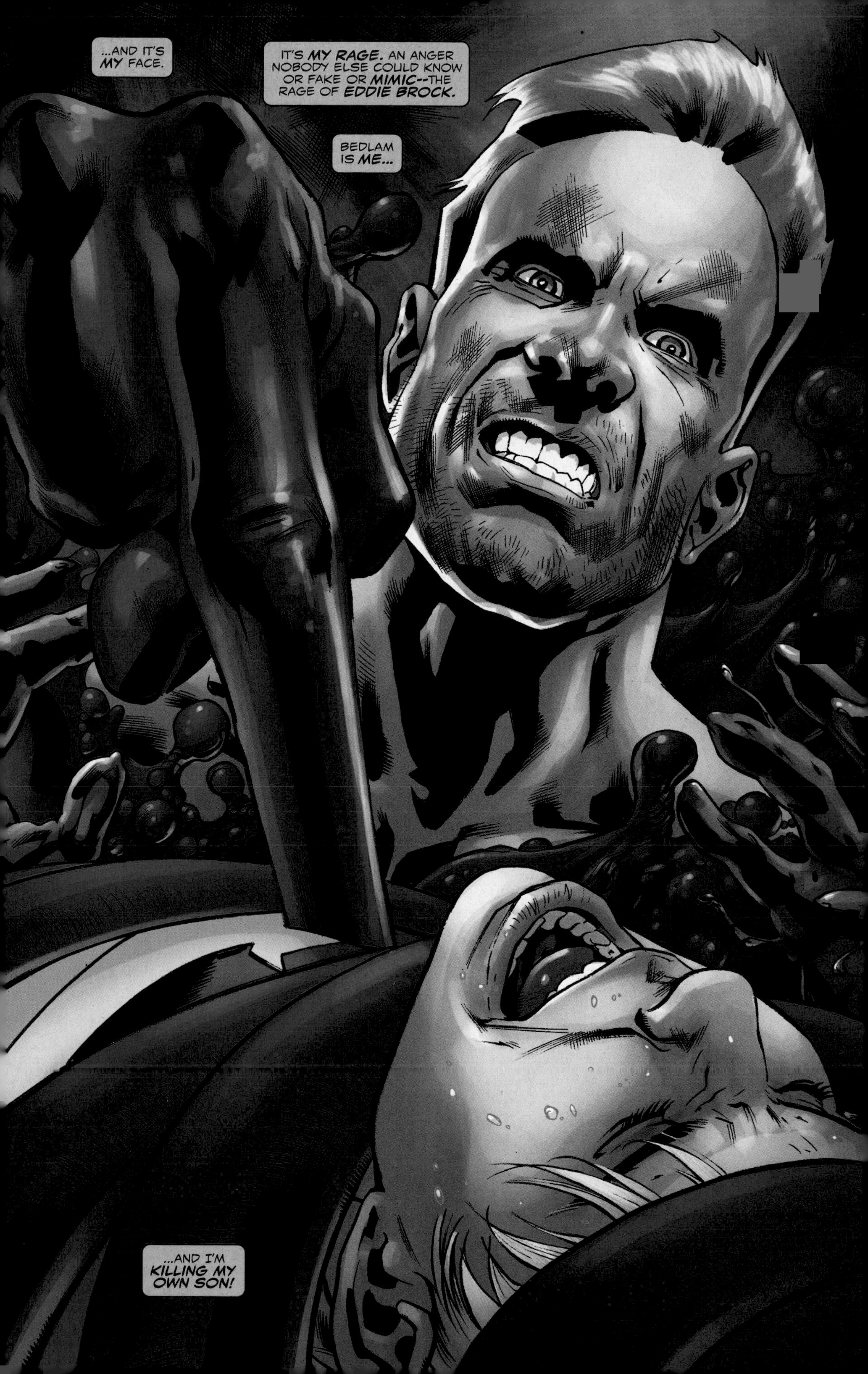
...AND IT'S MY FACE.
IT'S MY RAGE. AN ANGER NOBODY ELSE COULD KNOW OR FAKE OR MIMIC--THE RAGE OF EDDIE BROCK.
BEDLAM IS ME...
...AND I'M KILLING MY OWN SON!

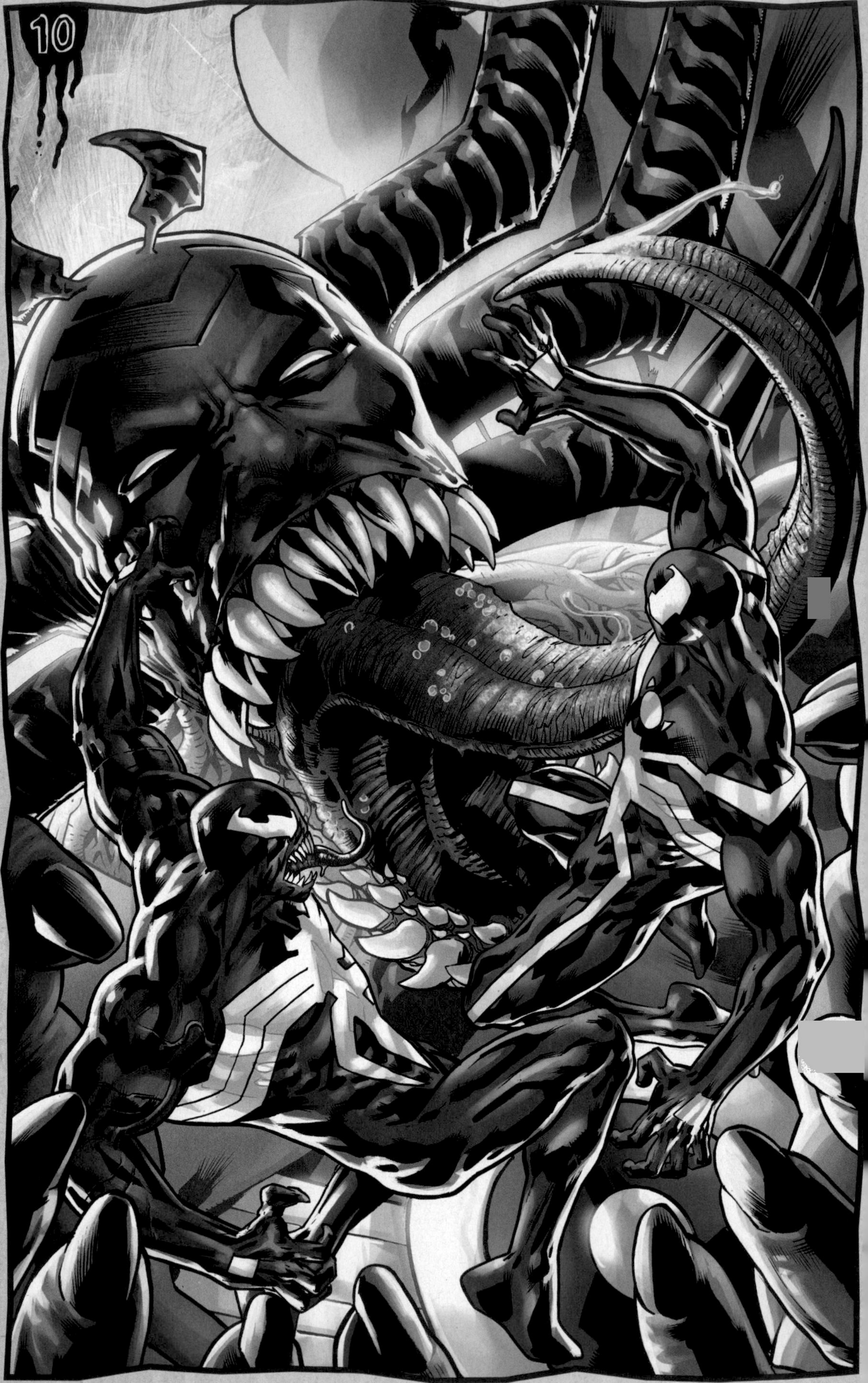
10

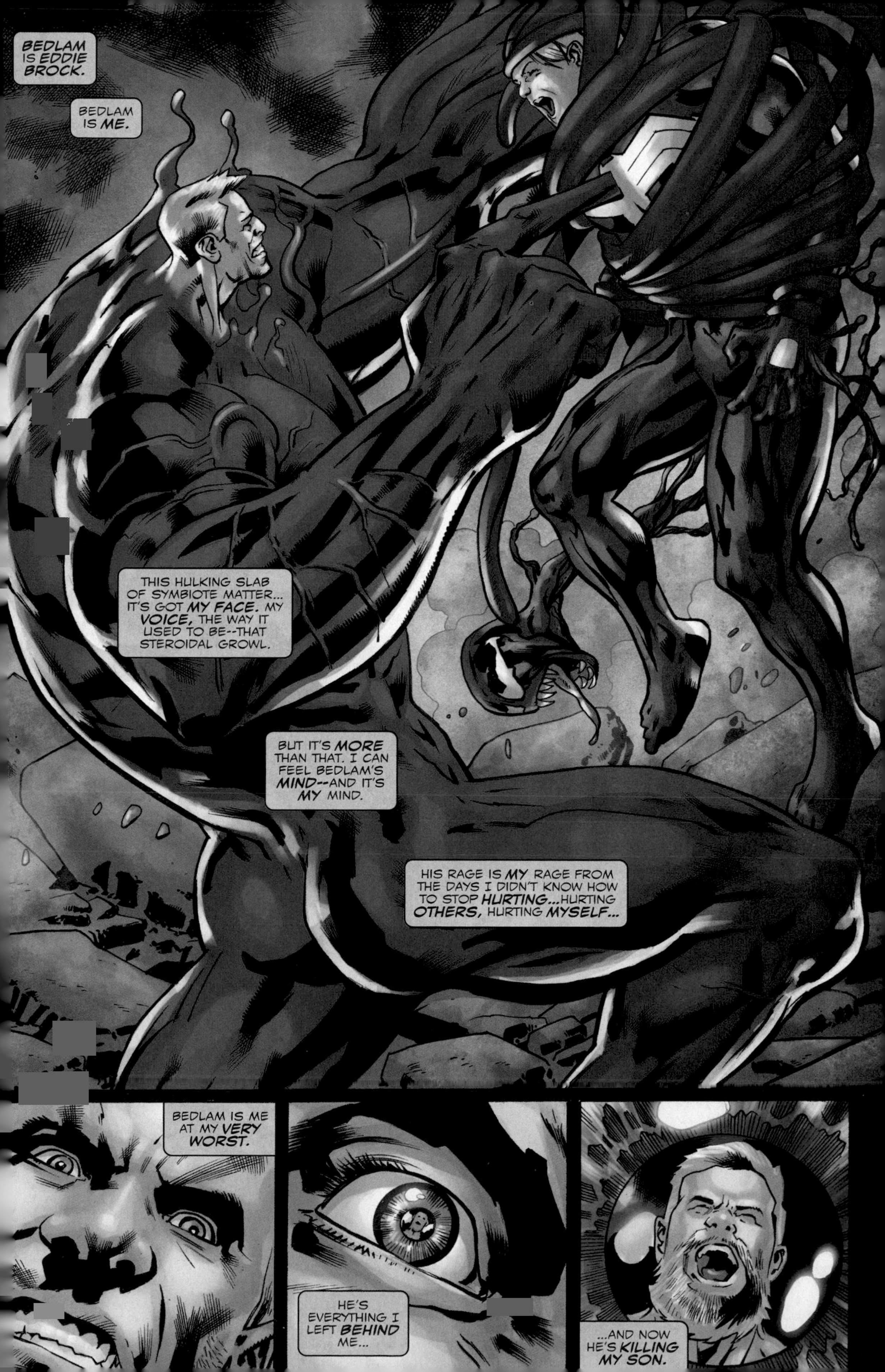
BEDLAM IS EDDIE BROCK.
BEDLAM IS ME.
THIS HULKING SLAB OF SYMBIOTE MATTER... IT'S GOT MY FACE. MY VOICE, THE WAY IT USED TO BE--THAT STEROIDAL GROWL.
BUT IT'S MORE THAN THAT. I CAN FEEL BEDLAM'S MIND--AND IT'S MY MIND.
HIS RAGE IS MY RAGE FROM THE DAYS I DIDN'T KNOW HOW TO STOP HURTING...HURTING OTHERS, HURTING MYSELF...
BEDLAM IS ME AT MY VERY WORST.
HE'S EVERYTHING I LEFT BEHIND ME...
...AND NOW HE'S KILLING MY SON.

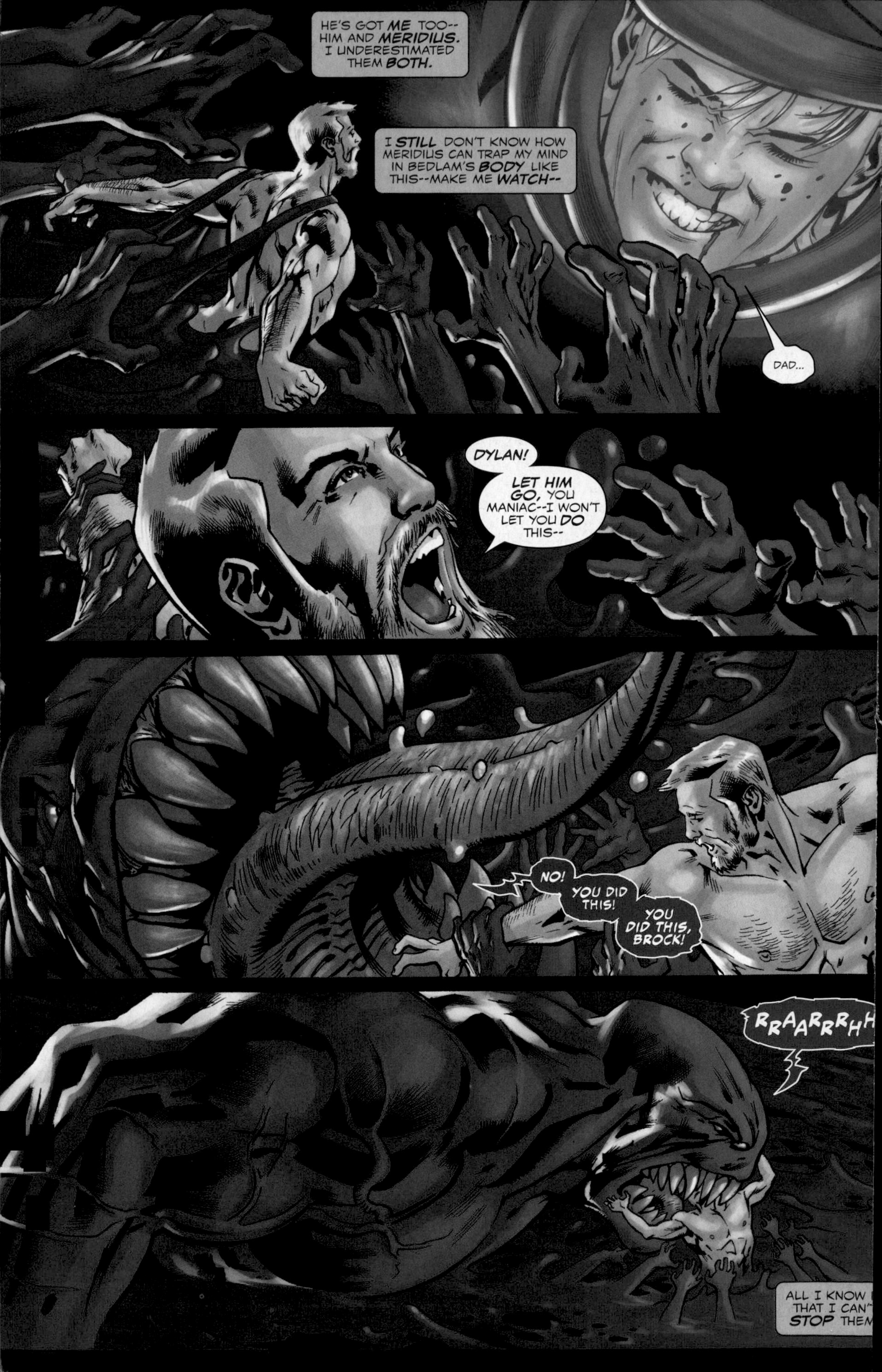
HE'S GOT ME TOO--HIM AND MERIDIUS. I UNDERESTIMATED THEM BOTH.
I STILL DON'T KNOW HOW MERIDIUS CAN TRAP MY MIND IN BEDLAM'S BODY LIKE THIS--MAKE ME WATCH--
DAD...
DYLAN!
LET HIM GO, YOU MANIAC--I WON'T LET YOU DO THIS--
NO!
YOU DID THIS!
YOU DID THIS, BROCK!
RRAARRRHH
ALL I KNOW
THAT I CAN'T
STOP THEM

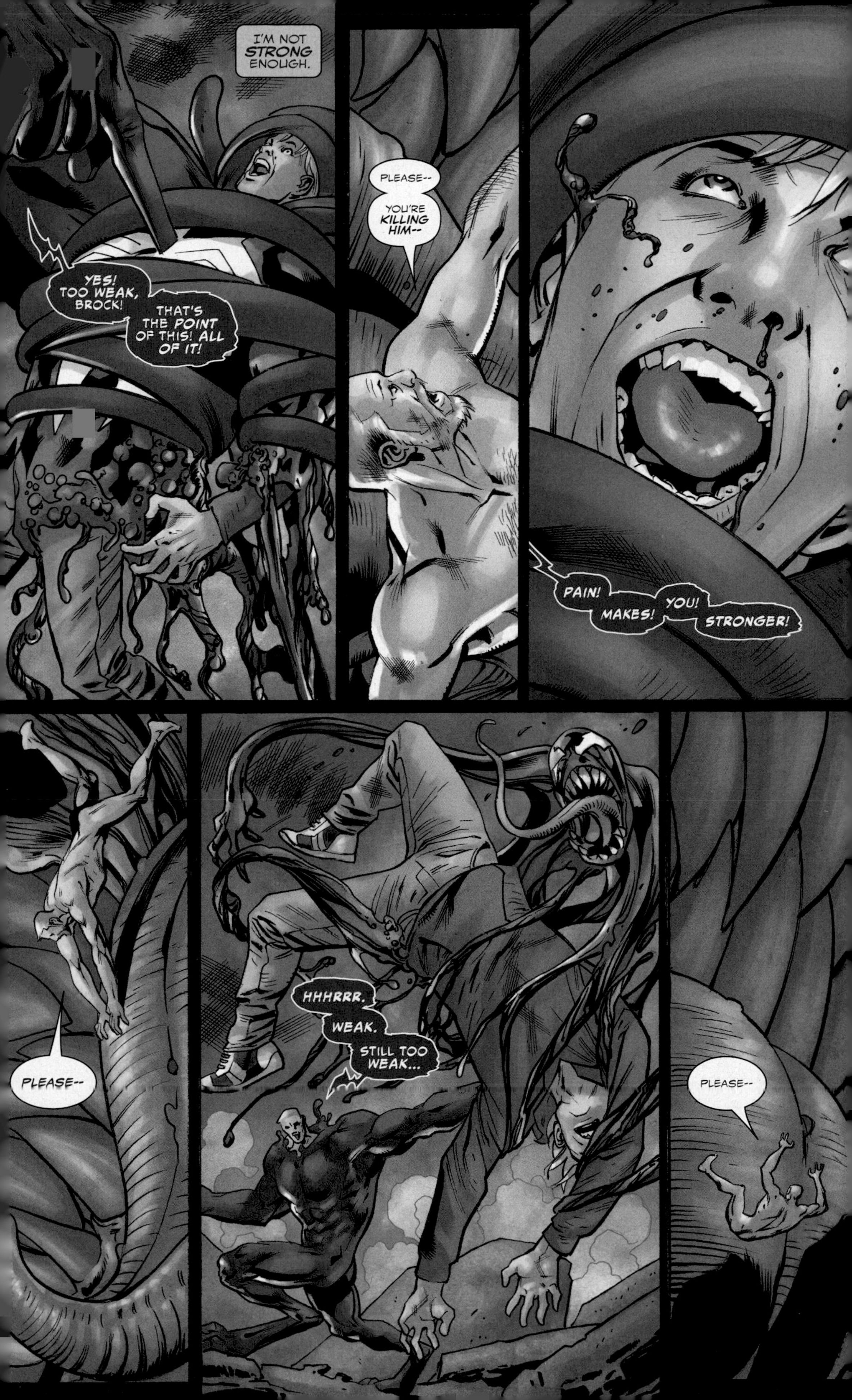
I'M NOT STRONG ENOUGH.
YES! TOO WEAK, BROCK!
THAT'S THE POINT OF THIS! ALL OF IT!
PLEASE--
YOU'RE KILLING HIM--
PAIN!
MAKES!
YOU!
STRONGER!
PLEASE--
HHHRRR.
WEAK.
STILL TOO WEAK...
PLEASE--

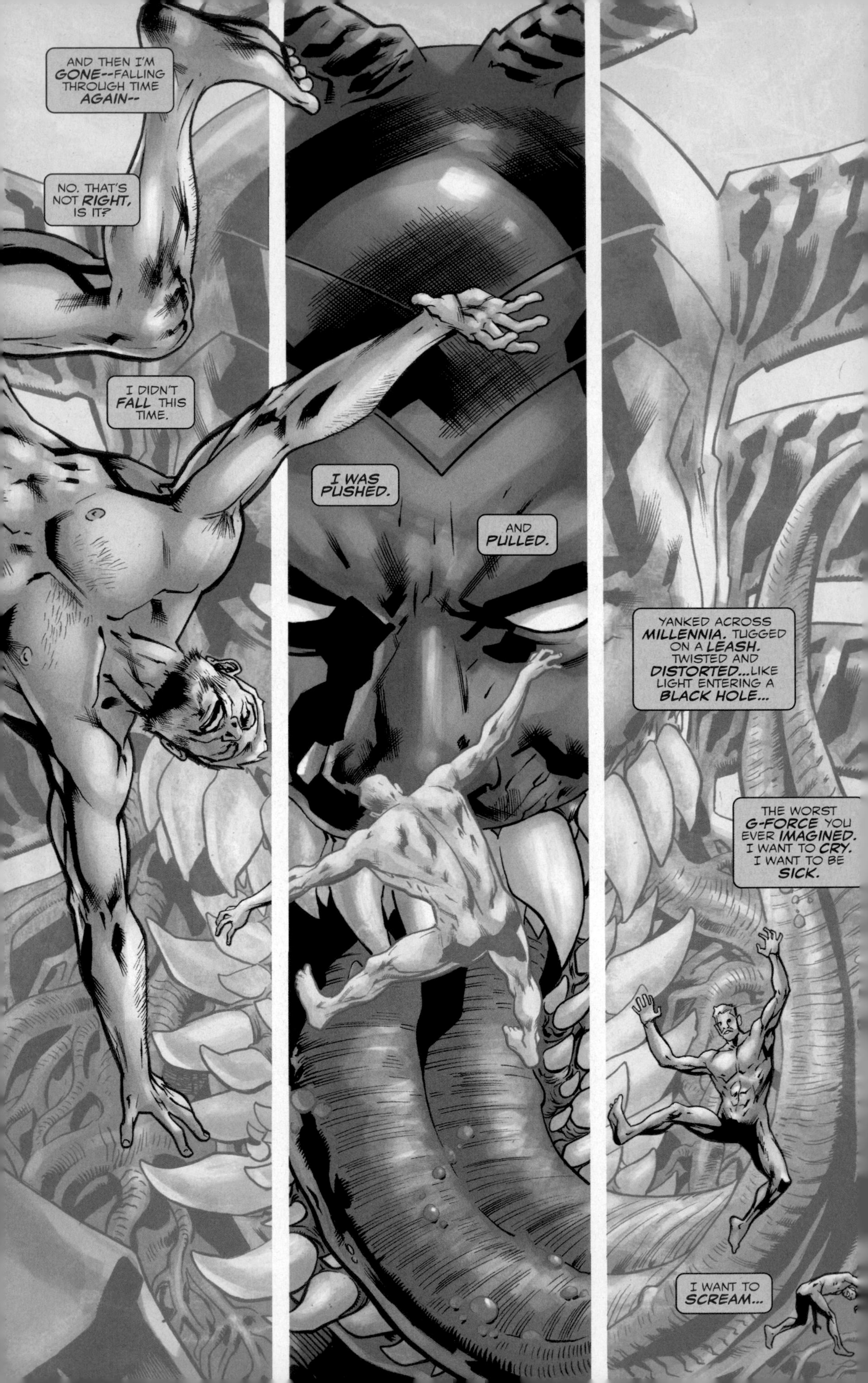
AND THEN I'M GONE--FALLING THROUGH TIME AGAIN--
NO. THAT'S NOT RIGHT, IS IT?
I DIDN'T FALL THIS TIME.
I WAS PUSHED.
AND PULLED.
YANKED ACROSS MILLENNIA. TUGGED ON A LEASH. TWISTED AND DISTORTED...LIKE LIGHT ENTERING A BLACK HOLE...
THE WORST G-FORCE YOU EVER IMAGINED. I WANT TO CRY. I WANT TO BE SICK.
I WANT TO SCREAM...

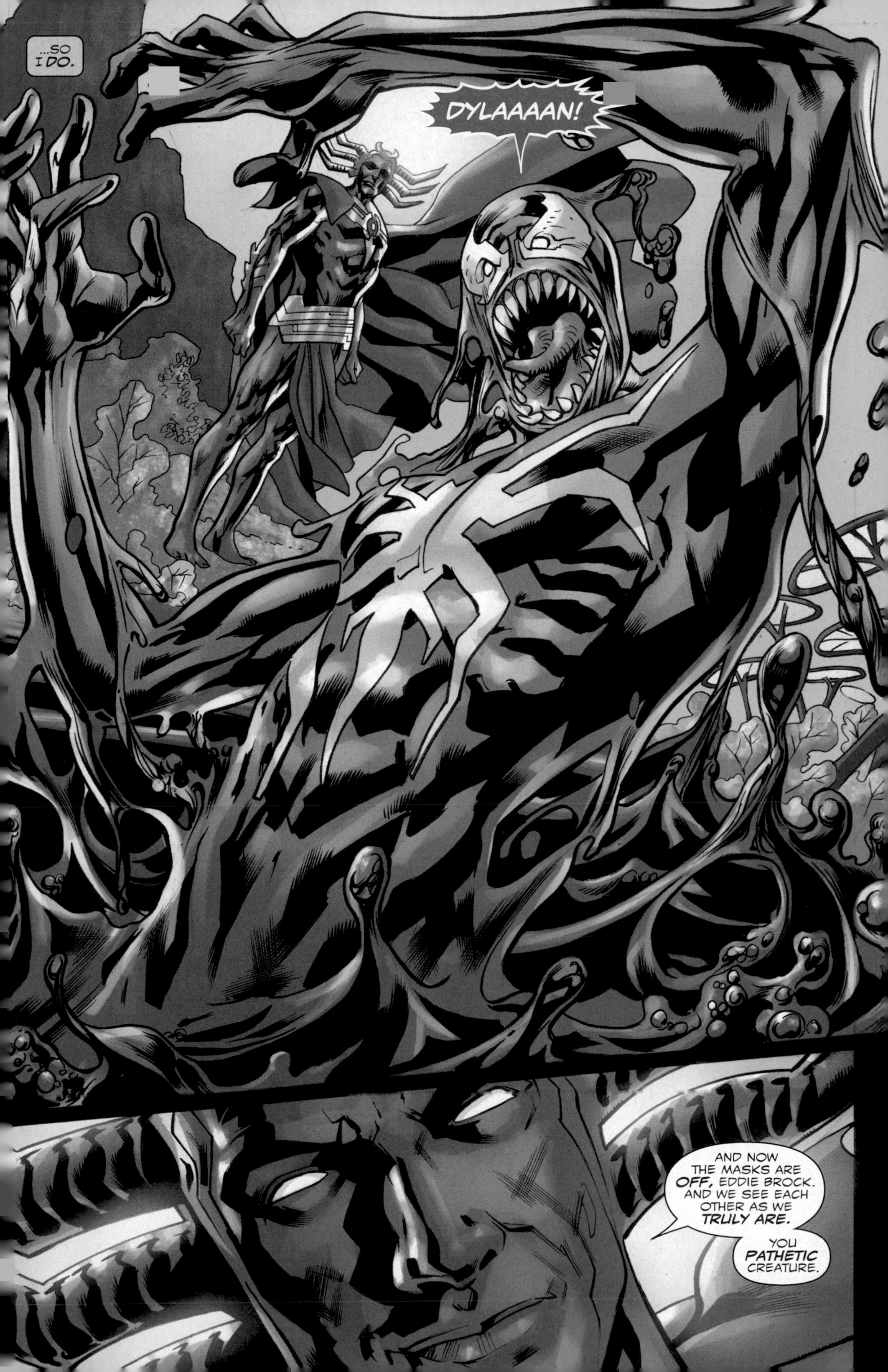
...SO I DO.
DYLAAAAN!
AND NOW THE MASKS ARE OFF, EDDIE BROCK. AND WE SEE EACH OTHER AS WE TRULY ARE.
YOU PATHETIC CREATURE.

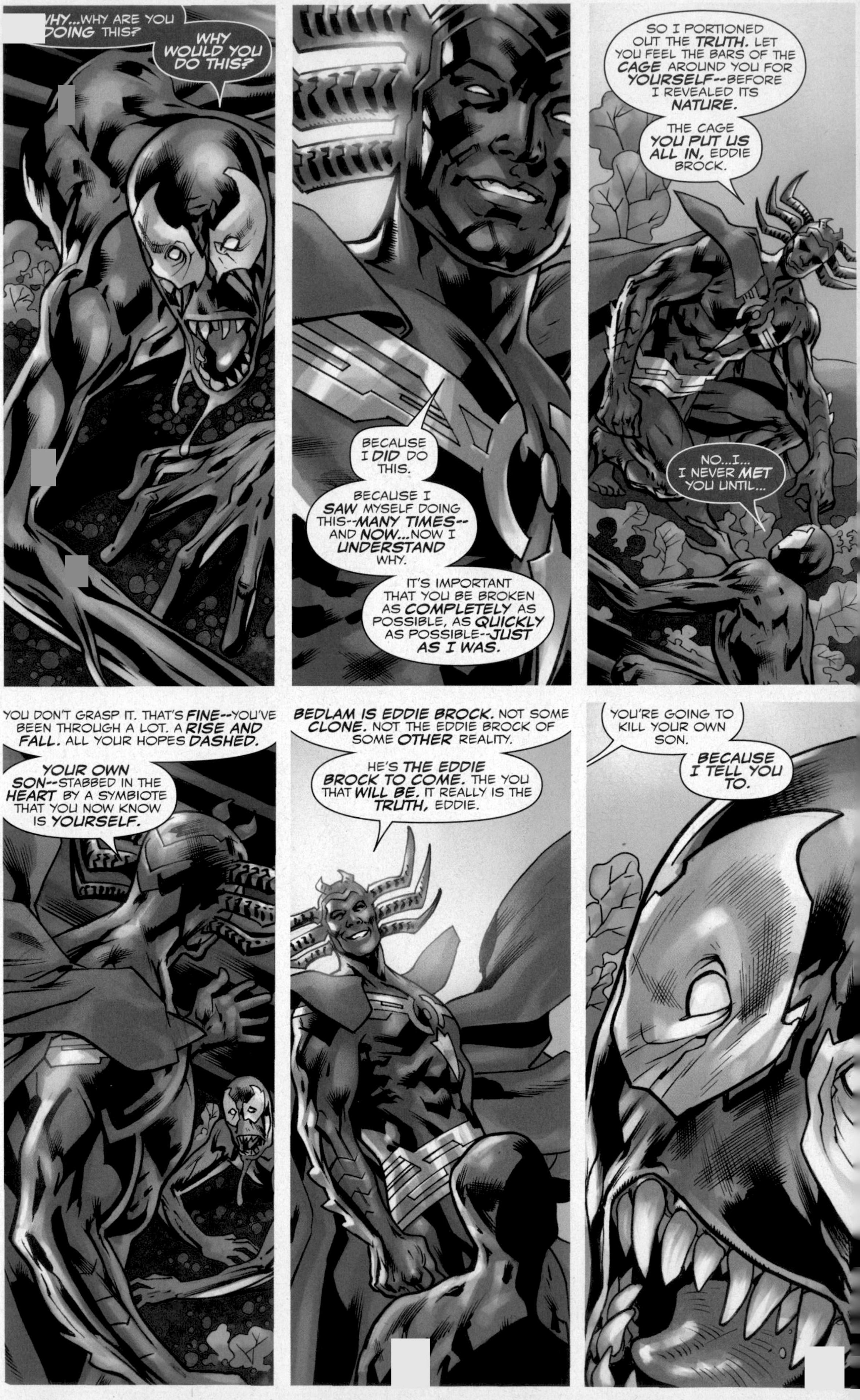
WHY...WHY ARE YOU DOING THIS?
WHY WOULD YOU DO THIS?
BECAUSE I DID DO THIS.
BECAUSE I SAW MYSELF DOING THIS--MANY TIMES--AND NOW...NOW I UNDERSTAND WHY.
IT'S IMPORTANT THAT YOU BE BROKEN AS COMPLETELY AS POSSIBLE, AS QUICKLY AS POSSIBLE--JUST AS I WAS.
SO I PORTIONED OUT THE TRUTH. LET YOU FEEL THE BARS OF THE CAGE AROUND YOU FOR YOURSELF--BEFORE I REVEALED ITS NATURE.
THE CAGE YOU PUT US ALL IN, EDDIE BROCK.
NO...I... I NEVER MET YOU UNTIL...
YOU DON'T GRASP IT. THAT'S FINE--YOU'VE BEEN THROUGH A LOT. A RISE AND FALL. ALL YOUR HOPES DASHED.
YOUR OWN SON--STABBED IN THE HEART BY A SYMBIOTE THAT YOU NOW KNOW IS YOURSELF.
BEDLAM IS EDDIE BROCK. NOT SOME CLONE. NOT THE EDDIE BROCK OF SOME OTHER REALITY.
HE'S THE EDDIE BROCK TO COME. THE YOU THAT WILL BE. IT REALLY IS THE TRUTH, EDDIE.
YOU'RE GOING TO KILL YOUR OWN SON.
BECAUSE I TELL YOU TO.

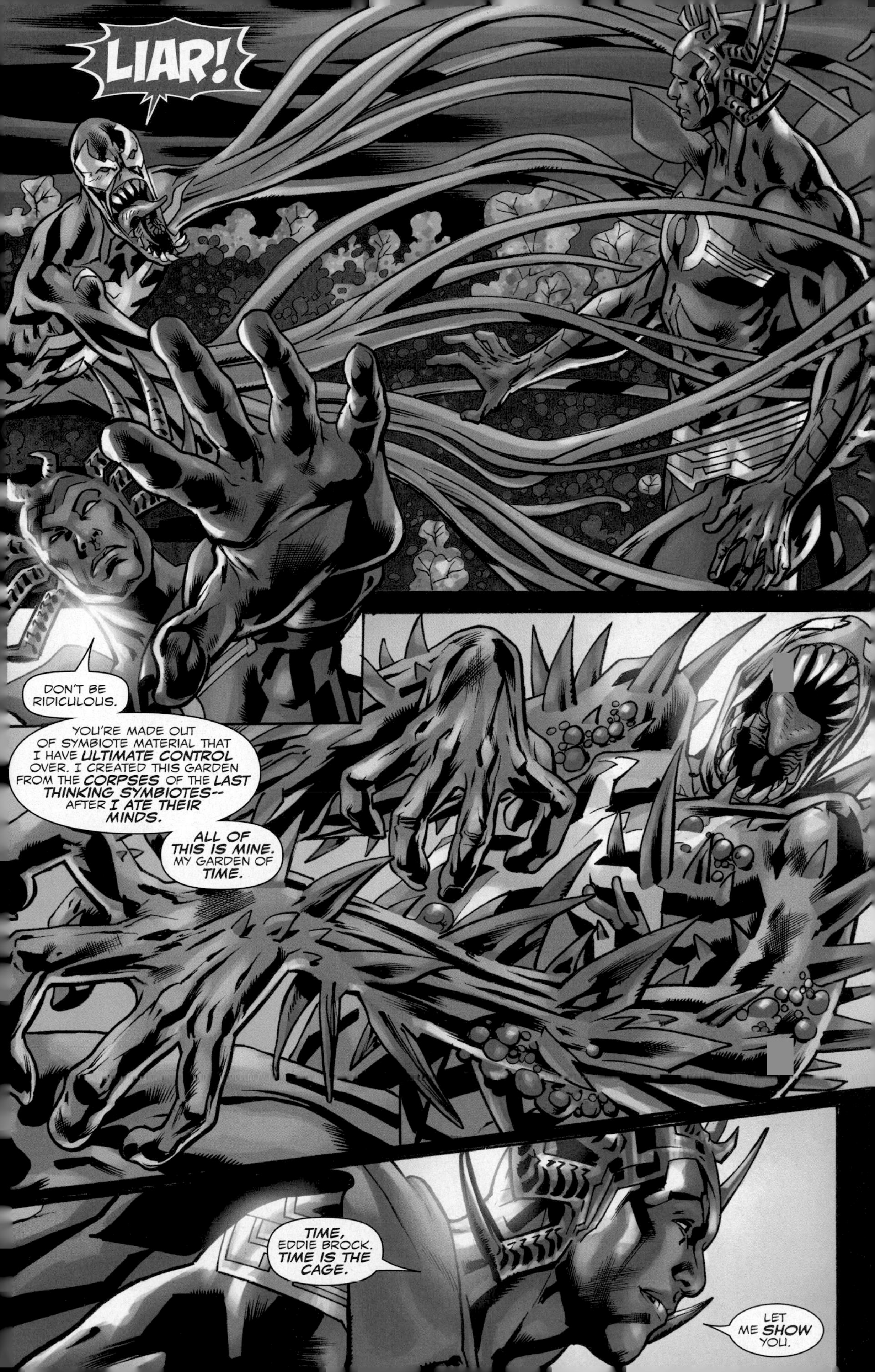
LIAR!
DON'T BE RIDICULOUS.
YOU'RE MADE OUT OF SYMBIOTE MATERIAL THAT I HAVE ULTIMATE CONTROL OVER. I CREATED THIS GARDEN FROM THE CORPSES OF THE LAST THINKING SYMBIOTES-- AFTER I ATE THEIR MINDS.
ALL OF THIS IS MINE. MY GARDEN OF TIME.
TIME, EDDIE BROCK. TIME IS THE CAGE.
LET ME SHOW YOU.

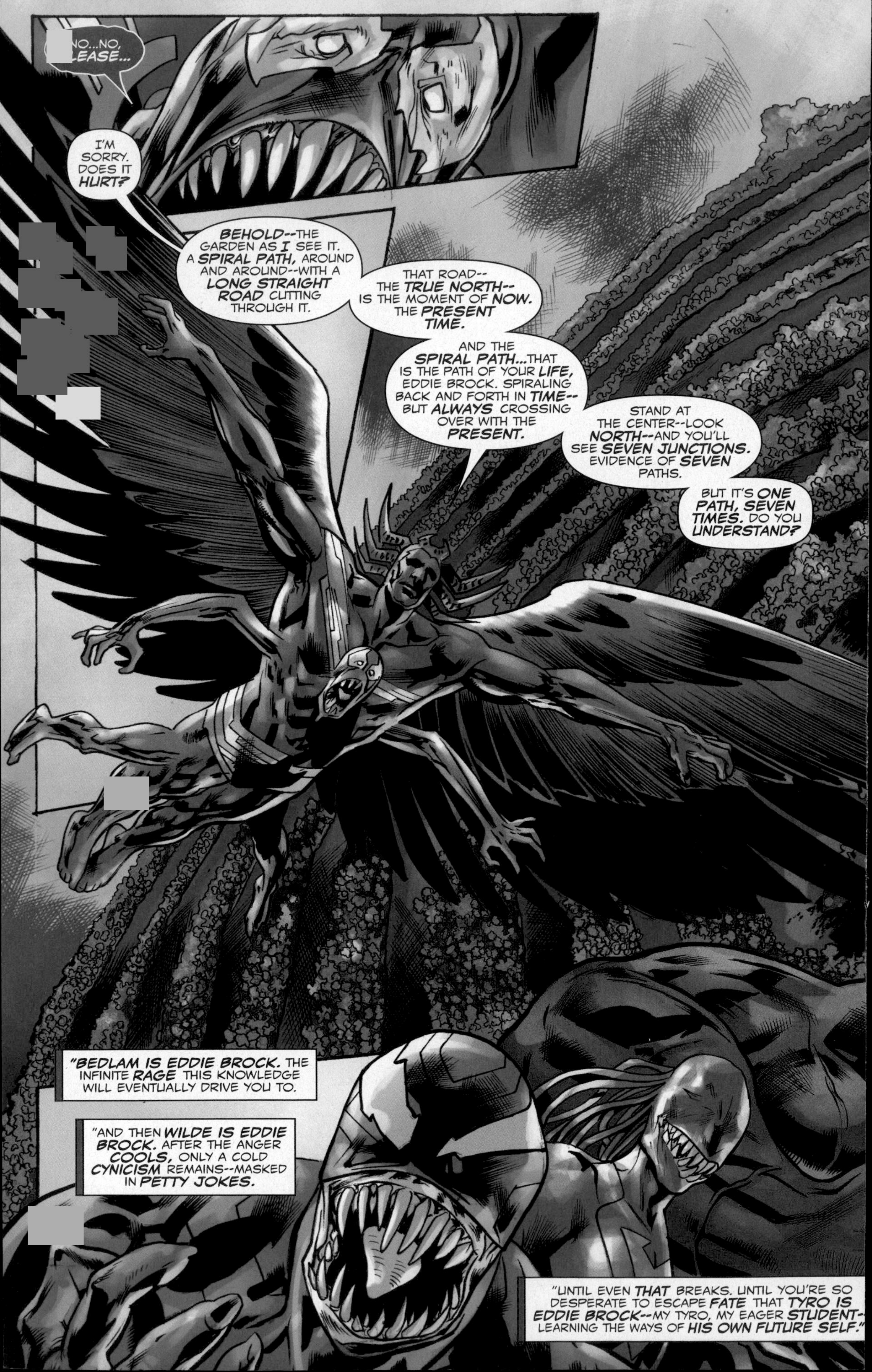
NO...NO, LEASE...
I'M SORRY. DOES IT HURT?
BEHOLD--THE GARDEN AS I SEE IT. A SPIRAL PATH, AROUND AND AROUND--WITH A LONG STRAIGHT ROAD CUTTING THROUGH IT.
THAT ROAD--THE TRUE NORTH--IS THE MOMENT OF NOW. THE PRESENT TIME.
AND THE SPIRAL PATH...THAT IS THE PATH OF YOUR LIFE, EDDIE BROCK. SPIRALING BACK AND FORTH IN TIME--BUT ALWAYS CROSSING OVER WITH THE PRESENT.
STAND AT THE CENTER--LOOK NORTH--AND YOU'LL SEE SEVEN JUNCTIONS. EVIDENCE OF SEVEN PATHS.
BUT IT'S ONE PATH, SEVEN TIMES. DO YOU UNDERSTAND?
"BEDLAM IS EDDIE BROCK. THE INFINITE RAGE THIS KNOWLEDGE WILL EVENTUALLY DRIVE YOU TO.
"AND THEN WILDE IS EDDIE BROCK. AFTER THE ANGER COOLS, ONLY A COLD CYNICISM REMAINS--MASKED IN PETTY JOKES.
"UNTIL EVEN THAT BREAKS. UNTIL YOU'RE SO DESPERATE TO ESCAPE FATE THAT TYRO IS EDDIE BROCK--MY TYRO, MY EAGER STUDENT--LEARNING THE WAYS OF HIS OWN FUTURE SELF."

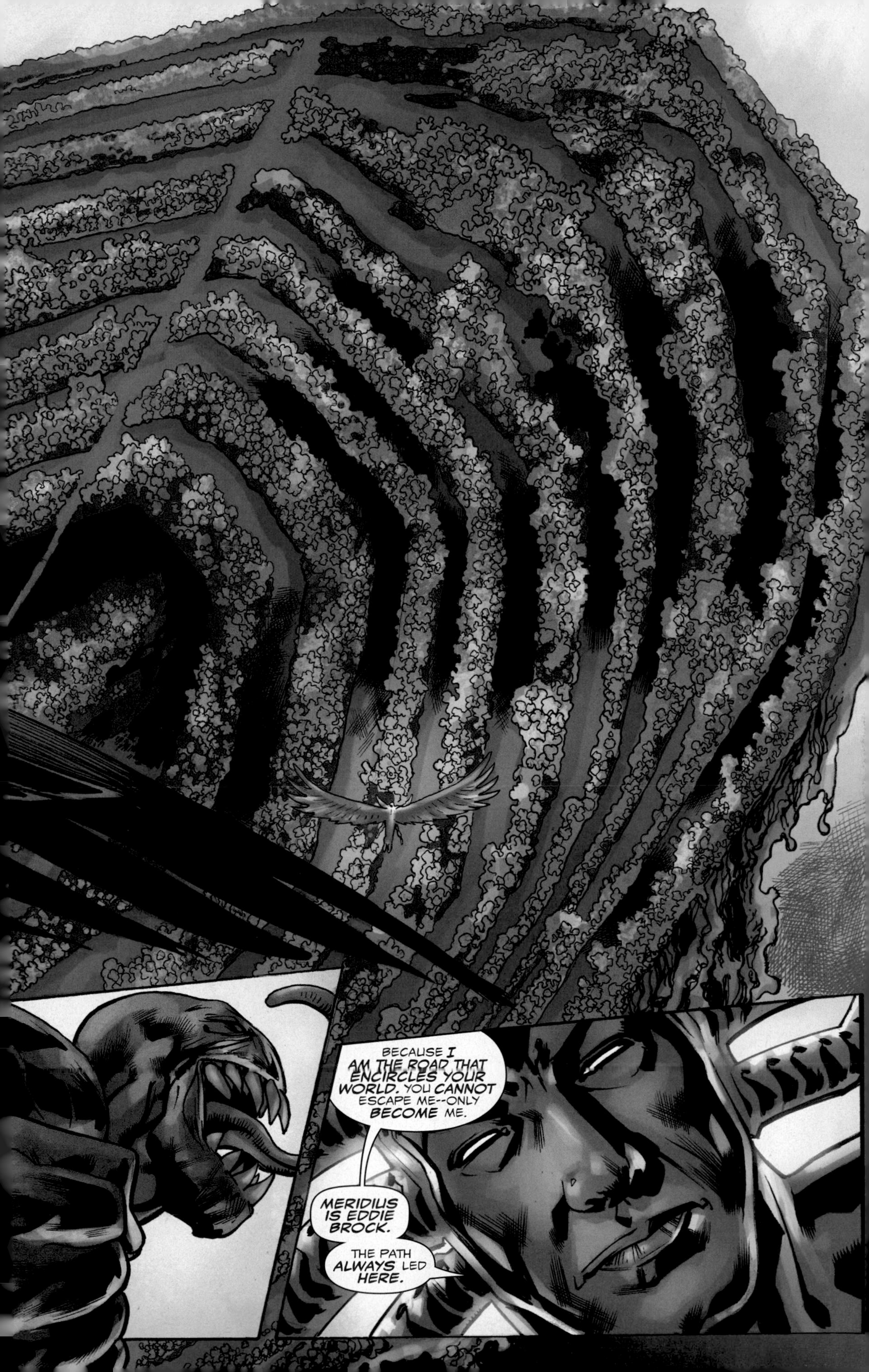
BECAUSE I AM THE ROAD THAT ENCIRCLES YOUR WORLD. YOU CANNOT ESCAPE ME--ONLY BECOME ME.
MERIDIUS IS EDDIE BROCK.
THE PATH ALWAYS LED HERE.

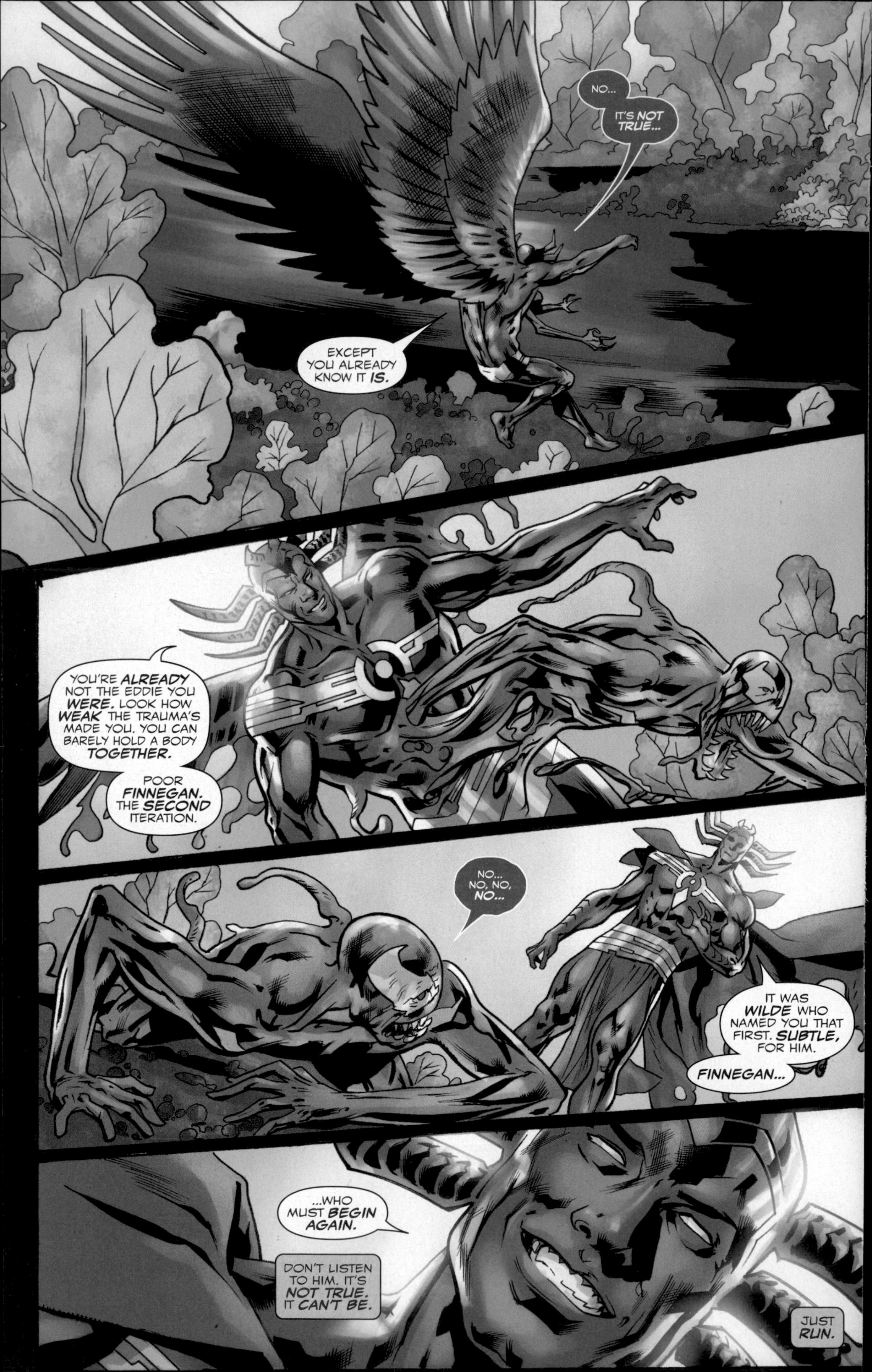
NO...
IT'S NOT TRUE...
EXCEPT YOU ALREADY KNOW IT IS.
YOU'RE ALREADY NOT THE EDDIE YOU WERE. LOOK HOW WEAK THE TRAUMA'S MADE YOU. YOU CAN BARELY HOLD A BODY TOGETHER.
POOR FINNEGAN. THE SECOND ITERATION.
NO... NO, NO, NO...
IT WAS WILDE WHO NAMED YOU THAT FIRST. SUBTLE, FOR HIM.
FINNEGAN...
...WHO MUST BEGIN AGAIN.
DON'T LISTEN TO HIM. IT'S NOT TRUE. IT CAN'T BE.
JUST RUN.

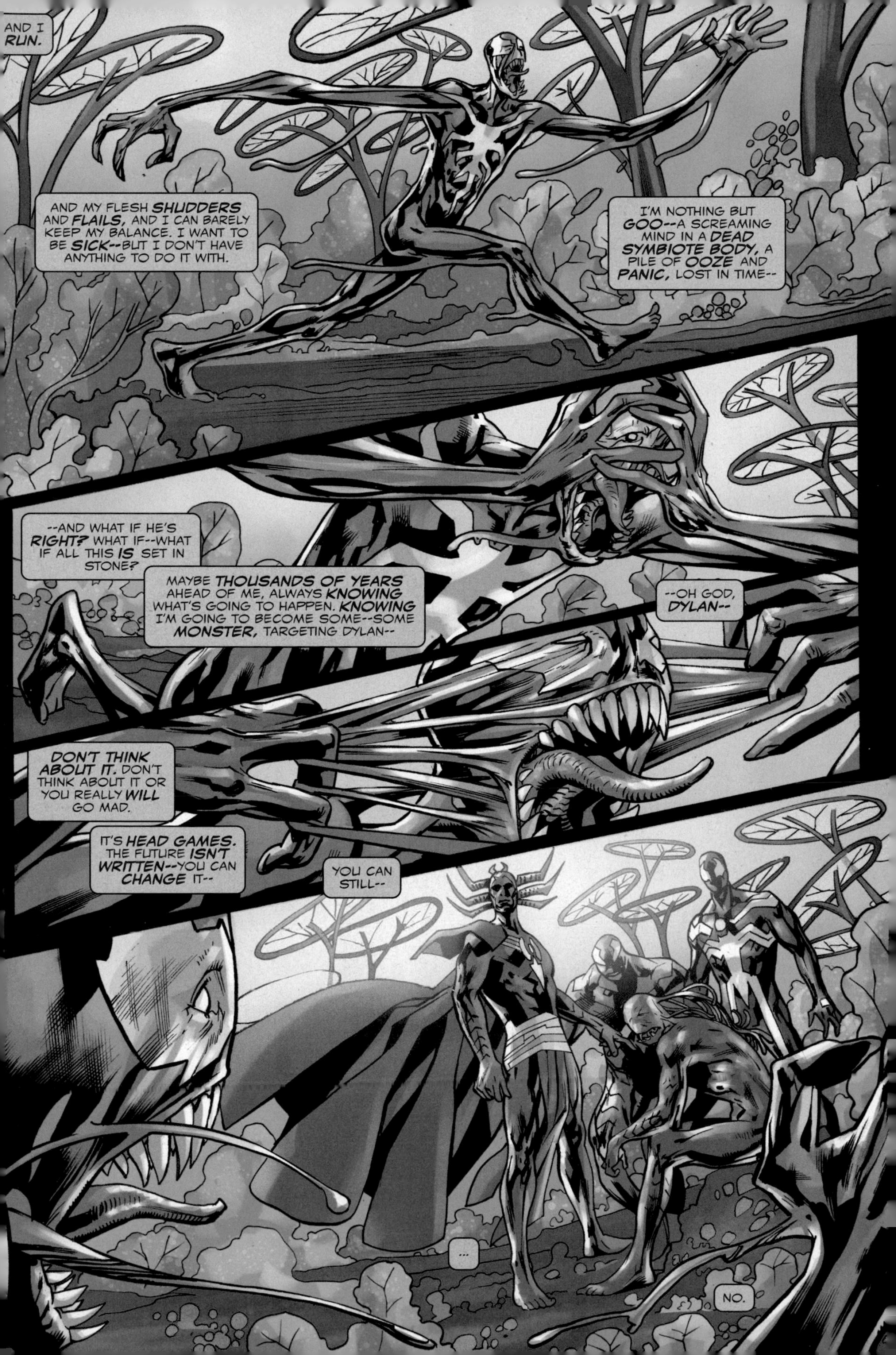
AND I RUN.
AND MY FLESH SHUDDERS AND FLAILS, AND I CAN BARELY KEEP MY BALANCE. I WANT TO BE SICK--BUT I DON'T HAVE ANYTHING TO DO IT WITH.
I'M NOTHING BUT GOO--A SCREAMING MIND IN A DEAD SYMBIOTE BODY, A PILE OF OOZE AND PANIC, LOST IN TIME--
--AND WHAT IF HE'S RIGHT? WHAT IF--WHAT IF ALL THIS IS SET IN STONE?
MAYBE THOUSANDS OF YEARS AHEAD OF ME, ALWAYS KNOWING WHAT'S GOING TO HAPPEN. KNOWING I'M GOING TO BECOME SOME--SOME MONSTER, TARGETING DYLAN--
--OH GOD, DYLAN--
DON'T THINK ABOUT IT. DON'T THINK ABOUT IT OR YOU REALLY WILL GO MAD.
IT'S HEAD GAMES. THE FUTURE ISN'T WRITTEN--YOU CAN CHANGE IT--
YOU CAN STILL--
...
NO.

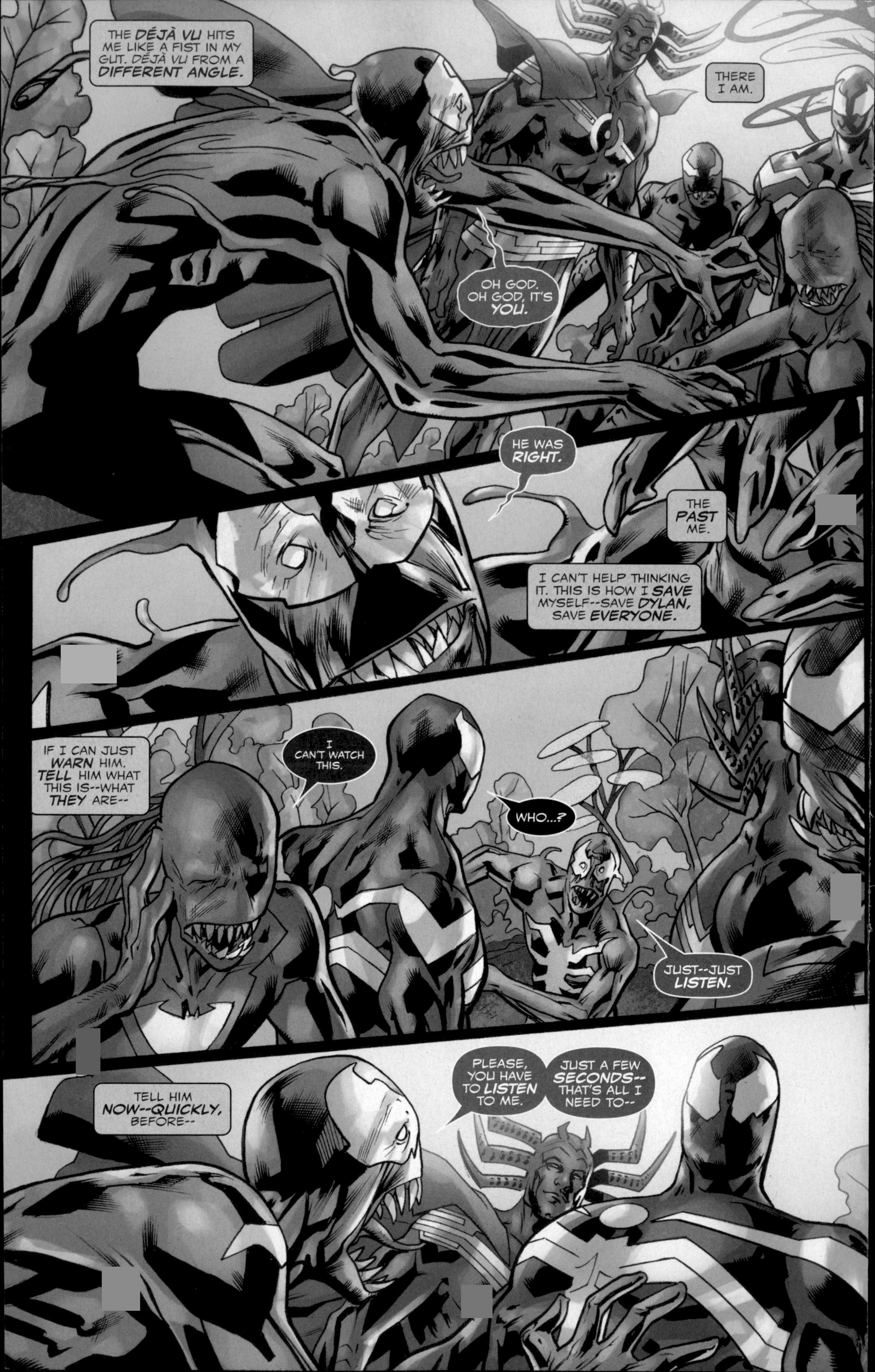
THE DÉJÀ VU HITS ME LIKE A FIST IN MY GUT. DÉJÀ VU FROM A DIFFERENT ANGLE.
THERE I AM.
OH GOD. OH GOD, IT'S YOU.
HE WAS RIGHT.
THE PAST ME.
I CAN'T HELP THINKING IT. THIS IS HOW I SAVE MYSELF--SAVE DYLAN, SAVE EVERYONE.
IF I CAN JUST WARN HIM. TELL HIM WHAT THIS IS--WHAT THEY ARE--
I CAN'T WATCH THIS.
WHO...?
JUST--JUST LISTEN.
TELL HIM NOW--QUICKLY, BEFORE--
PLEASE, YOU HAVE TO LISTEN TO ME.
JUST A FEW SECONDS--THAT'S ALL I NEED TO--

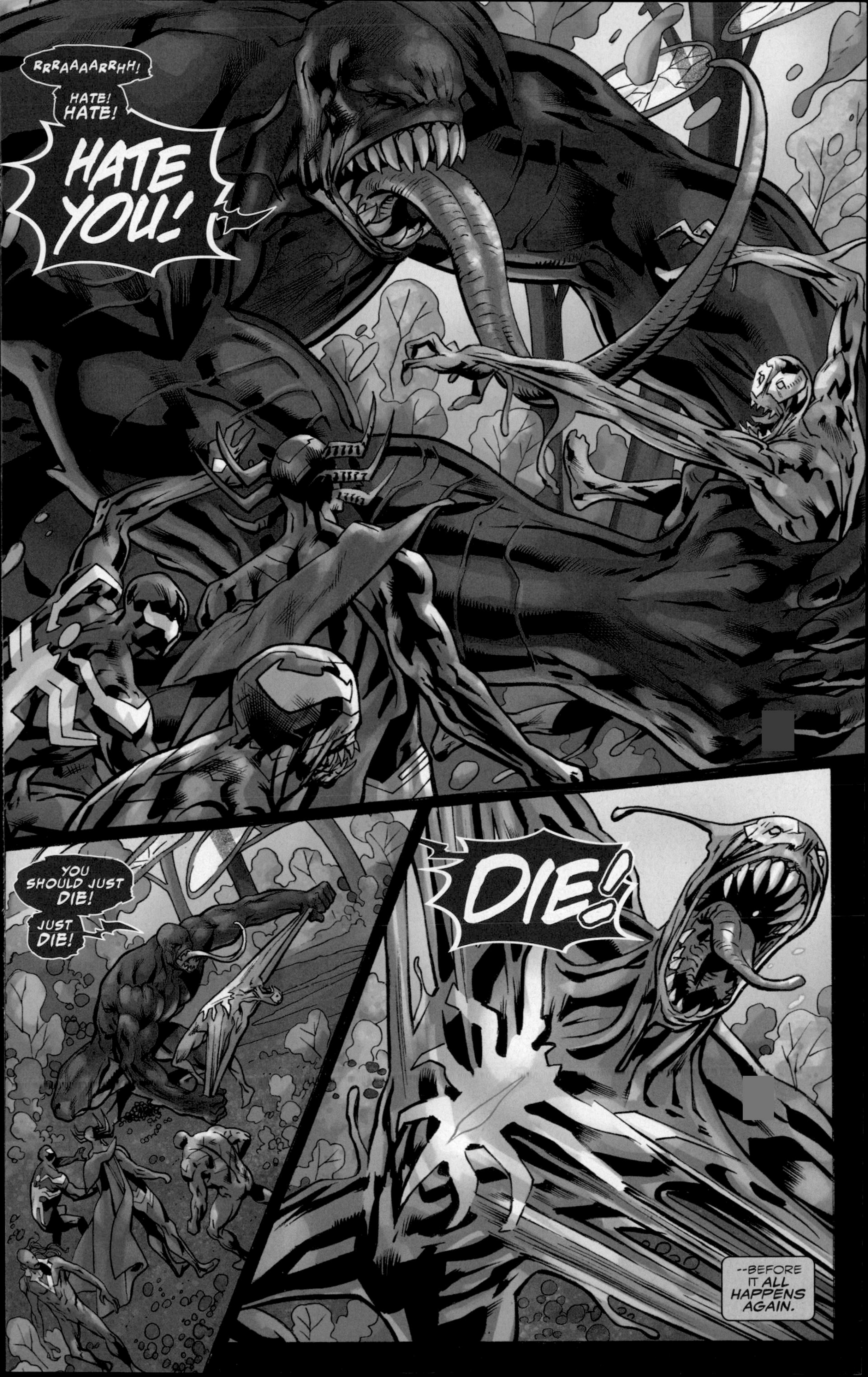
RRRAAAARRHH!
HATE! HATE!
HATE YOU!
YOU SHOULD JUST DIE!
JUST DIE!
DIE!
--BEFORE IT ALL HAPPENS AGAIN.

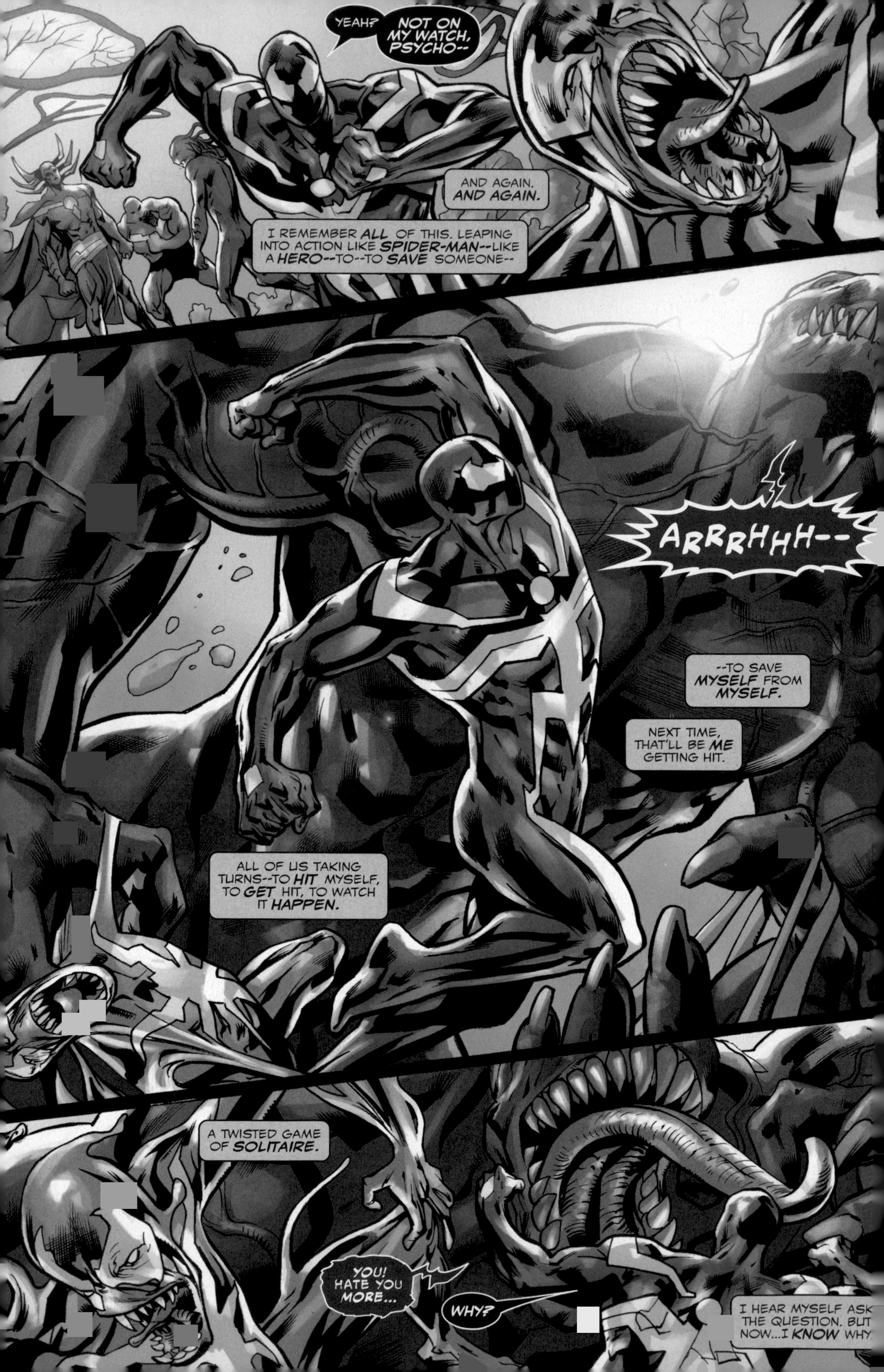
YEAH?
NOT ON MY WATCH, PSYCHO--
AND AGAIN. AND AGAIN.
I REMEMBER ALL OF THIS. LEAPING INTO ACTION LIKE SPIDER-MAN--LIKE A HERO--TO--TO SAVE SOMEONE--
ARRRHHH--
--TO SAVE MYSELF FROM MYSELF.
NEXT TIME, THAT'LL BE ME GETTING HIT.
ALL OF US TAKING TURNS--TO HIT MYSELF, TO GET HIT, TO WATCH IT HAPPEN.
A TWISTED GAME OF SOLITAIRE.
YOU! HATE YOU MORE...
WHY?
I HEAR MYSELF ASK THE QUESTION. BUT NOW...I KNOW WHY

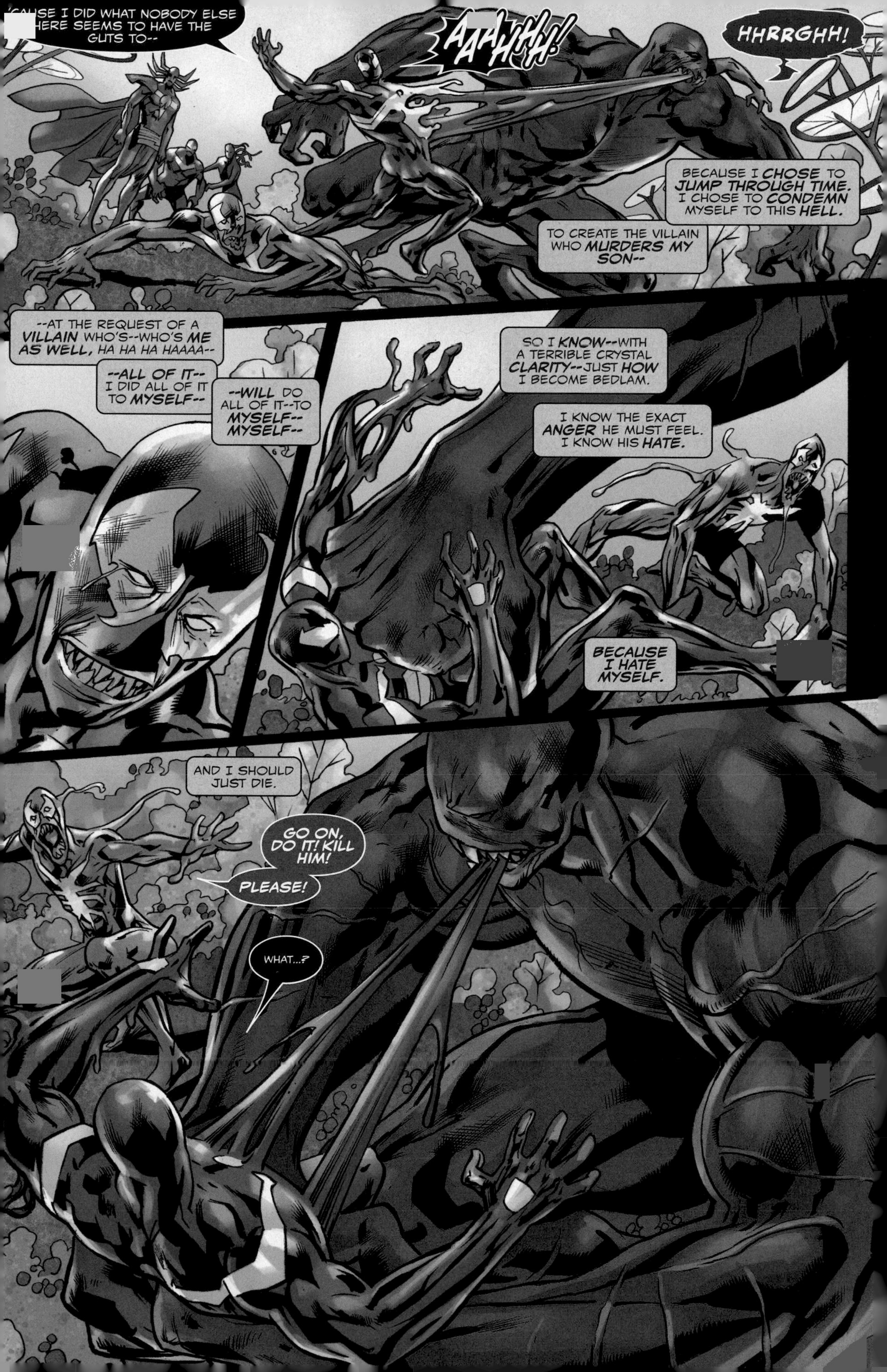
'CAUSE I DID WHAT NOBODY ELSE HERE SEEMS TO HAVE THE GUTS TO--
AAHHHH!
HHRRGHH!
BECAUSE I CHOSE TO JUMP THROUGH TIME. I CHOSE TO CONDEMN MYSELF TO THIS HELL.
TO CREATE THE VILLAIN WHO MURDERS MY SON--
--AT THE REQUEST OF A VILLAIN WHO'S--WHO'S ME AS WELL, HA HA HA HAAAA--
--ALL OF IT-- I DID ALL OF IT TO MYSELF--
--WILL DO ALL OF IT--TO MYSELF-- MYSELF--
SO I KNOW--WITH A TERRIBLE CRYSTAL CLARITY--JUST HOW I BECOME BEDLAM.
I KNOW THE EXACT ANGER HE MUST FEEL. I KNOW HIS HATE.
BECAUSE I HATE MYSELF.
AND I SHOULD JUST DIE.
GO ON, DO IT! KILL HIM!
PLEASE!
WHAT...?

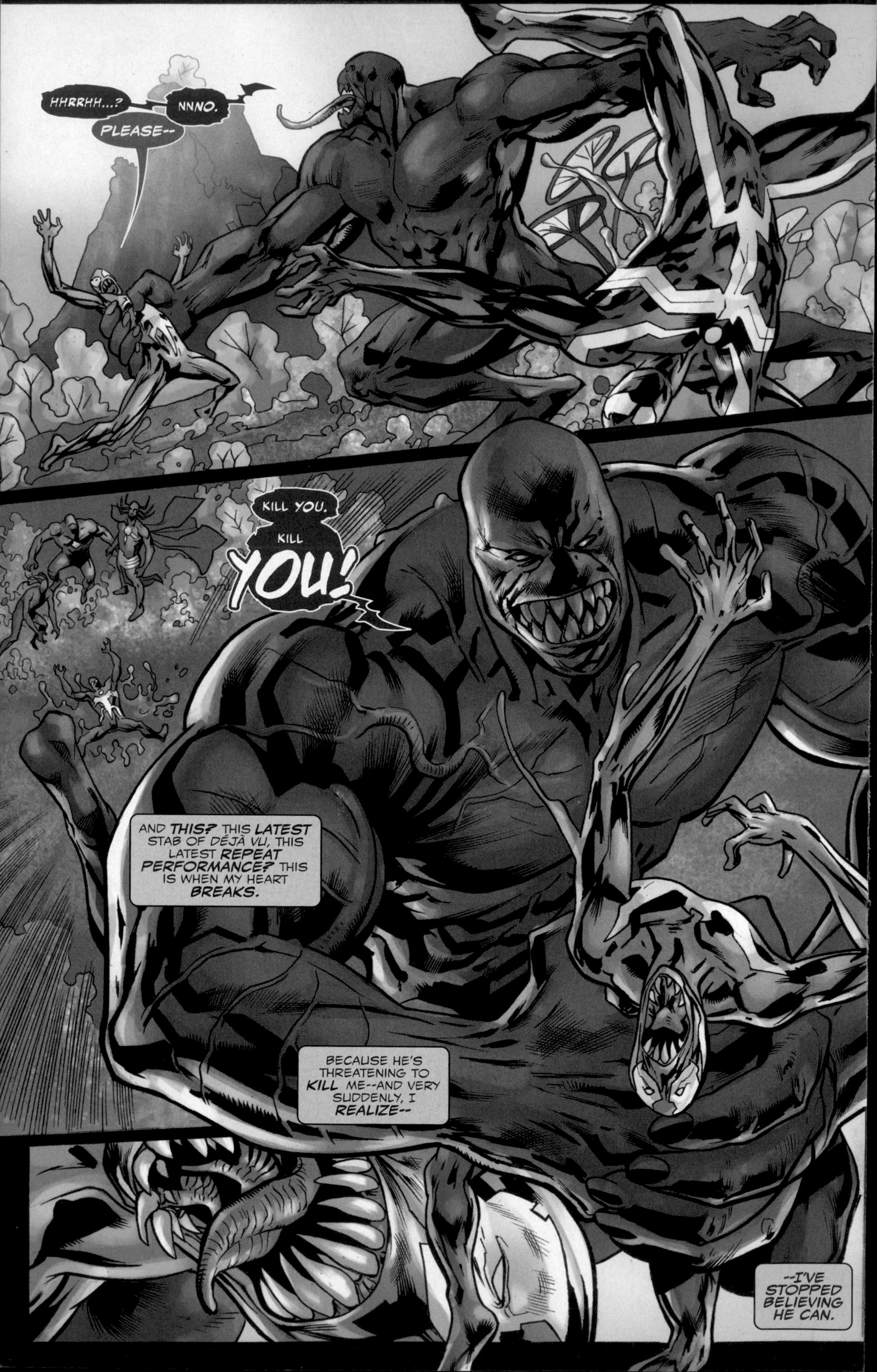

HHRRHH...?
NNNO.
PLEASE--
KILL YOU.
KILL
YOU!
AND THIS? THIS LATEST STAB OF DÉJÀ VU, THIS LATEST REPEAT PERFORMANCE? THIS IS WHEN MY HEART BREAKS.
BECAUSE HE'S THREATENING TO KILL ME--AND VERY SUDDENLY, I REALIZE--
--I'VE STOPPED BELIEVING HE CAN.

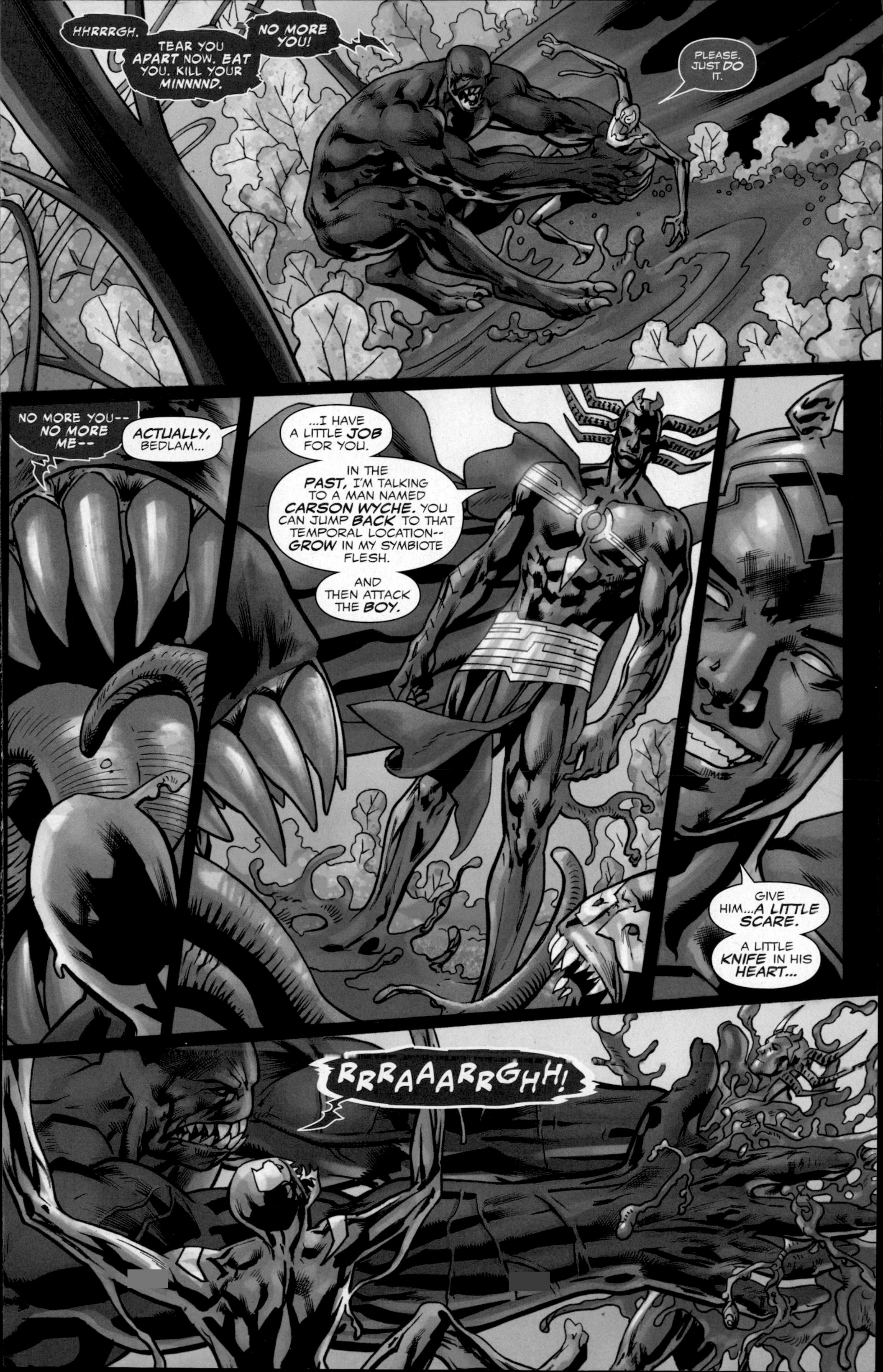
HHRRRGH.
TEAR YOU APART NOW. EAT YOU. KILL YOUR MINNNND.
NO MORE YOU!
PLEASE. JUST DO IT.
NO MORE YOU-- NO MORE ME--
ACTUALLY, BEDLAM...
...I HAVE A LITTLE JOB FOR YOU.
IN THE PAST, I'M TALKING TO A MAN NAMED CARSON WYCHE. YOU CAN JUMP BACK TO THAT TEMPORAL LOCATION--GROW IN MY SYMBIOTE FLESH.
AND THEN ATTACK THE BOY.
GIVE HIM...A LITTLE SCARE.
A LITTLE KNIFE IN HIS HEART...
RRRAAARRGHH!

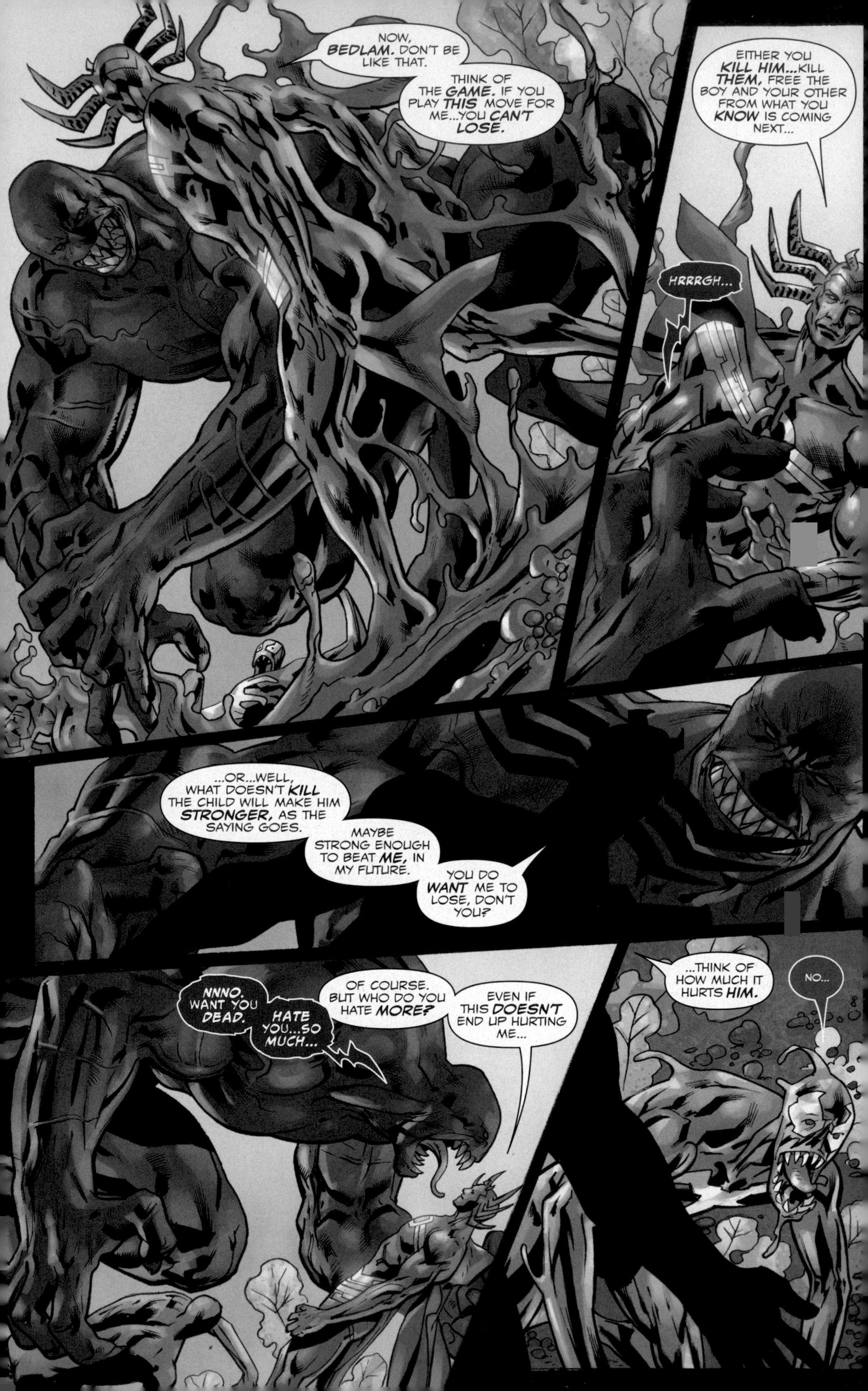
NOW, BEDLAM. DON'T BE LIKE THAT.
THINK OF THE GAME. IF YOU PLAY THIS MOVE FOR ME...YOU CAN'T LOSE.
EITHER YOU KILL HIM...KILL THEM, FREE THE BOY AND YOUR OTHER FROM WHAT YOU KNOW IS COMING NEXT...
HRRRGH...
...OR...WELL, WHAT DOESN'T KILL THE CHILD WILL MAKE HIM STRONGER, AS THE SAYING GOES.
MAYBE STRONG ENOUGH TO BEAT ME, IN MY FUTURE.
YOU DO WANT ME TO LOSE, DON'T YOU?
NNNO. WANT YOU DEAD.
HATE YOU...SO MUCH...
OF COURSE. BUT WHO DO YOU HATE MORE?
EVEN IF THIS DOESN'T END UP HURTING ME...
...THINK OF HOW MUCH IT HURTS HIM.
NO...

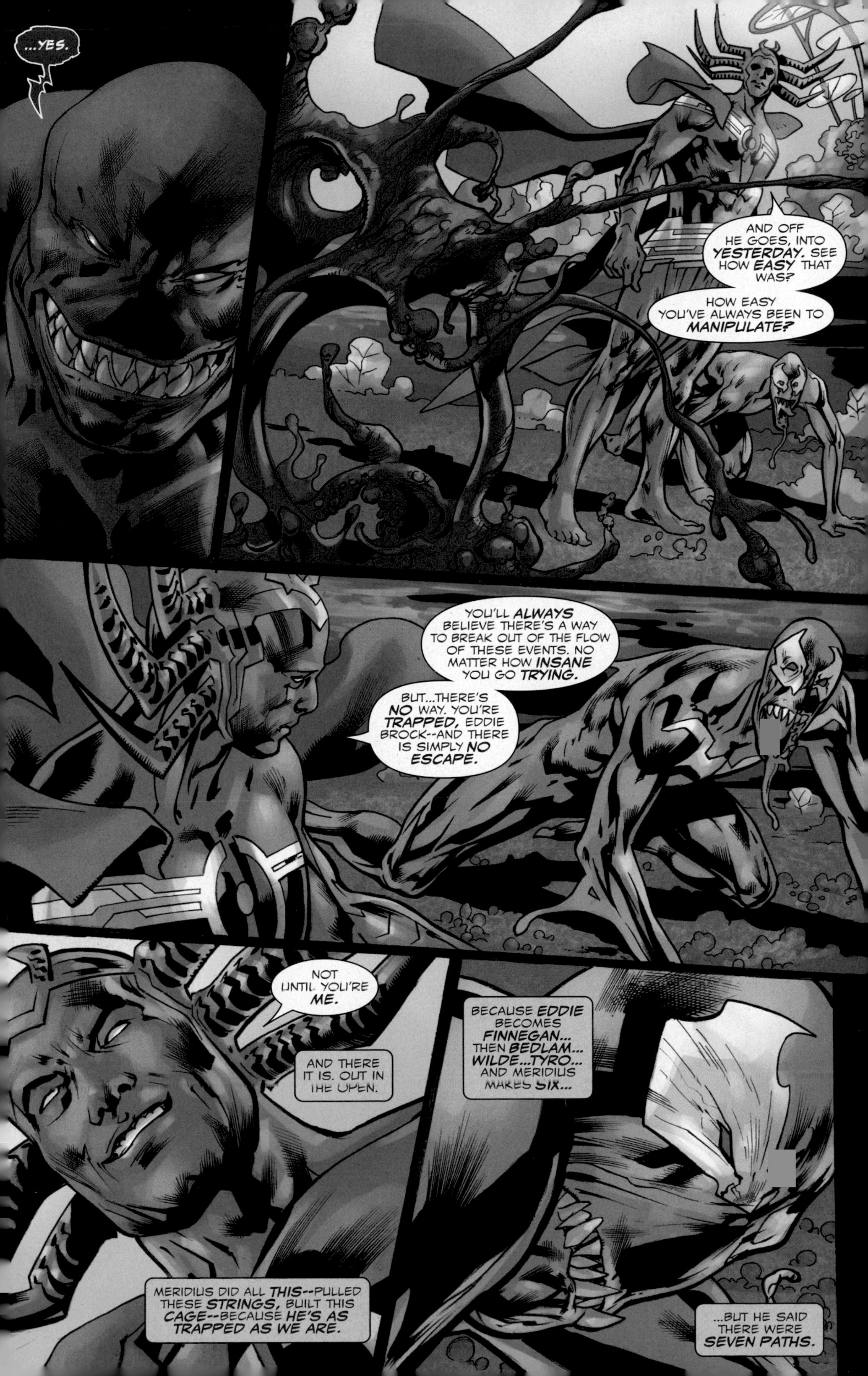

...YES.
AND OFF HE GOES, INTO YESTERDAY. SEE HOW EASY THAT WAS?
HOW EASY YOU'VE ALWAYS BEEN TO MANIPULATE?
YOU'LL ALWAYS BELIEVE THERE'S A WAY TO BREAK OUT OF THE FLOW OF THESE EVENTS. NO MATTER HOW INSANE YOU GO TRYING.
BUT...THERE'S NO WAY. YOU'RE TRAPPED, EDDIE BROCK--AND THERE IS SIMPLY NO ESCAPE.
NOT UNTIL YOU'RE ME.
AND THERE IT IS. OUT IN THE OPEN.
BECAUSE EDDIE BECOMES FINNEGAN... THEN BEDLAM... WILDE...TYRO... AND MERIDIUS MAKES SIX...
MERIDIUS DID ALL THIS--PULLED THESE STRINGS, BUILT THIS CAGE--BECAUSE HE'S AS TRAPPED AS WE ARE.
...BUT HE SAID THERE WERE SEVEN PATHS.

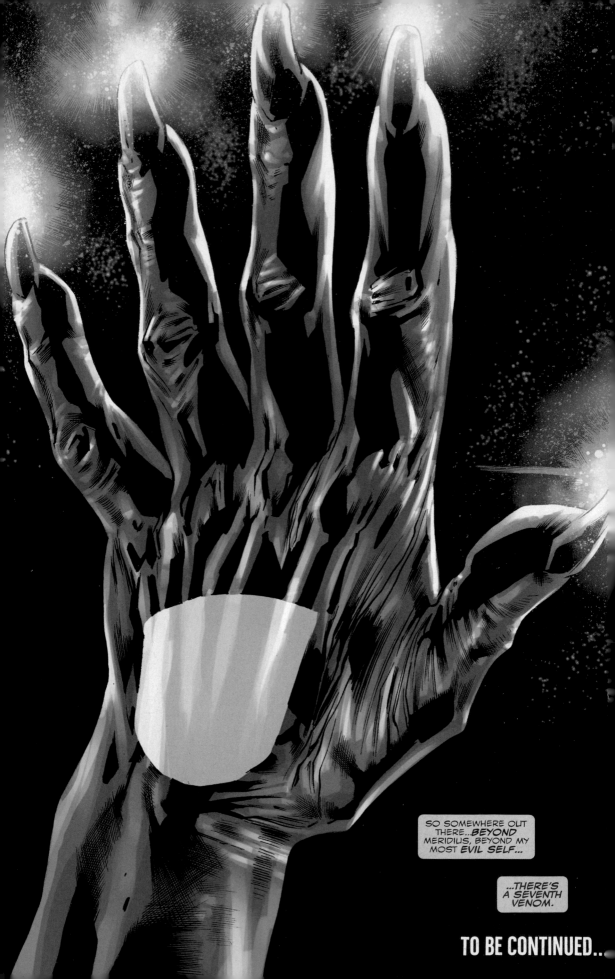

SO SOMEWHERE OUT THERE...*BEYOND* MERIDIUS, BEYOND MY MOST *EVIL SELF*...

...THERE'S A SEVENTH VENOM.

TO BE CONTINUED..

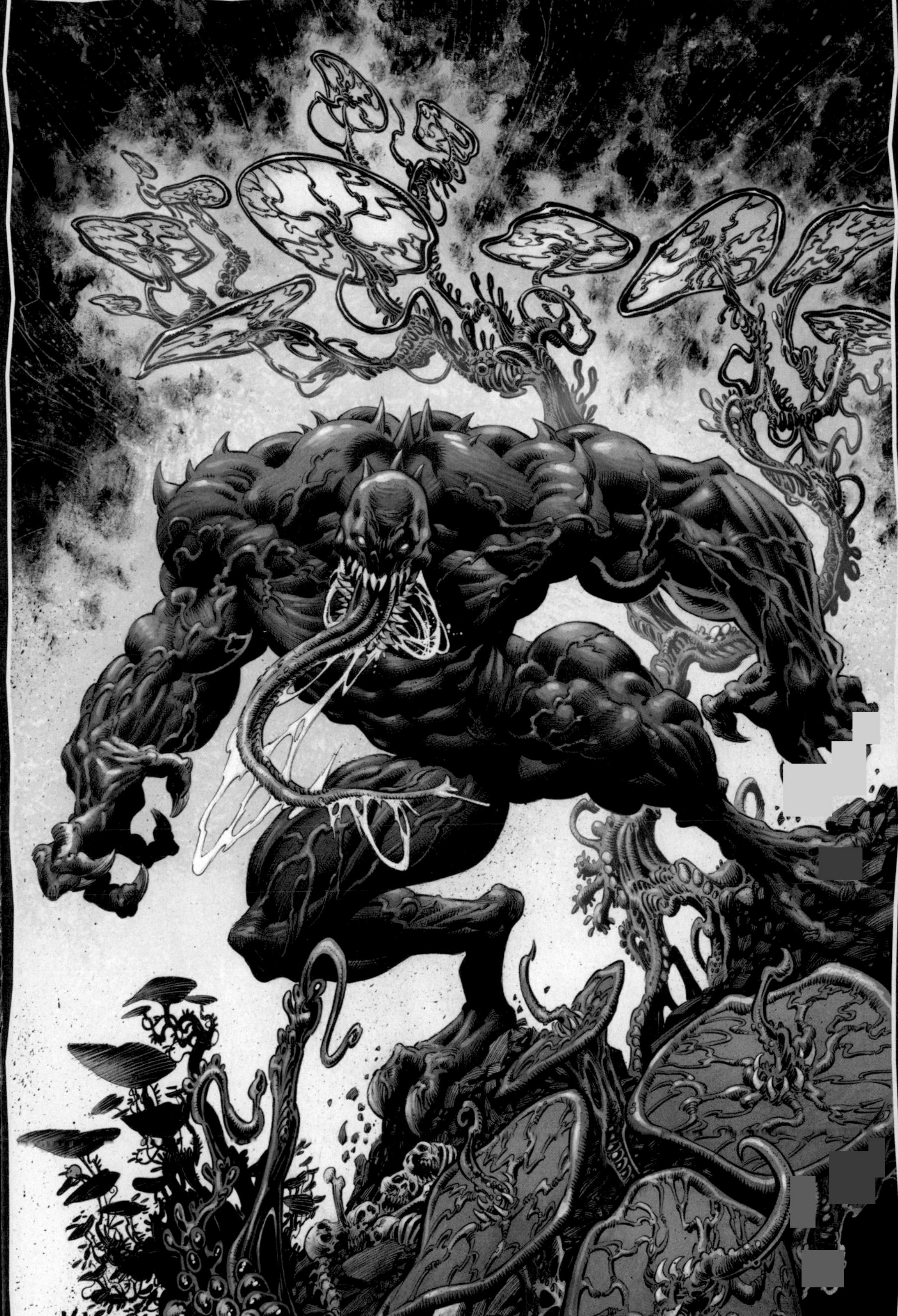

#9 variant by
KYLE HOTZ

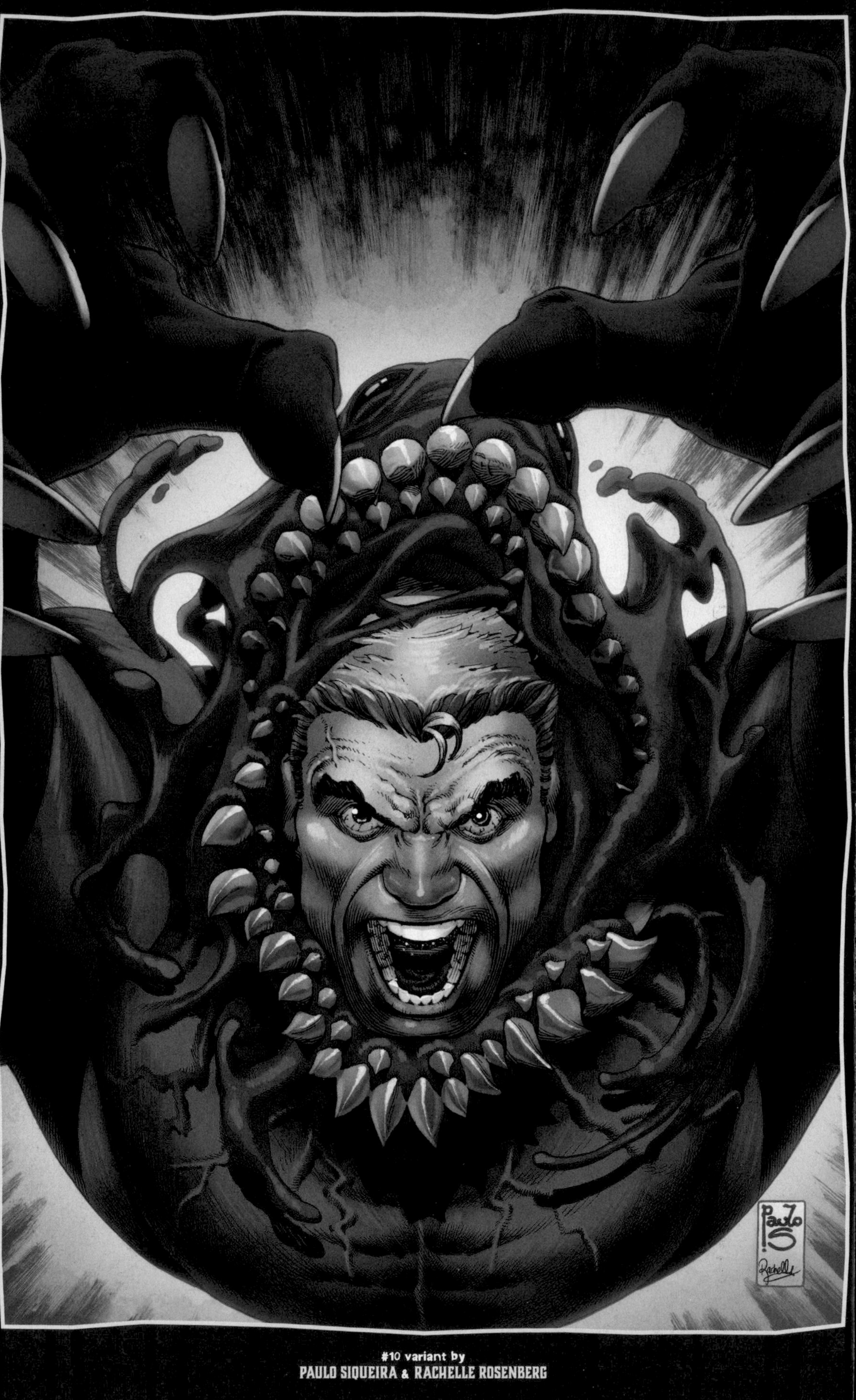

#10 variant by
PAULO SIQUEIRA & RACHELLE ROSENBERG